A Travel Guide to the War of 1812
in the Chesapeake

Johns Hopkins Books on the War of 1812

Donald R. Hickey, *Series Editor*

THE WAR OF 1812
IN THE CHESAPEAKE

Eighteen Tours in Maryland, Virginia,
and the District of Columbia

RALPH E. ESHELMAN

The Johns Hopkins
University Press Baltimore

© 2011 The Johns Hopkins University Press
All rights reserved. Published 2011
Printed in the United States of America on acid-free paper

9 8 7 6 5 4 3 2 1

The Johns Hopkins University Press
2715 North Charles Street
Baltimore, Maryland 21218-4363
www.press.jhu.edu

Library of Congress Cataloging-in-Publication Data
Eshelman, Ralph E.
 A travel guide to the War of 1812 in the Chesapeake: eighteen tours in
Maryland, Virginia, and the District of Columbia / Ralph E. Eshelman.
    p. cm. — (Johns Hopkins books on the War of 1812)
 Includes bibliographical references and index.
 ISBN-13: 978-0-8018-9836-5 (hardcover : alk. paper)
 ISBN-10: 0-8018-9836-6 (hardcover : alk. paper)
 ISBN-13: 978-0-8018-9837-2 (pbk. : alk. paper)
 ISBN-10: 0-8018-9837-4 (pbk. : alk. paper)
 1. United States—History—War of 1812—Campaigns. 2. Historic sites—
Chesapeake Bay Region (Md. and Va.)—Guidebooks. 3. Chesapeake
Bay Region (Md. and Va.)—History, Military—19th century. 4. Historic
sites—Maryland—Guidebooks. 5. Historic sites—Virginia—Guidebooks.
6. Historic sites—Washington (D.C.)—Guidebooks. 7. Maryland—
History—War of 1812. 8. Virginia—History—War of 1812. 9. Washington
(D.C.)—History—Capture by the British, 1814. I. Title.
 E355.1.C485E83 2011
 973.5'23—dc22   2010022519

A catalog record for this book is available from the British Library.

*Special discounts are available for bulk purchases of this book. For more
information, please contact Special Sales at 410-516-6936 or specialsales@
press.jhu.edu.*

The Johns Hopkins University Press uses environmentally friendly book
materials, including recycled text paper that is composed of at least 30
percent post-consumer waste, whenever possible. All of our book papers
are acid-free, and our jackets and covers are printed on paper with
recycled content.

CONTENTS

ABBREVIATIONS

Adm.	Admiral
Brig. Gen.	Brigadier General
Capt.	Captain
Col.	Colonel
Com.	Commodore
D.C.	District of Columbia
Gen.	General
HABS	Historic American Buildings Survey
H.M.	His or Her Majesty's
Hon.	Honorable
Lieut.	Lieutenant
Lt.	Lieutenant
Maj.	Major
NHD	National Historic District
NHL	National Historic Landmark
NHS	National Historic Site
NRHP	National Register of Historic Places
Pvt.	Private
Rev.	Reverend
Sgt.	Sergeant
&c.	etc.

A Travel Guide to the War of 1812
in the Chesapeake

OVERVIEW

Nearly all Americans have heard about the bombardment of Fort McHenry in 1814. Observing that event inspired Francis Scott Key to write the lyrics that later became our national anthem. But how many citizens living near Chesapeake Bay, let alone Americans in general, have ever heard of the battles of Caulks Field or Pungoteague? How many Americans know the Chesapeake Bay region suffered more raids and skirmishes than any other theater during the War of 1812? The Chesapeake Bay region has an amazing wealth of history related to this poorly understood conflict—most of it sadly unfamiliar and underappreciated. This guide will help the user explore a fascinating era, discover its importance in American history, and better appreciate the Chesapeake region's significant contributions to the outcome of that war.

The conflict broke out thirty years after the United States had won its independence, when—despite that fact—the British imposed unfavorable trade restrictions, impressed American sailors on the high seas (that is, compelled them to serve in the British navy by force and without notice), continued to occupy American territory along the Great Lakes, and apparently supported Indian raids on the western American frontier. For citizens in the Chesapeake, maritime issues loomed especially large. Between 1807 and 1812, the British seized more than four hundred American ships and their cargoes and forced some six thousand American citizens into the Royal Navy. Among the impressed were John Strachan and William Ware of Maryland, two of four seamen whom the British seized during the notorious *Chesapeake–Leopard* affair, which took place near the mouth of Chesapeake Bay in June 1807 and incited raucous calls for American action.

Hostilities formally broke out five years later, on June 18, 1812. Congress then declared war on Great Britain by votes of 79–49 in the House and 19–13 in the Senate—the closest margins in American history. As armed forces went after each other, it became clear that fighting would take place in four theaters: on the oceans; along the Atlantic coast, including the Chesapeake Bay; on the American-Canadian border; and in the Gulf of Mexico.

The war arrived quickly in the Chesapeake. In early February 1813, a British squadron established a blockade at the mouth of Chesapeake Bay. Raiding parties from these ships hoped to draw American troops away from the Canadian border and stir up so much unrest that local populations would clamor for peace. The Potomac region provided the scene for what surely was the lowest point in the war for the United States: humiliating defeat at the Battle of Bladensburg followed by British occupation of the nation's capital and the burning of many public buildings. Tidewater towns—Havre de Grace and Fredericktown, Maryland, and Tappahannock, Virginia—went up in flames during British raids, and many communities and plantations experienced the indignity of enemy occupation and the abuses of looting. In at least one town, Hampton, Virginia, there was rape and murder, as well.

As many as 159 military actions took place in the Chesapeake during the war—11 battles, 61 skirmishes, and 87 raids (for purposes of this guide, "battles" involved one hundred or more troops engaged on both sides). Although other areas, most notably the Niagara region, were the scene of significant campaigning and extensive property losses, the

1

Chesapeake suffered more enemy raids, and sustained more property damage and other losses, than any other theater of operations in the war. But there were also American successes: the small but sharp engagement at Craney Island in late June 1813 and, of course, in mid-September 1814, the two-day Battle for Baltimore. The latter demonstrated the spirit of citizen soldiers, when well led, and by happenstance produced the lyrics that became the national anthem in 1931. The flag of Fort McHenry and the music had been enshrined in public memory well before that year.

* * *

This travel guide focuses on War of 1812 places related to Chesapeake Bay—but not all of the known sites in Maryland, Virginia, and the District of Columbia—and those historic routes and sites that are accessible to the public. In many cases, war-related places remain in private hands. When possible, the guide supplies photographs of privately owned structures and sites not visible from public roads.

The guide is divided into two broad categories—historic route tours and historic city, town, and regional tours—and focuses on driving and walking between sites. Throughout the guide, sites designated as National Historic Landmarks (NHL) or those listed on the National Register of Historic Places (NRHP) or in a National Historic District (NHD) are identified. (*See the list of abbreviations for a complete guide.*)

Historic route tours in part 1 follow as closely as possible the pathways participants took during the war. In some cases, one can no longer track portions of original routes because railroads, modern roads, or interstate highways have cut into them or highway authorities have realigned them for safety issues. Optional side trips to nearby war-related sites are occasionally recommended in the historic route tours section.

The five tours are arranged in the order that the events occurred. The two most important routes trace the British landing at Benedict on the Patuxent River and the march to Washington and the British landing at North Point on the Patapsco River and campaign against Baltimore. The British Invasion Tour is approximately 55 miles long and traces the British landing at Benedict to the Bladensburg Battlefield. The culmination of the British Invasion Tour is the Battle of Bladensburg Tour, separated from the invasion tour for the convenience of those who wish to visit only the battlefield. The battlefield tour also includes the British route, in the aftermath, to the District of Columbia and Capitol Hill. It provides information on the route of the American retreat from the battlefield, the rendezvous point at Montgomery Court House (present-day Rockville), and route to Baltimore to defend that city from the anticipated next logical British attack. Finally, it supplies information on the British return route to Benedict, which differed from the route to Bladensburg.

The First Family Flight Tour describes the independent routes President James Madison and First Lady Dolley Madison took in escaping Washington and seeking safety during the British foray into the city. President Madison's flight route is approximately 41 miles long (Washington, D.C., via Virginia to Brookeville, Maryland); that of the First Lady runs approximately 29 miles.

The Saving the Declaration of Independence Tour extends some 36 miles and follows the route used by U.S. State Department personnel as they saved some of the most important official records from certain destruction.

Note that both these tours will interest only the keenest travelers. They have few surviving structures, and most of those are privately owned and not open to the public. Some are not even visible from public roads.

Chesapeake Bay Region

The approximately 8-mile-long Battle of North Point Tour follows the British landing at North Point, the march route to the battlefield, and the battlefield itself. It includes information about the British route from the battlefield to the outskirts of Baltimore.

* * *

To make trip planning easier, the historic city, town, and regional tours in part 2 are grouped as sites in Maryland, Virginia, and the District of Columbia. These have been arranged according to jurisdiction or region. Baltimore and Washington, D.C., lend themselves to a day or more of walking, biking, or using public transportation to visit their numerous War of 1812 sites. Where city or town sites appear in the historic route tours, cross references refer the traveler to the appropriate tour.

The Maryland section includes tours of Annapolis, Baltimore, Southern Maryland, Maryland's Eastern Shore, and sites and towns at the head of Chesapeake Bay—including an optional side tour to the site of the Du Pont Gunpowder Company in Delaware. Although located outside the Chesapeake region, the Du Pont facility played an important role in supplying gunpowder to the region. A tour of Frederick is also included because of its significance as home to the Francis Scott Key grave and one of his monuments.

Virginia, a huge state in comparison to Maryland, contains numerous sites that do not necessarily fall into historic routes or make convenient regional tours. In addition to tours of Alexandria, Norfolk, Richmond and Petersburg, and Tappahannock there is a tour of sites in Central Virginia encompassing the homes of significant persons including Presidents Jefferson and Madison, then-Secretary of State and War James Monroe, and Virginia war Governor Barbour. An optional side trip to Organ Cave (originally in Virginia but now in West Virginia), shows where saltpetre was mined to make gunpowder. The final tour in Virginia includes significant sites that are scattered about the Tidewater region of the state, such as Irvington, New Point Comfort, and Fort Boykin.

Two of the four largest and most important battlefields in Virginia, the Battle of Craney Island and the Battle of Hampton, retain little or no historic integrity. The Craney Island site now resides inside the boundaries of a military installation and is not accessible to the public. Another site on the Virginia side of the Potomac, White House (no relation to the President's House in Washington), is also within the boundaries of a military installation but is currently accessible to the public with photo ID. Thus the guide offers only a summary of the Battle of Craney Island in the Greater Norfolk Tour and but a brief discussion of the Battle of White House in the Southern Maryland Tour (*see* Fort Washington *in* Southern Maryland Tour *in part 2*) and Alexandria Tour. Hampton was burned during the War of 1812 and again in the Civil War but still has several surviving historic sites (*see* Hampton *under* Greater Norfolk Tour *in part 2*) worth visiting. Virginia's fourth significant battlefield, the site of the Battle of Pungoteague, lies on the Eastern Shore. It retains much of its original appearance but stands on private property. No structures related to the battle survive, and one can view the site only from the water. A summary of this battle appears under "Pungoteague" among the water routes in appendix C.

A WORD ABOUT THE SOURCES

Whenever possible the words of the participants in the war are used to impart the spirit and opinions of the time. Primary sources such as diaries, journals, newspapers, contemporary accounts, and other documents from the period have been quoted. For the more significant entries, such as battlefields, the perspective from both the British and American sides are given when possible. Any contemporary quotation used to explain a site is reproduced (even with misspelled words, incorrect punctuation, or lack of punctuation) exactly as it appears in the document to retain the original voice of the authors. Any changes made to the text and any additional information supplied have been given in square brackets. For those quotes not identified or not fully identified and for a detailed bibliographical essay see Ralph E. Eshelman, Scott S. Sheads, and Donald R. Hickey, *The War of 1812 in the Chesapeake: A Reference Guide to Historic Sites in Maryland, Virginia, and the District of Columbia* (Johns Hopkins University Press, 2010). Please refer to the suggested reading at the end of this guide for additional information about the War of 1812 in the Chesapeake.

A CAUTIONARY NOTE

In these days of instant communication change is quick and often. Although every effort has been made to ensure the information

National Historic Trail and Maryland Scenic Byway

The Star-Spangled Banner National Historic Trail was designated by Congress in 2008. Administered by the National Park Service, the trail is being developed in cooperation with state and local governments, nonprofit organizations, and the private sector. Once complete, the 290-mile-long land and water trail through tidewater Maryland, the District of Columbia, and portions of Virginia will connect the places, people, and events that led to the birth of the national anthem. Most of the sites on the Star-Spangled Banner National Historic Trail, along with many more, are included in this guide. For further information on this trail *see:* www.nps.gov/stsp.

The Star-Spangled Banner Byway, a Maryland Scenic Byway for which America's Byway designation is being actively pursued, is a 130-mile-long driving tour from Solomons to Baltimore that follows the most significant portions of the British invasion route in Maryland. The Maryland Byways map and guide and a brochure, "Star-Spangled Banner Trail: War of 1812 Chesapeake Campaign," are worth obtaining from www.starspangled200.org.

in this guide is accurate and up to date, it is suggested you call or check the Web page of a site before visiting. Days and hours of operation often change depending on season.

As our nation prepares for the bicentennial celebration of the War of 1812, numerous societies, towns, cities, counties, and states and the federal government are gearing up to mark this anniversary. Many are in the process of creating new tours, preparing pamphlets, restoring sites, and erecting and updating interpretive panels. Reenactments are being planned here and in Canada. This guide is intended to help you plan for your 1812 travels in the Chesapeake Region; but be alert to the new and exciting programs and other aides to understanding the significance of this region in the war that were not available to be included in this guide.

Some of the sites in this guide are located in high congestion areas, such as Bladensburg, Annapolis, Baltimore, Norfolk, or Washington, D.C., while others are located on narrow, winding, or hilly rural roads. Those wishing to visit these sites, whether on foot, by bicycle, or by car, should exercise caution. Keep valuables out of sight and lock your car at all times. Many sites are located on private property. Some cannot be seen from public roads; others can be seen from public roads but no parking is available. Please respect private property and only pass by such sites. *Do not trespass.* Finally, remember that it is against the law to relic hunt on public property or on any lands submerged below the high water mark. It is also against the law to relic hunt or trespass on private property without the permission of the owner. Please take nothing but photographs and leave only with good memories.

PART 1 | Historic Route Tours

British Invasion Tour

Particulars This tour is approximately 55 miles long and offers another 14 miles of optional side trips. At least five hours should be allowed to complete the entire trail, although the amount of time you spend will vary depending on how long you linger at individual sites, looking at exhibits, viewing river vistas, eating, etc. To make your tour as enjoyable and leisurely as possible, I recommend you spend the preceding night in the Prince Frederick area so you can have a full day for your journey the next morning. There are numerous dining options and overnight accommodations nearby. Pack a picnic lunch or stop at the several eateries along the tour.

Historical Background The British Invasion Tour takes the traveler along the route (and in many places, along the same roads) used by the British during their successful invasion of Maryland and occupation of Washington after defeating the Americans at the Battle of Bladensburg. This campaign marks the only time in our history that a foreign army invaded the United States and captured our capital. Come and retrace the route along the Patuxent River that was used by the British in their invasion of Maryland. Explore the sites where history was made. Learn fascinating tales related to this invasion, such as how nineteen-year-old Henry Canter retrieved his horse from the British; and how Francis Scott Key, attempting to seek the release of an American doctor, ended up observing the bombardment of Fort McHenry and writing the lyrics that became our national anthem.

Fifteen-year-old Royal Navy Midshipmen Robert J. Barrett, aboard H.M. frigate *Hebrus,* described the Patuxent River in the summer of 1814: *The fleet at length proceeded, with a fair wind, under all sail, up the lovely and romantic river of the Patuxent, whose verdant and picturesque banks attested to the spectator of this rural scene how bountiful had Nature been in her gifts to this favoured country.*

Eighteen-year-old British Army Lt. George Robert Gleig, aboard H.M. transport *Golden Fleece,* also described the Patuxent: *The sail up* [the Patuxent] *surpasses even that up the Thames, the woods are so fine, the cottages so beautiful, and the cultivation so rich.* The Patuxent, surprisingly, retains much of this same quality today.

The Maryland *Gazette* reported on March 31, 1814: *A large British force coming to America. Preparations have been made on a large scale to enable Sir A. Cochrane* [Vice Adm. Alexander Cochrane, British Commander-in-Chief of the North American Station] *to take with him a very large force, both naval and military. Sir Alexander takes with him about 4000 marines . . . also . . . a strong body of riflemen, battering artillery, Congreve rockets, Shrapnel shells, with all the ammunition, &c. necessary to give effect to these engines of destruction.*

Rear Adm. George Cockburn, Second-in-Command, wrote to Vice Adm. Alexander Cochrane on June 17, 1814: *I feel no hesitation in stating to you that I consider the town of Benedict in Patuxent, to offer us advantages for this purpose beyond any other spot within the United States . . . Within forty-eight hours after the arrival in the Patuxent of such a force as you expect, the City of Washington might be possessed without difficulty or opposition of any kind.*

American Secretary of War, Gen. John Armstrong, stated the following opinion during a department head meeting on July 1, 1814: *That the navigation of the Potomac is long and sinuous, and if not doubtful, as to practicability, by large ships, is at least uncertain in relation to the time its ascent may occupy; while that of the Patuxent is short and safe, and may be calculated with sufficient precision for military purposes; that, should the enemy ascend the former, his object is unmasked—he at once declares his destination, and of course leaves us at liberty to concentrate our whole force against him; that, on the other hand, should he ascend the Patuxent (or South River), his object is uncertain—it may be the [Chesapeake] flotilla, or Baltimore, or Washington; and that, as long as his point of attack is unknown, so long must our force remain divided; that these considerations suggest the preference he will probably give the Patuxent.*

On the morning of August 14, 1814, twenty-two British vessels from Bermuda, carrying over three thousand seasoned troops fresh from fighting Napoleon in Europe, joined the British forces already in the Patuxent. The total British force, consisting of forty-five large vessels and numerous smaller craft, ascended the river. On August 19 and 20, about forty-four hundred troops landed at Benedict, roughly 40 miles from Washington. The population of Benedict in 1814 is unknown, but the total population of Charles County from the Third Census of 1810 was 20,245. Only 7,398 were white, including men, women, and children (37% white and 63% nonwhite). Thus the British invasion force outnumbered the total white male population of the entire county.

The British army began its land invasion on the afternoon of August 20. Smaller vessels of the fleet shadowed the marching troops, moving by sail and oar north along the Patuxent River to Nottingham, reaching it on the evening of August 21.

British Vice Adm. Alexander Cochrane wrote to American Secretary of State James Monroe on August 18, 1814: *Sir, Having been called upon by the Governor General of the Canadas to aid him in carrying into effect, measure of retaliation against the inhabitants of the United States, for the wanton destruction committed by their army in Upper Canada, it has become Imperiously my duty, conformably with the nature of Governor General's application, to issue to the naval force under my command, an order to destroy and lay waste such towns and districts upon the coast, as may be found assailable.* Delivery of this communication was delayed until after the capture of Washington.

Invasion Route Itinerary Begin your British Invasion Tour at **BENEDICT,** located on the Patuxent River only 6 miles west of Prince Frederick.

BENEDICT. Parking: free. **Facilities:** waterfront restaurants; no public restrooms. **Comment:** Benedict has no overnight facilities although nearby Prince Frederick does; other than a roadside historical marker, there is presently no interpretation on the War of 1812 at this important site.

From the west end of the Benedict Bridge, drive 0.3 mile west on Prince Frederick Road (Route 231) to the intersection with Benedict Avenue on the left (south). Turn left and drive 0.3 mile to the waterfront at Benedict.

Here at Benedict on June 16, 1814, a British raid consisting of one hundred sixty marines and a thirty-man detachment of the Colonial Marines (former slaves) took Benedict without a fight despite the nearby presence of the Charles County Militia under the command of Brig. Gen. Philip Stuart. During the raid, at least one barrel of whiskey, intentionally

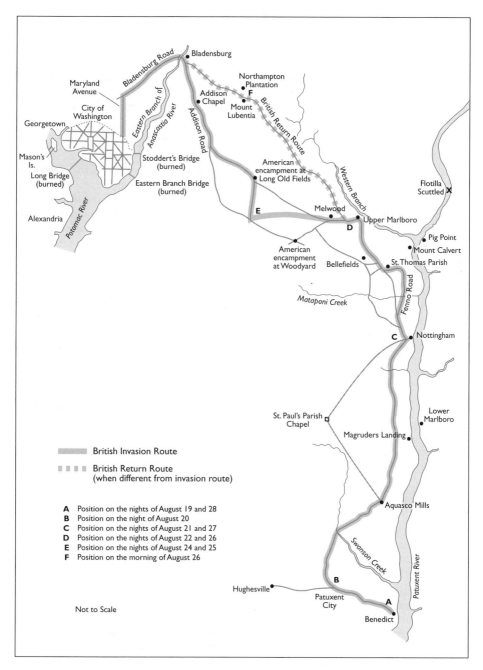

British Invasion Route: Benedict to Washington (updated, corrected, and redrawn from 1814 sketch map by Robert Smith, "Sketch of the march of the British army under M. Genl. Ross . . ."; courtesy of Beinecke Rare Book and Manuscript Library, Yale University)

laced with arsenic, was left for the British troops to discover and drink. An American, however, warned the British of the ploy.

Capt. Robert Barrie reported his account of the raid to Rear Adm. George Cockburn on June 19, 1814: *arrived at Benedict here a party of Regulars were stationed who fled on our approach leaving several Musquets, Knapsacks and part of their Camp Equipage behind them, they also left a 6 pr. Field Piece which was spiked—The Inhabitants deserted the Town and removed their Effects.—We found a Store containing about 360 Hogsheads of Tobacco.*

The British attempted a second landing at Benedict on June 21, 1814, but were successfully driven off by District of Columbia Dragoons (militia cavalry) assisted by artillery. About 2 p.m. the British landed a small party of marines to conduct reconnaissance. Two British naval officers and a Sergeant Mayo (also spelled Mayeaux and Mahiou) were separated from the patrol and encountered the militia under Brig. Gen. Philip Stuart. The general led his horsemen in the direction of the British to cut them off from their ships. Six members of the British patrol were captured. The British officers jumped a hedge and escaped but Sergeant Mayo was attacked. Trooper Francis Wise of the District of Columbia Dragoons first approached Sergeant Mayo but overrode him and was shot and killed by the sergeant. Then, with his bayonet, Mayo took on Trooper Alexander Hunter who, with his pistol, slightly wounded the sergeant, spooking his horse in the process. Sergeant Mayo turned on General Stuart with his bayonet as Hunter, now dismounted, rejoined the fight. The sergeant dropped his rifle and ran to the nearby swamp. Hunter, borrowing Stuart's sword, pursued Mayo with two other cavalrymen and mortally wounded him. The remaining British forces hurriedly took to their ships.

Capt. Thomas Brown reported his account of the raid to Rear Adm. George Cockburn on June 23, 1814: *I dispatched the St. Lawrence* [18-gun schooner] *with the Launches and part of the Marines of the Frigate up to St. Benedict, to load with the remaining Tobacco. After getting on board seventeen Hogsheads, the Party were surprised and attacked by several hundred Infantry and Cavalry, with four field Pieces* [cannon], *a Sergeant, four Marines and one Seaman, retreating to the Boats were cut off and made Prisoners, but I am happy to learn no lives have been lost, or any person wounded* [despite Brown's claim, the sergeant was killed].

Beginning August 19 until late on the afternoon of August 20, 1814, the British landed 4,370 men at Benedict without a shot fired in resistance. Lieutenant and diarist George Robert Gleig wrote on August 19, 1814, that the British troops, recently embarked from Bermuda, had been held up in their ships for such a long time that, upon landing at Benedict, some were: *lying at full length upon the grass, basking in the beams of a sultry sun, and apparently made happy by the very feeling of the green sod under them. Others were running and leaping about, giving exercise to the limbs which had so long been cramped and confined onboard ship.*

Gleig also described the area: *The banks of the river covered with fields of Indian corn and meadows of the most luxuriant pasture, the neat wooden houses, white and surrounded with orchards and gardens, with backgrounds of boundless forest, differed in every respect from the country in France* [the last country most of the British troops had seen; while fighting Napoleon], *the furze, heath and underwood skirting the similar pine forests as if there had not been time to grub and clear the ground. When we landed it was totally deserted by its inhabitants. The furniture however had not been removed, at least not wholly, from any of the houses, and not a few of the dairies were garnished with dishes of exquisite milk and delicate new cheese.*

Gleig described the inhabitants of Benedict as *surly beasts, sneering at our troops, refusing to even return a greeting, and spitting in a way that showed their detestation.* Benedict served as the main anchorage for the British naval forces during the invasion, August 19–30, 1814.

Return to Prince Frederick Road and turn left (west) 0.5 mile to Indian Creek Tract, Patuxent River Natural Resource Management Area on left (south) and the colorful pastel-colored barns of the Serenity Farm entrance on right (north). Parking is available at the Indian Creek Tract for those who wish to observe this area in more detail.

From the nearby heights, about 3 miles to the northwest, Secretary of State James Monroe reconnoitered the British fleet and troop strength around 10 a.m., August 20, 1814. On the morning of August 21, 1814, Monroe counted twenty-three British square-rigged vessels lying just below Benedict. The British encampment was along this very road below the heights ahead (west). Three cannon were placed on the road at the top of these heights and pickets were placed on both sides up to 2.5 miles inland. Because of these pickets and British vessels on the river, the British encampment was protected from American attack.

Lieutenant Gleig described the scene: *This little army was posted upon a height which rises at the distance of two miles from the river. In front of a valley cultivated for some way and intersected with orchards; at the farther extremity of which the advanced piquets took their ground; pushing forward a chain of sentinels to the very skirts of the forest. The right of the position was protected by a farm-house with its enclosure and outbuildings, and the left rested upon the edge of the hill, or rather mound, which there abruptly ended. On the brow of the hill, and above the centre of the line, were placed the cannon, ready loaded, and having lighted fusees beside them; whilst the infantry bivouacked immediately under the ridge, or rather upon the slope of the hill which looked towards the shipping, in order to prevent their disposition from being seen by the enemy, should they come down to attack. But as we were now in a country where we could not calculate upon being safe in rear, any more than in front, the chain of piquets was carried round both flanks, and so arranged, that no attempt could be made to get between the army and the fleet, without due notice, and time given to oppose and prevent it . . . Such is the little army with which we invade America.*

Nearby British Raids

Hollowing Point, a white house on the opposite shore just north of the Benedict Bridge, can be seen from the waterfront at Benedict facing the river (east). Here the British made a landing on July 21, 1814, and destroyed the home of Col. Benjamin Mackall. One account claims the Mackall home was burnt in retaliation for its use by Maj. Michael Taney as his headquarters for the local militia. The present house occupies the location of the original house. Sheridan Point, about 3 miles downstream (south) on the Patuxent River on the Calvert County side, was the site of another British raid on July 16, 1814, where the home of Dr. John Gray was burned.

South of Benedict 3 miles, on the St. Mary's County side, the British raided Trent Hall in July 1814. Landing a force of about five hundred troops including sailors armed with pikes, they marched inland in pursuit of tobacco and other property belonging to Mr. W. Kilgour. Kilgour, in an attempt to hide his tobacco from the British, had moved it about 3 miles inland to a barn and covered it with wheat. The British, having found it, gave the owner of the property four hogsheads of tobacco and then burnt the barn with all its remaining contents. The British also found and destroyed eight hogsheads of tobacco concealed in the woods near the water. The local militia, although summoned, were apparently unable to defend the property due to the overwhelming numbers of the enemy.

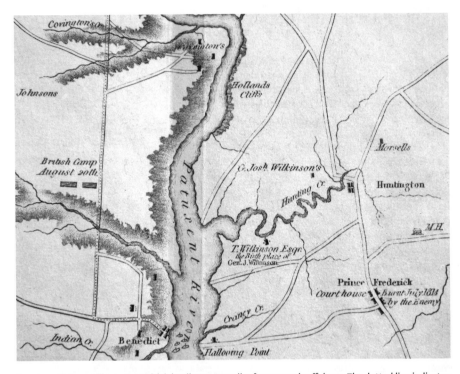

American 1816 map illustrates British landing at Benedict from vessels offshore. The dotted line indicates the route taken by the British invasion troops to their first and second night encampments after departing Benedict. The first encampment is north of that position shown in a contemporary British map drawn in 1814. Map also depicts the towns of Prince Frederick and Huntingtown (then Huntington). (Detail of James Wilkinson map; Fort McHenry National Historic Monument collections)

During the British march on Washington, advance pickets and flanking squadrons spread out into the fields and woods to ensure the safety of the main column. The British made good use of local sympathizers who gave the British directions and/or served as guides. Meanwhile, shallow draft British vessels on the Patuxent River paralleled the land troops in support. Finally, guard troops and ships were left at Benedict to safeguard their base. The British invasion force triumphantly returned to Benedict on August 29 and 30, 1814, to re-embark on their ships.

As you pass up this hill, imagine the British cannon placed here and the over four thousand men camped below. Travel approximately 5.0 miles (0.7 mile west of intersection with Route 381) to **OLDFIELDS CHAPEL** on the left (south). Pull into the church driveway.

OLDFIELDS EPISCOPAL CHURCH. Address: 15837 Prince Frederick Road, nearly opposite Goode Road. **Parking:** free. **Hours:** daylight hours. **Fees:** none. **Facilities:** none. **Contact:** 301-274-3796. **Comment:** The church is usually locked so only exterior views are possible.

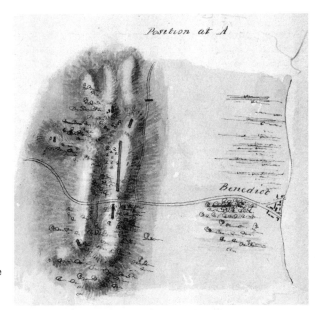

British 1814 sketch map depicts the Patuxent River to the right and the village of Benedict and the British defensive position on the heights to the extreme left. The British encampment was below the heights on both sides of what today is Prince Frederick Road. (Lt. Robert Smith, 44th Regiment, "Sketch of the march of the British army under M. Genl. Ross from the 19th to the 29th Augt 1814"; courtesy Beinecke Rare Book and Manuscript Library, Yale University)

Present-day view of British encampment site looking east from heights toward Benedict and Patuxent River. (Ralph Eshelman 2005 photograph)

Oldfields Chapel was established in 1753 and is now called Oldfields Episcopal Church. The present structure dates from 1769. During the British march on Washington, some British pickets may have camped on the grounds of this chapel.

Backtrack 0.7 mile from Oldfields Chapel to the intersection with Brandywine Road (Route 381). Here, at what today is called Patuxent City, the British made their first camp after leaving Benedict.

The redcoats began their march about 4 p.m., but owing to the heat and the poor condition of the men, most of whom had been cramped onboard ships for weeks, stragglers were everywhere. After marching only approximately 4 miles, they camped here without shelter, getting soaked in a thunderstorm about 7 p.m.

Lt. George Robert Gleig wrote in his diary on the evening of August 20, 1814: *Our march today was extremely short, the troops halting when they had arrived at a rising ground distant not more than six miles from the point where they set out; and having stationed the piquets, planted the sentinels, and made such other arrangements as the case required, fires were lighted, and the men were suffered to lie down. It may seem strange, but it is nevertheless true, that during this short march of six miles a greater number of soldiers dropped out of the ranks, and fell behind from fatigue, than I recollect to have seen in any march in the Peninsula* [Iberian Peninsular Campaign] *thrice its duration . . . The ground upon which we bivouacked . . . was a gentle eminence, fronted by an open and cultivated country, and crowned with two or three houses, having barns and walled gardens attached to them. Neither flank could be said to rest upon any point peculiarly well defended, but they were not exposed; because, by extending or condensing the line, almost any one of these houses might be converted into a protecting redoubt. The outposts, again, were so far arranged differently from those of yesterday, that, instead of covering only the front and the two extremities, they extended completely round the encampment, enclosing the entire army within a connected chain of sentinels; and precluding the possibility of even a single individual making his way within the line unperceived . . . The effect of the lightning, as it glanced for a moment upon the bivouac, and displayed the firelocks piled in regular order, and the men stretched out like so many corpses beside them, was extremely fine.*

Truth or Fiction?

Henry Canter (1795–1866) lived on his father's farm near Benedict and is buried at Oldfields Chapel. A family story holds that the British bought a horse from the Canter farm for $28. Henry supposedly was able to get his horse back by sneaking up on the British encampment and whistling for his horse. When it obediently came to him, he rode the horse home. Henry is buried in the church graveyard near the parking area north of the entrance to the church. Local tradition claims that two British soldiers who died of heatstroke are also buried here in unmarked graves.

Continue north on Route 381 about 3.0 miles to the town of Aquasco, then known as Aquasco Mills. Near here is the site where Secretary of State James Monroe and a handful of dragoons stood on a hill reconnoitering the British fleet and troop strength about 10 a.m., August 20, 1814. In order to expedite communication of British activities to the U.S. government, Monroe ordered dragoons to be placed every 12 miles between Aquasco Mills and Washington.

Monroe dispatched the following information on August 20, 1814: *I had a view of their ships but being at a distance of three miles, and having no glass, we could not count them . . . they are still debarking their troops* [at Benedict], *of the number of which I have not obtained any satisfactory information.*

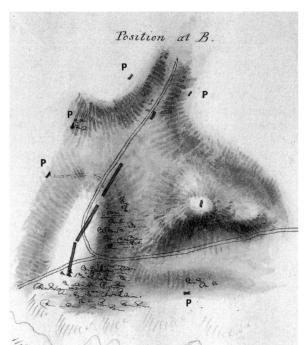

British 1814 sketch map showing the position of British troop deployment during their encampment at what today is Patuxent City. Prince Frederick Road runs east and west, and what today is called Brandywine Road runs north. Note the numerous piquet positions indicated by squares and keyed by the letter *P* added to the original sketch. (Lt. Robert Smith, "Sketch of the march of the British army under M. Genl. Ross . . ."; Beinecke Rare Book and Manuscript Library, Yale University)

Photograph of the road conditions at Patuxent City circa 1917, probably little changed from those experienced by the British forces encamped there in 1814. (*The Road to Washington*, 1919)

Forgotten War Hero

Brig. Gen. Leonard Covington was born near Aquasco on October 30, 1788. A hero of the War of 1812, he was wounded in the Battle of Crysler's Farm (near Cornwall, Ontario, Canada), on November 11, 1813, and died three days later. Fort Covington, in Baltimore, which played a critical role in defeating a British flanking night attack on Fort McHenry, is named for him. At least twenty-one cities, towns, and counties in Alabama, Kentucky, Mississippi, Oklahoma, Texas, and Virginia are also named for Leonard Covington.

Brig. Gen. Leonard Covington (*Memoir of Leonard Covington* by B.L.C. Wailes 1861; courtesy of C. Segert Wailes)

The general idea also is, that Washington is their objective, but of this I can form no opinion at this time.

Stay on Route 381 for 6.5 miles and turn right onto Croom Road north (Route 382). Croom Road was in existence by 1739. A good rest stop along the Patuxent River is at the **CLYDE WATSON BOATING AREA.** After going 2.2 miles north on Route 382 turn right (east) at the intersection with Magruders Ferry Road. Near the end of this 1.2-mile-long road is the entrance to Clyde Watson Boating Area on your right (south). Magruders Landing is located at the end of Magruders Ferry Road, but it is gated. Views of the landing can be seen from the end of the pier at Clyde Watson Boating Area.

CLYDE WATSON BOATING AREA. Address: 17901 Magruders Ferry Road. **Parking:** free. **Hours:** 8 a.m. to 8 p.m. **Fees:** none. **Facilities:** picnic tables, restrooms, boat ramp, and pier. **Contacts:** 301-627-6074; www.pgparks.com/ Things_To_Do/Nature/Clyde_Watson_Boating_ Area. **Comment:** permit required for trailered boats; no permit required for launch of canoes and kayaks transported by car rooftop (*see* appendix C).

Here is the site where the British burned three hundred hogsheads of tobacco in the Moil and Magruder warehouse on June 17, 1814. Walk to the end of the pier on the Patuxent River and look upriver (north). At the first point on the same side of the river, pilings off the end of Magruders Ferry Road are visible at low tide. These are the remains of a late-nineteenth-century steamboat wharf built near where the 1814 tobacco warehouse was once located.

Exit the park and turn left (west) on Magruders Ferry Road to Croom Road. Turn right (north) and continue another 1.8 miles to the intersection with Whites Landing Road. Whites Landing served as a temporary base for the Chesapeake Flotilla.

There is no public access at this landing so continue north on Croom Road another 2.3 miles (4.1 miles from Magruders Ferry Road intersection) to the intersection with Tanyard Road on your right (east). Tanyard Road existed by 1739. Take Tanyard Road 1.8 miles to Nottingham.

As the British neared Nottingham, a few shots were fired at the advance guard resulting in one American casualty before the Americans fled.

Rear Adm. George Cockburn wrote his account of the taking of Nottingham on August 21, 1814: *On approaching the Town a few shots were exchanged between the leading Boats and some of the Enemy's Cavalry, but the appearance of our army advancing caused them to retire with precipitation.*

Lt. George Robert Gleig wrote on August 21, 1814: *We came in at dusk to a good-sized village called Nottingham, where the enemy's flotilla had been, but on our approach they moved higher up the river. The boys caught a parcel of turkeys and geese on which we made a capital supper and slept under the shade of an old barn full of Tobacco.*

At the intersection of Tanyard Road and Nottingham Road go left (north) on Nottingham Road 0.1 mile to a dirt driveway on the right (east). Turn onto this drive and park near the historic **NOTTINGHAM SCHOOL.** Here you will find interpretive signage about Nottingham and the War of 1812. Note the ravine just to the south of the school. This trace was once a "rolling road." Hogsheads of tobacco were rolled down to the water on the road to be shipped to Europe. Several remains of rolling roads still survive along the Patuxent River.

NOTTINGHAM SCHOOL INTERPRETIVE AREA. Address: 17412 Nottingham Road. **Parking:** free. **Hours:** daylight hours. **Fees:** none. **Facilities:** interpretive signage. **Contact:** 301-627-6074. **Comment:** Nottingham was once a bustling river port but today it is a sleepy residential village. Please respect private property.

Surprised Militiamen Pose as Squirrel Hunters

During the British advance, reports were received that American troops were lurking in the woods and preparing an ambush. The British increased their flanking patrols. Lt. George Robert Gleig wrote the following humorous account on August 21, 1814:

I thought I could perceive something like the glitter of arms a little farther towards the middle of the wood. Sending several files of soldiers in different directions, I contrived to surround the spot, and then moving forward, I beheld two men dressed in black coats, and armed with bright firelocks, and bayonets, sitting under a tree; as soon as they observed me, they started up and took to their heels, but being hemmed in on all sides, they quickly perceived that to escape was impossible, and accordingly stood still. I hastened towards them and having got within a few paces of where they stood, I heard the one say to the other, with a look of the most perfect simplicity, "Stop, John till the gentlemen pass." There was something so ludicrous in this speech, and in the cast of the countenance which accompanied it, that I could not help laughing aloud; nor was my mirth diminished by their attempts to persuade me that they were quiet country people, come out for no other purpose than to shoot squirrels. When I desired to know whether they carried bayonets to charge the squirrels, as well as muskets to shoot them, they were rather at loss to a reply; but they grumbled exceedingly when they found themselves prisoners, and conducted as such to the column.

Nottingham served as the naval base for the American Chesapeake Flotilla during July and August 1814. This important port town had a much larger population during the War of 1812 than it does today. Here the Georgetown Dragoons passed through Nottingham about noon, June 20, 1814, on their way to unsuccessfully defend Benedict from a British landing. Nottingham was abandoned as an American naval base after a brief skirmish between thirty dragoons under Secretary of State James Monroe and British expeditionary forces under Maj. Gen. Robert Ross. From about 6 p.m. on August 21 to about 8 a.m. on August 22, 1814, the British troops established their third camp here (the first was at Benedict and the second was at Patuxent City) while thirty to forty British barges were anchored close by offshore. The inhabitants of Nottingham fled in such haste that it is said baking bread was left in the ovens.

Camped here early on the morning of August 22, 1814, Major General Ross, as he did again at Upper Marlboro, hesitated about continuing farther into the interior of enemy ter-

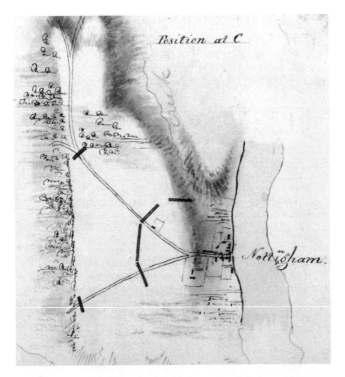

British 1814 sketch map showing the position of British troop deployment during their encampment at Nottingham. The bottom road leading to Nottingham is now called Tanyard Road. The upper road leading to Nottingham is now called Nottingham Road. The uppermost fork in this road shows Fenno Road branching to the right. It is this fork that the British are believed to have used to march toward Upper Marlboro. The lower left fork is what today is called Candy Hill Road. (Lt. Robert Smith, "Sketch of the march of the British army under M. Genl. Ross . . ."; Beinecke Rare Book and Manuscript Library, Yale University)

ritory before finally pursuing his march on Washington. The British rearguard that remained at Nottingham could see the red glow in the sky from the burning of Washington the night of August 24, 1814. Upon the victorious return of the British forces from Washington, vessels took on the wounded, artillery, and spoils of war from August 27 through 29. They sailed back to Benedict early in the morning of the 29th.

> ### "Flux & Measles"
>
> When the Nottingham militia was called to muster, only six appeared. In a letter dated July 12, 1814, local farmer Clement Hollyday, embarrassed by the poor showing, asked Urban Hollyday to tell no one for, "It would give them [the British] a bad opinion of our part of the county . . . Nottingham has been & is now very sickly. The inhabitants has the flux & measles."

Lt. George Robert Gleig wrote on August 28, 1814: *A gun-brig, with a number of ships' launches and long-boat, had made their way up the stream* [river], *and were at anchor opposite to the town. On board the former were carried such of the wounded as had been able to travel, whilst the later were loaded with flour and tobacco, the only spoil which we found it practicable to bring off . . . to our no small surprise we saw our friend Dr. Bean* [William Beanes] *brought in as a prisoner. On enquiring into the cause we learned that as soon as our troops had left the village* [Upper Marlboro] *he had armed his slaves, and sallied forth cutting off all our stragglers. As soon as the General heard of it, he sent back our Cossacks* [expert horsemen] *who took him out of his bed, and brought him off a prisoner.*

William Hill, who was also taken prisoner with Beanes, wrote his account that was published in 1890: *After the British had left Marlboro, I rode into town to see Dr. Beanes with whom I dined with General* [Robert] *Bowie and some others. Whist at the Doctor's we saw several stragglers belonging to the army of the enemy passing through town to join the army. We determined on making prisoners of them, and succeeded in taking five. I staid at the Doctor's that night, and about one o'clock we were taken out of our beds by the artillery drivers, consisting of about eighty-five men, all mounted, and with two lead horses for the doctor and myself. We were carried to Nottingham to General* [Robert] *Ross, who ordered us to be sent to the fleet . . . I was taken with Dr. Beanes and confined in the same ship with him as long as I remained a prisoner. The day of my discharge Gen. Ross sent for me on board the* Tonnat, *Admiral Cochran's flagship, and when I convinced him he addressed me in the following manner: . . . your detention was in consequence of an injustice that you were one of those who had met us with a flag on our entrance into* [Upper] *Marlboro, and in consequence your property had been protected. I thought you and Dr. Beanes were alike in trouble, . . . I shall let you return to your friends and family . . . He pointed to Mr. Weems, who was with me, and said that he could return with me, as he was under age and not found in arms.*

Turn right (northwest) back onto Nottingham Road and follow it out of Nottingham 0.7 mile to a fork. Turn right at the fork (north) staying on Nottingham Road. After another 0.4 mile, take a right (north) on Fenno Road (note: the two bridges over Mataponi Creek on Fenno Road are closed for replacement but are scheduled to reopen during the summer of 2011. Road signs will warm you if the bridges are still closed. If so, stay on Nottingham Road and turn right (north) on Croom Road and then right (east) on St. Thomas Church Road. By following this route you may reach the unpaved sunken section of Fenno Road discussed below).

Follow Fenno Road 1.6 miles to St. Thomas Church Road. Fenno Road has existed since at least 1729. The age of the road can also be appreciated by the extreme depth of the roadbed caused by hundreds of years of erosion. As they do today, large trees hung over the road providing welcome shade to the woolen-clad British soldiers who marched in the August heat of southern Maryland in 1814. Lt. George Robert Gleig wrote in his diary on August 22, 1814: "The road was well wooded, so the rays of the sun did not oppress us so much as usual."

Slow down where Fenno Road turns sharply to the left (west) and becomes St. Thomas Church Road. Look at the unpaved sunken road that continues to the north. This section of the road gives an impression of the conditions over which the British marched in 1814. Please note this road is private; do not trespass. At one time, Fenno Road apparently connected with Duvall and Chew roads.

Turn left (west) on St. Thomas Church Road and follow it 3.7 miles to St. Thomas Church on the right (north). South 0.2 mile off St. Thomas Church Road is Mattaponi (*see sidebar*) the former home of Governor Robert Bowie who assisted in rounding up British looters at Upper Marlboro following the burning of Washington.

ST. THOMAS EPISCOPAL PARISH is at the intersection of St. Thomas Church Road and Croom Road. Pull into the church parking lot on the right (east).

Mattaponi, Home of Governor Bowie

Located at 11000 Mattaponi Road, Mattaponi, which means "where the waters meet," is now owned by the Catholic Church. It can be seen from the parking area. The house was constructed circa 1745 for William Bowie and greatly altered in 1820 when one-story wings were added and the finishings on the central block were changed. Here lived Robert Bowie (1750–1818), governor of Maryland from 1803 to 1806 and 1811 to 1812 and a major general of the 1st Division, Maryland Militia, in 1812. When British stragglers began stealing on their way back to their ships on the Patuxent, Bowie was one of the citizens who seized them and placed them in custody. Upon learning of this incident, a contingent of British troops was sent back to Upper Marlboro and took Dr. William Beanes, who had orchestrated the capture (*see sidebar* Upper Marlboro and the Story of "The Star-Spangled Banner" *in this tour*), and two others who were later released, into custody. It was Francis Scott Key's attempt to secure the release of Dr. Beanes that led to the writing of the lyrics for "The Star-Spangled Banner." Bowie was born and died at Mattaponi. He is believed to be buried in the family graveyard located in a field across the road south of the house, although no marker for him is known.

Sunken unpaved road off Fenno Road illustrating the probable road conditions in 1814. (Ralph Eshelman 2005 photograph)

ST. THOMAS EPISCOPAL PARISH. NRHP. **Address:** 14300 St. Thomas Church Road. **Parking:** free. **Hours:** daylight hours. **Fees:** none. **Facilities:** historic graveyard. **Contacts:** 301-627-8469; http://stthomascroom.edow.org/history.shtml. **Comment:** Seven British soldiers are said to be buried adjacent to the Berry family plot on the north side of the church. They are marked by modern flat concrete squares along the east side of the Berry plot fence. The church is usually locked so only exterior views are possible.

St. Thomas Episcopal Parish, then called Page's Chapel, is on the route used by the British to advance toward Upper Marlboro.

American Brig. Gen. William Winder mentions this Chapel several times in his Committee of Investigation narrative of September 26, 1814: *intelligence was brought that the enemy was moving on from Nottingham in force toward the Chapel. I immediately proceeded, . . . to gain an observation of the enemy, and came within view of the enemy's advance about two miles below the Chapel. The observation was continued until the enemy reached the Chapel.*

St. Thomas Church was the home church of Anglican Bishop Thomas John Claggett, the first Episcopal Bishop consecrated in the United States. The bishop also established Trinity Church in Upper Marlboro in 1810 (*see optional side trip, below*). Claggett is buried at the National Cathedral in Washington. In 1812, President James Madison declared that the third Thursday in August be observed as a fast day of prayer and humiliation because of the recent declaration of war. Bishop Claggett ordered church services throughout the Diocese of Maryland and called for repentance and fasting so that the nation might be spared divine vengeance. On the presidential fast day the following year, September 9, 1813, Bishop Claggett instructed his followers to ignore the boycott of such services proposed by antiwar newspaper editors in Maryland and the District of Columbia: "Trusting that a call thus sanctioned by God, by the Church and by the Civil authority, will not be lightly regarded, I do direct and require the members of the said Church to repair to their respective parish churches on that day."

Continue on St. Thomas Church Road 0.1 mile to Croom Road. Turn right (north) on Croom Road and travel 0.3 mile north to the intersection with Duley Station Road. Duley Station Road came into use sometime between 1740 and 1762 and was known as the Woodyard Road during the War of 1812. Just before the entrance to Duley Station Road, the trace of the original road can be seen in the woods along a fence line on the left (west) side of Croom Road. This road trace joins present-day Duley Station Road a short distance from this intersection. Turn left (west) on Duley Station Road and drive 0.7 mile to the intersection with Bellefield Road (this road loops back onto Duley Station Road). Turn

Page's Chapel Pews

Many War of 1812 figures worshiped at Page's Chapel. Maj. Benjamin Oden, owner of nearby Bellefields, purchased pew no. 1; William Beanes (presumably Dr. William Beanes, not his half brother William Bradley Beanes) purchased pew no. 7 on the southeast square; and Governor Robert Bowie purchased pew no. 7 on the northwest square.

right (northwest) onto Bellefield Road, which is part of the original Woodyard Road. **BELLEFIELDS** is visible immediately ahead.

BELLEFIELDS. NRHP. Address: 13104 Duley Station Road. **Parking:** none. **Facilities:** none. **Comment:** this is private property; drive by only. Please respect private property and do not trespass.

Bellefields, also called Bellefields Estate, was Benjamin Oden's home (altered today from its 1814 appearance) where American Brig. Gen. William Winder and his army, along with Secretary of State James Monroe, marched from the American encampment at the Woodyard (*see* Woodyard Encampment *sidebar below*) to intercept Maj. Gen. Robert Ross and his British troops. It was believed that if the British advance went north on Croom Road

Secretary of State James Monroe and Brig. Gen. William H. Winder reportedly observed the British advance from the upper gable window at Bellefields. (John. O. Brostrup 1936 photograph; HABS, Library of Congress)

it was headed for the Chesapeake Flotilla and possibly north to Baltimore. If it turned left (west) on Duley Station Road the advance was probably headed toward Fort Washington and the capital. As the British came to this fork about 8:30 a.m., August 22, 1814, they saw American horsemen and swung left (along Duley Station Road) to attack. Lt. George Robert Gleig wrote in his diary on August 22, 1814: "Our advanced people had some little affair with the enemy's Cavalry, in which no one was killed."

The Americans withdrew toward Long Old Fields (*see below*). Major General Ross halted his British troops, then reversed his course and marched to Upper Marlboro along Croom Road. This confused the Americans who had thought the British were heading west toward either Fort Washington or the capital via that route.

Tradition holds that Oden gave his cattle to General Winder rather than be forced to sell them to the British. Reputedly, when these cattle where driven into Winder's camp about 2 a.m. on August 23, 1814, they caused a false alarm, the sentries mistaking them for British troops.

Continue on Bellefield Road 0.3 mile back to Duley Station Road. Turn left (east) and return 0.9 mile to the intersection with Croom Road. Turn left (north) on Croom Road. After traveling 1.3 miles, you will come to Mount Calvert Road on the right (east).

Optional Side Trip **MOUNT CALVERT.** Follow Mount Calvert Road 2.8 miles northeast.

Escaped Slave Mortally Wounded at Fort McHenry

African American William Williams was a slave who escaped Oden's farm in the Spring of 1814. He changed his name from Frederick Hall and enlisted in the U.S. Army at age 21, serving as a private in the 38th U.S. Infantry at Fort McHenry during the Battle for Baltimore. Williams's leg was blown off by a bomb fragment during the bombardment of Fort McHenry, and he later died from this wound. Before learning of this Oden advertised for his return:

Forty Dollars Reward

For apprehending and securing in jail

so that I can get him again,

NEGRO FREDERICK;

Sometimes calls himself FREDERICK HALL *a bright mulatto; straight and well made; 21 years old; 5 feet 7 or 8 inches high, with a short chub nose and so fair as to show freckles; he has no scars or marks of any kind that is recollected; his clothing when he left home, two months since, was home made cotton shirts, jacket, and Pantaloons of cotton and yarn twilled, all white. It is probable he may be in Baltimore, having a relation there, a house servant to a Mr. Williams, by the name of Frank, who is also a mulatto, but not so fair as Frederic.*

Benjamin Oden
Prince George's County, may 12ᵗʰ

(Baltimore *American and Commercial Daily Advertizer,* May 18, 1814)

MOUNT CALVERT HISTORICAL AND ARCHAEOLOGICAL PARK. Address: 16302 Mount Calvert Road. **Parking:** free. **Hours:** grounds open 8 a.m. to dusk year round; house and exhibits open April through October: Saturday, 8:30 a.m. to 5 p.m., Sunday, noon to 4 p.m., weekdays, by appointment. **Fees:** none. **Facilities:** small boat landing (no put in or takeout), restrooms open during house hours. **Contacts:** 301-627-1286; pgparks.com/places/parks/mtcalvert. html. **Comment:** this location provides an impressive view of the Patuxent River.

Mount Calvert is the site where Rear Adm. George Cockburn landed his seamen and Royal Marines to join the march on Washington following the destruction of the Chesapeake Flotilla further up the river above Pig Point. Just offshore, on the evening of August 22, 1814, Cockburn, aboard a tender from the H.M. brig *Resolution,* wrote a report detailing "the complete destruction of this Flotilla of the Enemy which has lately occupied so much of our time."

Rear Adm. George Cockburn reported to Vice Adm. Alexander Cochrane on August 27, 1814: *I instantly sent orders for our marine and naval forces at Pig Point to be forthwith moved over to Mount Calvert, and for the marines, marine artillery, and a proportion of the seamen to be there landed, and with the utmost expedition to join the army, which I also most readily agreed to accompany.*

Bristol Landing, originally called Pig Point, can be seen across the river, toward the northeast. Pig Point is named for bars of pig iron made at the Snowden Iron Furnace, barged downriver and from there transported to sailing ships.

Rear Admiral Cockburn reported to Vice Adm. Alexander Cochrane on August 22, 1814: *As we opened the reach above Pig Point I plainly discovered Commodore Barney's broad pendent in the headmost vessel, a large sloop, and remainder of the Flotilla extending in a long line astern of her. Our boats now advanced toward them as rapidly as possible, but on nearing them we observed the sloop to be on fire, and she very soon afterward blew up. I now saw clearly that they were all abandoned and on fire with trains to their magazines, and out of the 17 vessels which composed this formidable and so much vaunted Flotilla, 16 were in quick succession blown to atoms, and the 17th, in which the fire had not taken, was captured. I found laying above the Flotilla under its protection 13 merchant schooners, some of which not being worth bringing away I caused to be burnt. Such as were in good condition I directed to be moved to Pig Point.*

Retrace your way back to Croom Road by following Mount Calvert Road 2.8 miles to the intersection with Mount Calvert Road Spur. Turn right (northwest) on Mount Calvert Road Spur and continue 0.1 mile to the intersection with Croom Road and make another right (north).

Continue 0.8 mile on Croom Road to the intersection with Croom Station Road. Turn right (north) on Croom Station Road and follow it 1.6 miles to Blue Star Memorial Highway (U.S. Route 301). Croom Station Road is another early road (in use by 1739). Cautiously take a right (north) on U.S. Route 301; as soon as possible, move to the left-hand lane; continue 0.3 mile to the intersection with Chew Road. Chew Road once connected with Duval Road. This is the route the British used to march to Upper Marlboro. Chew Road may have been in use as early as 1706 but certainly was by 1739. Rear Admiral Cockburn and his contingent of marines and sailors from Mount Calvert also probably used Chew Road when they marched to Upper Marlboro on August 23, 1814.

Cautiously turn left (west) across U.S. Route 301 (this is a busy and dangerous intersection) and follow Chew Road 0.4 mile to the intersection with Croom Station Road. After traveling 0.2 mile you will come to an intersection with Old Croom Station Road on the right (north). This road once joined with Old Crain Highway, but Route 4 now truncates that route. British troops took this route to Upper Marlboro. Continue 0.3 mile on Croom Station Road and turn right (north) onto Old Crain Highway.

About 0.1 mile on the left (northwest) is William Beanes Road, named after the doctor whose imprisonment by the British led, indirectly, to our national anthem. It was while securing Dr. Beanes's release that Francis Scott Key viewed the bombardment of Fort McHenry. Continue 0.1 mile over the Route 4 overpass. About 0.1 mile on the right (east), you can catch a glimpse of the old original road trace of Croom Station Road. Continue 0.5 mile on Old Crain Highway, which becomes Main Street at **UPPER MARLBORO**. Continue east on Main Street 0.2 mile and turn left (north) on Water Street. Follow Water Street 0.1 mile north to the intersection with Governor Oden Bowie Drive. Turn right (east) and follow Governor Oden Bowie Drive 0.3 mile to the entrance of Darnall's Chance on left (north). Park here.

Upper Marlboro was established in 1706 on the Western Branch of the Patuxent River. Because two towns on the Patuxent River were named for the first Duke of Marlborough, one became Upper Marlboro and the other Lower Marlboro (*see optional side trip under Southern Maryland Tour in part 2*).

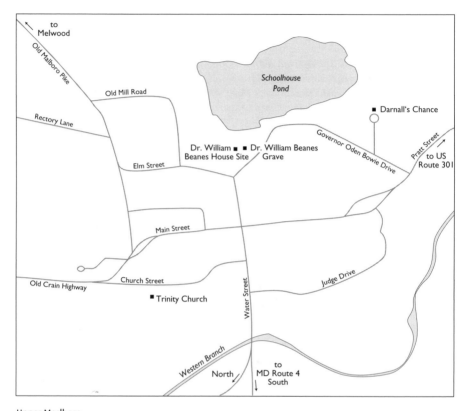

to
Melwood

Old Malboro Pike

Old Mill Road

Rectory Lane

Elm Street

Schoolhouse
Pond

Darnall's Chance

Dr. William ■ ■ Dr. William Beanes
Beanes House Site / Grave

Governor Oden Bowie Drive

Pratt Street

to US
Route 301

Main Street

Old Crain Highway

Church Street

Water Street

Judge Drive

■ Trinity Church

Western Branch

North

to
MD Route 4
South

Upper Marlboro

On August 22, 1814, after abandoning their boats above Pig Point, American Com. Joshua Barney and nearly 400 Chesapeake Flotillamen passed through Upper Marlboro. They joined Brigadier General Winder's troops assembling at an encampment known as Long Old Fields. Later that same day, Rear Adm. George Cockburn and approximately 400 marines and sailors, who had debarked at Mount Calvert on the Patuxent River, joined Maj. Gen. Robert Ross and approximately 4,400 British regulars who had landed at Benedict. The combined British force encamped here from August 22 until noon August 23 before continuing its march to Washington.

British Lt. George Robert Gleig's memory of entering Upper Marlboro was published in 1821: *several bodies of the enemy's horse occasionally showing themselves, and what appeared to be the rear-guard of a column of infantry evacuating* [Upper] *Marlborough, as our advance entered. There was, however, little or no skirmishing, and we were allowed to remain in the village all night without molestation.*

Gleig wrote in his diary August 22, 1814: *Came in at one o'clock to a nice village called* [Upper] *Marlboro, where we bivouacked in a large green field. Got plenty of fowls and for once ate a hearty dinner undisturbed. Chose a snug situation with some trees, where we brought some hay, and passed the night very comfortably.*

Gleig published his memory of Upper Marlboro in 1847: *The village itself lies in a valley formed by two green hills; the distance from the base of one hill to the base of the other may be about two miles, the whole of which was laid out in fields of corn, hay, and tobacco; whilst the slopes themselves were covered with sheep, for whose support they furnished ample means . . . the houses are scattered over the plain, and along the sides of the hills, at considerable intervals from one another, and are all surrounded by orchards and gardens, abounding in peaches and other fruits of the most delicious flavour. To add to the beauty of this place, a small rivulet makes it way though the bottom, and winding round the foot of one of these ridges, falls into the Patuxent* [Western Branch] *, which flows at its back.*

After capturing Washington, the British returned to Upper Marlboro, encamping here from late afternoon August 26 to early morning August 27. Lt. George Robert Gleig reported that near here many slaves offered to serve as either soldiers or sailors, if given their liberty. Maj. Gen. Robert Ross refused, probably fearing they would delay the march back to the ships. The Maryland State records were moved here from Annapolis for protection during the war. Ironically, Annapolis was never attacked while Upper Marlboro was occupied by British troops. By this time, however, the public records had been moved again to nearby Mount Lubentia (*see* Mount Lubentia *sidebar in* Battle of Bladensburg Tour *in part 1*).

Begin your tour at **DARNALL'S CHANCE**, built between 1741 and 1742, remodeled in 1857, and restored to its original appearance in 1986.

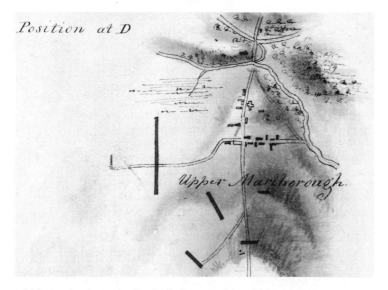

Position at D

Upper Marlborough.

British 1814 sketch map showing the deployment of the British troops encamped at Upper Marlboro. This sketch is not oriented with north at top of the map. Main Street runs top (northeast) to bottom (southwest) and Water Street is the cross road running to the right (southeast) terminating at the Western Branch of the Patuxent River. Water Street becomes Old Mill Road and Old Marlboro Pike to the left (northwest). British troops encamped along what today are Old Crain Highway and Old Marlboro Pike to the west and southwest of the village. (Lt. Robert Smith, "Sketch of the march of the British army under M. Genl. Ross . . ."; Beinecke Rare Book and Manuscript Library, Yale University)

Upper Marlboro and the Story of "The Star-Spangled Banner"

When the British withdrew through Upper Marlboro, stragglers plundered the nearby farms. Several men, including Dr. William Beanes, seized them and confined them at nearby Queen Anne's Town. One of the prisoners managed to escape and take word of the captures to his comrades. When Major General Ross learned of the captures, he ordered a contingent of mounted horsemen to seek their release and to arrest Beanes, whom he held responsible. The British search party seized several Americans (including Beanes), holding them as hostages and threatening to torch Upper Marlboro if the British prisoners were not returned. With little choice, the townsmen released their captives, but the British took three American citizens, including Doctor Beanes, to the British flagship, H.M. ship-of-the-line *Tonnant*, but only Beanes was ultimately confined.

A friend of Beanes's, Richard E. West, hurried to Georgetown to urge his brother-in-law, Francis Scott Key, a prominent attorney in the District of Columbia, to seek Beanes's release. Key consulted with President James Madison, who sent the young attorney to Brig. Gen. John T. Mason, the U.S. commissioner for prisoners. Mason gave Key a letter addressed to the British asking for Beanes's release on the grounds that he was a civilian noncombatant. Mason then sent Key to Baltimore to meet John Stuart Skinner, the U.S. agent for the exchange of prisoners, who was to join Key on his mission. The two men set sail in a flag-of-truce boat down the Patapsco River into Chesapeake Bay, where on September 7, 1814, they met the British fleet at the mouth of the Potomac River and boarded *Tonnant*.

Vice Adm. Alexander Cochrane graciously invited the American visitors to dinner. To buttress their case for Beanes's release, Skinner presented letters from wounded British soldiers left behind after the Battle of Bladensburg giving testimony to the kind treatment that they had received from their American captors, including Doctor Beanes. Major General Ross was moved by these letters and informed Skinner and Key that the doctor could return with them, but only after a planned attack on Baltimore was over, lest the Americans share any intelligence that they might have picked up during their visit.

Aboard the flag-of-truce boat during the bombardment of Fort McHenry, Key paced the deck, and the next morning saw that the British assault squadron had called off its attack and was heading back down the Patapsco River toward Chesapeake Bay. The successful defense of Fort McHenry so moved him that he composed lyrics to a tune to commemorate the occasion. The tune was a gentlemen's drinking song, called "Anacreon in Heaven," written in 1780. The three Americans soon returned to Baltimore, and Key spent the night perfecting his work. "The bombs bursting in air" refers to the British 190-pound mortar shells, many of which exploded over the fort. The "rockets red glare" refers to the Congreve rockets (similar to modern sky rockets) that were fired at the fort.

The lyrics were published as a handbill under the title "Defence of Fort M'Henry," but were soon re-titled "The Star-Spangled Banner." It was an instant hit and remained popular throughout the nineteenth century. On March 3, 1931, Congress proclaimed the tune and the lyrics the national anthem.

DARNALL'S CHANCE. Address: 14800 Governor Oden Bowie Drive. **Parking:** free. **Hours:** open tours available Friday and Sunday, noon to 4 p.m.; tours by appointment Tuesday through Thursday, 10 a.m. to 4 p.m. **Fees:** $3 adults, $2 seniors, $1 children 18 and under. **Facilities:** house museum, museum store, restrooms, and tourist information. **Contacts:** 410-952-8010; www.pgparks.com/places/eleganthistoric/darnalls_history.html. **Comment:** it is a pleasant 0.3 mile walk partially along a mill pond to Dr. William Beanes's tomb. It is another 0.3 mile walk from the gravesite to Trinity Church. Bicycles are an alternative method of transportation for touring Upper Marlboro.

When a detachment of British troops returned to Upper Marlboro to retrieve straggling soldiers incarcerated by local citizens, John Hodges, who lived here from 1800 until 1825, reluctantly released them from nearby Queen Anne's Town (Queen Anne). For his actions, Hodges was tried for treason. Defended by William Pinkney, Attorney General of Maryland in 1805 and Attorney General of the United States from 1811 until 1814, Hodges was found not guilty. In Darnall's Chance is a small diorama on the second floor correctly depicting Dr. Beanes, John Stuart Skinner, and Francis Scott Key, all observing the bombardment of Fort McHenry.

From Darnall's Chance, walk, bike, or ride to **WILLIAM BEANES'S GRAVE AND HOUSE SITE.**

DR. WILLIAM BEANES'S GRAVE AND HOUSE SITE. Location: Academy Hill at the corner of 14518 Elm Street and Governor Oden Bowie Drive. **Parking:** limited meter parking. **Hours:** daylight hours. **Fees:** none. **Facilities:** none. **Comment:** it is recommended that you walk to this site from Darnall's Chance.

Dr. William Beanes's Grave, located in what was probably the former garden of his home, was restored in 1914, partially from contributions from Prince George's County public school children during a centennial celebration sponsored by the National Star-Spangled Banner Centennial Commission. The inscription on a plaque on Beanes's grave claims Key wrote the national anthem when inspired by the defense of Fort McHenry. In fact, Key wrote lyrics to a song that after his death became the words to the national anthem in 1931. This plaque omits the fact that John Stuart Skinner, U.S. Agent for Prisoner Exchange, was also present, and that both negotiated the release of Beanes.

Dr. William Beanes's House Site is located just west of the tomb under an abandoned building, on Academy Hill, that served as a schoolmaster's house. Beanes's house burned down on July 25, 1855. British officers used Dr. Beanes's home as a headquarters during their occupation of the town. On the night of August 22, 1814, Maj. Gen. Robert Ross reportedly had dinner with Beanes. Rear Adm. George Cockburn met here with Ross on the morning of August 23, 1814, and persuaded him to attack Washington despite the lack of cavalry and limited artillery.

Cockburn reported the incident to Vice Adm. Alexander Cochrane on August 27, 1814: *I proceeded by Land . . . to Upper Marlborough, to meet and confer with Major General Ross as to our further operations against the Enemy, and we were not long in agreeing on the propriety of making an immediate attempt on the City of Washington.*

Dr. William Beanes, a Federalist, loathed President James Madison's administration, although in 1812 he was commissioned a lieutenant colonel in the 2nd Maryland Cavalry District, Prince George's County. Beanes and Major General Ross became acquainted during the British occupation of Upper Marlboro. Ross, however, became furious when Beanes later retained some British stragglers and a deserter, believing Beanes had betrayed him.

Francis Scott Key wrote to his mother, Anne Carlton Key, on September 2, 1814: *I am going in the morning to Balt^e. to proceed in a flag-vessel to Genl [Robert] Ross. Old D^r [William] Beanes of [Upper] Marlboro' is taken prisoner by the Enemy, who threaten to carry him off— Some of his friends have urged me to apply for a flag & go & try to procure his release. I hope to return in about 8 or 10 days, though it is uncertain, as I do not know where to find the fleet.*

Key wrote his father, John Ross Key, the same day: *I cannot go [to Frederick] yet, as I have to make a journey to the Fleet to try to get Dr. Beanes released from the Enemy—I hope I may succeed but think it very doubtful.*

Optional Side Trip **TRINITY CHURCH**

TRINITY EPISCOPAL CHURCH. Address: 14519 Church Street. **Contact:** 301-627-2636. **Comment:** the present church building dates from 1846 and 1896.

Anglican Bishop Thomas John Claggett established Trinity Church in 1810. Parish records confirm that British soldiers entered the church and tore pages from the parish register book.

The Parish Register reads: *No meeting from 21st May 1814 to 27 March 1815 owing to the situation into which the country was thrown by the invasion of the British army in August. . . . Several leaves here and some other parts of this book were torn out by some of [Maj. Gen. Robert] Ross's soldiers who found the book in the Church where it [was] put for safe keeping. To their eternal disgrace be it recorded, John Read Magruder, clerk of the vestry.*

This concludes the sites in Upper Marlboro. You can either take the optional side trip to Patuxent Wetlands Park or follow Old Marlboro Pike west to the next site at Melwood. To continue directly onto Melwood, travel back to Main Street (west) and turn right (north) at the intersection with Old Marlboro Pike (Route 725), one of the earliest roads in the area. Follow Old Marlboro Pike 3.7 miles to Melwood.

Optional Side Trip **PATUXENT WETLANDS PARK.** The scuttling of the Chesapeake Flotilla, under orders of the Secretary of Navy William Jones to prevent its capture, took place upstream from here on August 22, 1814. This park is the closest public access point to the scuttling site. Travel east on Route 4 approximately 1.5 miles past the Robert S. Crain Highway intersection (U.S. Route 310) and take the Waysons Corner exit on right (south). At stop sign turn left (north), cross over the overpass and exit left (west) to Patuxent Wetlands Park. A historical roadside marker (now missing) claims a cutter, gunboats, and thirteen barges were found near the bridge in the early 1900s. In fact, only one positively identified vessel from the flotilla scuttled above the bridge has been identified and that was in 1980. In 1998, two additional flotilla vessels were identified in St. Leonard Creek, Calvert County.

The remaining vessels of the flotilla are believed to lie under marshland since the river later changed its channel.

PATUXENT WETLANDS PARK. Location: northeast side of bridge that carries Southern Maryland Boulevard (Route 4) over Patuxent River, Anne Arundel County. **Parking:** free. **Hours:** daylight hours. **Fees:** none. **Facilities:** canoe, kayak landing. **Comment:** there is currently no War of 1812 interpretation at this site. This is a good location to see the upper tidal Patuxent River near where the Chesapeake Flotilla was scuttled. Keep valuables in your vehicle out of sight and lock all doors. *See* **Mount Calvert** for additional information on the flotilla scuttling. Launch a canoe or kayak and explore the river (*see* appendix C).

For those who took the optional side trip, return to Upper Marlboro and exit right (north) on Water Street, left (west) on Main Street, and turn right (north) at the intersection with Old Marlboro Pike (Route 725). For those who did not take the side trip, continue back to Main Street (west) and turn right (north) at the intersection with Old Marlboro Pike (Route 725), one of the earliest roads in the area. Follow Old Marlboro Pike 3.7 miles to **MELWOOD**.

MELWOOD. NRHP. Address: 11008 Old Marlboro Pike. **Comment:** no access; pass by only; views of the historic house can be seen on the right (north) side. Use caution as Melwood is located just beyond a blind curve.

Maj. Gen. Robert Ross and Rear Adm. George Cockburn reportedly invited themselves for dinner here at Melwood. (John O. Brostrup 1936 photograph; HABS, Library of Congress)

Melwood, also called Mellwood Parke, portions of which were built in 1714, became the home of William and Ignatius Digges (second son of Col. William Digges of Warburton Manor, the location of Fort Washington) in 1729. Tradition holds that British officers, including Maj. Gen. Robert Ross, invited themselves to a dinner hosted by widow Mary Carroll Digges. American scout Thomas McKenny stated that Major General Ross and Rear Admiral Cockburn slept in a small shed at the estate on the night of August 23, 1814. It is more likely that these officers rested or napped at Melwood after dinner while their troops passed by on their way to their next encampment near Belle Chance (now Andrews Air Force Base).

Continue 0.5 mile on Old Marlboro Pike to the intersection with Woodyard Road. North 2.4 miles at the intersection with Rosaryville Road is the site of the American encampment at Darnall's Delight, built prior to 1711 and later called Woodyard. Due to development there is little to see so only the most enthusiastic traveler will find it rewarding. But a brief overview of the encampment is in order as it was located at the strategic crossroad leading to the capital and Fort Washington. In July Brig. Gen. William H. Winder visited the Woodyard and reported that it would make a good encampment because any troops there would be within two hours travel of the Patuxent or Potomac rivers. On August 21, 1814, Woodyard served as a mustering site for Winder's troops.

Secretary of State James Monroe wrote to President Madison on the morning of August 22, 1814: *The enemy are advanced six miles on the road to the Wood Yard, and our troops are retiring. Our troops were on the march to meet them, but in too small a body to engage. General Winder proposes to retire til he can collect them in a body. The enemy are in full march for Washington. Have the material prepared to destroy the bridges. You had better remove the records.*

Colonel Allen McClane wrote that same night that he, *arrived at the woodyard . . . discovered that the enemy was also in motion. Question—what road he would take—that to Marlborough or that to Washington. Decided to watch both. The enemy soon after taking the former, the General* [Winder] *fell back on the Battalion's Old fields* [Long Old Fields is another encampment encountered later on the tour].

Marlboro Pike was truncated by the construction of Pennsylvania Avenue (Route 4). Therefore it is necessary to take a left (south) onto Woodyard Road, pass under Route 4, and make the first right (west) on to Marlboro Pike. Near Melwood Mall, 1 mile west on Marlboro Pike, on a little rise, a small unit of American volunteer artillery, attached to the District of Columbia militia, positioned six cannon flanked by militiamen. Before the British arrived, however, the Americans were ordered by Brigadier General Winder to pull back. They had barely begun to vacate the area when Major General Ross and other British officers appeared. The Americans fired two or three rounds of artillery and muskets at the approaching British before withdrawing; the first artillery to fire on the enemy in five days. Maj. George Peter, in command of the American forces, believed his men could have picked off Major General Ross and avoided the battle at Bladensburg had his men been armed with rifles instead of muskets, which were unreliable at that distance.

Maj. Gen. Robert Ross's report of the skirmish was reprinted in the Annapolis *Maryland Republican* December 10, 1814: *Having advanced to within sixteen miles of Washington, and ascertaining the force of the enemy to be such as might authorize an attempt at carrying his capitol, determined to make it and accordingly put the troops in movement on the evening of the 23rd. A corps of about 1200 men, appeared to oppose us, but retired after firing a few shot.*

Lt. George Robert Gleig wrote on August 23, 1814: *some Americans whom we could not see*

Woodyard Encampment

Woodyard was the home of Richard E. West. Reputedly, Com. Joshua Barney offered his services to Brigadier General Winder at this home. Gen. Stephen West, father of Richard West, was the commanding general of the Prince George's County Militia. Thus Woodyard was a major mustering ground and encampment for those units. West is buried in an unmarked grave at Woodyard. Poplar Hill, or His Lordship's Kindness, is within a mile of the encampment. This historic plantation was owned by Robert Sewall, who also owned the Sewall-Belmont House in the District of Columbia, which was torched by the British after shots had been fired from it, killing Maj. Gen. Robert Ross's horse.

This drawing of Woodyard depicts how the house appeared after the War of 1812 but before it was destroyed by fire in 1867. (Attributed to John Ross Key circa 1860s; courtesy Prince George's County Historical Society)

fired a volley at the General [Ross], *the balls of which came about us. We pushed on and saw a party drawn up on some heights, from which they threw* [fired] *two round shot* [cannonballs] *very correctly at us. They did not wait for us, but made off, the moment we advanced.*

Just before Melwood Mall, turn left (west) and continue 1.0 mile on Old Marlboro Pike that approximately follows the route of the old Eastern Branch Bridge Road. Old Marlboro Pike abruptly ends at the intersection with Dower House Road. The road originally continued beyond the gate on what today is called Fechet Avenue, within Andrews Air Force Base, before turning north. The British encamped there on the evening of August 23, 1814. The original road would have continued north to what today is Old Marlboro Pike, north of Suitland Parkway. To get back on the British route, turn right (north) on Dower House Road and travel 0.3 mile to the intersection with Route 4 (second traffic light) and turn left (west). Follow Route 4 for 2.0 miles under the Capital Beltway (I-495/95) to the intersection with Forestville Road. Turn right (north) on Forestville Road and travel for 0.2 mile before turning left on Marlboro Pike. You are now back on the British route. Follow Marlboro Pike

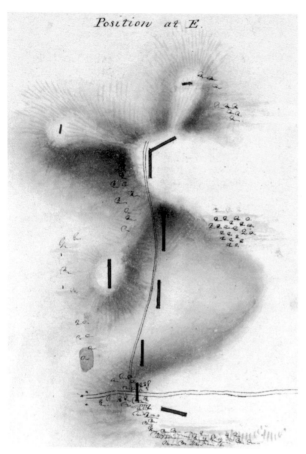

Position at E.

British 1814 sketch map showing the deployment of the British troops during their encampment on the evening of August 23, 1814. The road at the bottom is believed to represent a road that led west to the Alexandria ferry over the Potomac River and east to Upper Marlboro. The road to the north is believed to represent what was later called Old Marlboro Pike before Andrews Air Force Base was established. (Lt. Robert Smith, "Sketch of the march of the British army under M. Genl. Ross . . ."; courtesy of Beinecke Rare Book and Manuscript Library, Yale University)

0.5 mile to Boones Lane. Between here and Donnell Drive, at the present-day site of Penn-Mar Shopping Center, was the approximate site of the American encampment of **LONG OLD FIELDS,** also called Old Fields, and Battalion Old Field from August 22 to very early in the morning of August 24, 1814.

LONG OLD FIELDS [Penn-Mar Shopping Center]. **Address:** 7000 block of Marlboro Pike and Donnell Drive. **Parking:** free; no long-term or overnight parking allowed. **Comment:** this area is heavily developed and retains no historic integrity. There is no interpretation about the American encampment. There are several restaurants and fast food options here.

Long Old Fields was strategically located about midway between the 16 miles separating Washington and Upper Marlboro. Secretary of State James Monroe later wrote on November 13, 1814: "General Winder retired by the Woodyard to a place called the Old Fields, which covered equally Bladensburg, the bridges on the Eastern Branch [Anacostia River], and Fort Washington."

About thirty-two hundred men, including cavalry, encamped here. The army was supported by seventeen pieces of artillery. President James Madison, accompanied by three cabinet members, rode out from Washington to gauge the situation on August 22, 1814.

The already tired troops were roused by a false alarm at about 2 a.m. on the morning of August 23, 1814, possibly caused by cattle, given by Benjamin Oden from Bellefields, being driven into the camp. The awakened and exhausted troops were ordered to stay in readiness for troop formation at a moment's warning.

Gen. James Wilkinson described the night of August 22, 1814: *The camp was as open all night as a race-field, and the sailors and militia were as noisy as if at a fair; you might hear the countersign fifty yards when a sentry challenges. I made up my mind that if Ross, whose camp I had reconnoitred in the evening, was a man of enterprise, he would be upon us in the course of the night, and, being determined to die like a trooper's horse, I slept with my shoes on.*

The American army retired from the camp during the late hours of August 23 into the early hours of August 24, just before the British advance units arrived from Upper Marlboro.

Brig. Gen. William Henry Winder gave the following explanation for abandoning the camp: *My reason for not remaining at the Old Fields during the night [August 23, 1814] was, that, if an attack should be made in the night, our own superiority, which lay in artillery, was lost, and the inexperience of the troops would subject them to certain, infallible, and irremediable disorder, and probably destruction, and thereby occasion the loss of a full half of the force which I could hope to oppose, under favorable circumstances, to the enemy.*

Lead British patrols literally occupied the ground the Americans had just abandoned. Major General Ross and his troops passed through Long Old Fields on their way to Bladensburg about 4 a.m., August 24, 1814.

Lt. George Robert Gleig wrote of his remembrance of that morning published in 1821: *various fields on each side of the high road where smoking ashes, bundles of straw, and remnants of broken victuals were scattered about, indicated that considerable bodies of troops had passed the night in this neighbourhood. The appearance of the road itself, likewise, imprinted as it was with fresh marks of many feet and hoofs, proved that these troops could be no great way before us.*

During the early morning, the British could see a red glow in the western sky. The Benning Road Eastern Branch Bridge over the Anacostia River had been set on fire by the Americans.

In 1814, Addison Road probably connected directly to Marlboro Pike. The development of District Heights has altered this alignment so that today one must continue west on Marlboro Pike 0.8 mile to County Road on the right (not hard right on Gateway Street but soft second right). Turn right (north) on County Road and follow it 0.6 mile to the intersection with Walker Mill Road. Turn right (northeast) on Walker Mill and continue 0.3 mile to the intersection with Addison Road.

Bear left on Addison Road (north) and continue 2.2 miles to the intersection with Martin Luther King Highway (Route 704). There are two left-hand turn lanes; stay in the right so you can immediately turn back onto Addison Road after the jog to the left. Continue north on Addison Road 0.2 mile to the intersection with 62nd Place. Immediately after 62nd Place turn right into **ADDISON CHAPEL** (now St. Matthew's Anglican Catholic Church).

ADDISON CHAPEL. NRHP. **Address:** 5610 Addison Road. **Parking:** free. **Hours:** daylight hours. **Fees:** none. **Facilities:** none. **Comment:** the driveway into the property circles the chapel.

Addison Chapel was founded in 1696. The present structure was built between 1809 and 1816 and retains its original appearance except for the pitch of the roof altered in 1902. This chapel served as a temporary rest stop for the British troops during their march on Washington August 24, 1814. Francis Scott Key served as one of the lay readers at the chapel.

Exit the chapel drive and turn right (north) on Addison Road. Continue 0.5 mile to the intersection with Sheriff Road and turn right (east). Addison Road originally intersected with River Road, now essentially Kenilworth Avenue (Route 201). Addison Road has become truncated because of the construction of a railroad line, John Hanson Highway (U.S. Route 50), and Kenilworth Avenue. Thus the actual route the British took from here to Upper Marlboro is impossible to follow and a detour is necessary via Sheriff Road. Continue 0.8 mile on Sheriff Road to a traffic light at the intersection with Cabin Branch Drive on the left. Turn left (north) on Cabin Branch Drive and continue 0.7 mile to Columbia Park Road. Turn left (west) on Columbia Park Road and travel 0.5 mile over the overpass with John Hanson Highway. Just after crossing over John Hanson Highway turn right (northeast) onto Cheverly Avenue. Immediately on your right 0.1 mile is a small brick monument at **MAGRUDER SPRING** (also called Cheverly Spring).

MAGRUDER SPRING. Location: Cheverly Avenue and Arbor Street. **Parking:** free. **Hours:** daylight hours. **Fees:** none. **Facilities:** interpretive sign. **Comment:** there is no parking on Cheverly Avenue directly in front of the marker. Parking may be found further north on Cheverly Avenue and on Arbor Street at the next intersection.

The spring is actually located just below the embankment. The British reputedly stopped here to replenish their canteens. However, this location is about 0.5 mile east of River Road (Kenilworth Avenue) and seems too far out of the way from the known march route to be a logical watering stop. The original Addison Road crossing at Beaverdam Creek about 0.5 mile to the west is a more logical stop. This area is now completely disturbed by the construction of I-295 and U.S. Route 50.

Lt. George Robert Gleig wrote about his memory of this watering stop in his narrative published in 1821: *Numbers of men had already fallen to the rear, and many more could with difficulty keep up; consequently, if we pushed on much further without resting, the chances were that at least one half of the army would be left behind. To prevent this from happening, and to give time for the stragglers to overtake the column, an halt was determined upon and being led forward to a spot of ground well wooded, and watered by a stream which crossed the road, the troops were ordered to refresh themselves.*

Turn around and travel south 0.2 mile on Cheverly Avenue and turn right (west) at the intersection with Arbor Road (not to be confused with Arbor Street). Follow Arbor Road, which becomes Tuxedo Road, until it joins Kenilworth Avenue (Route 201). Follow Kenilworth

Avenue north toward Bladensburg. About 0.8 mile north from the Tuxedo Road and Kenilworth Avenue intersection, bear north on 52nd Avenue. Near the intersection with Inwood Street, the mausoleum at Fort Lincoln Cemetery can be seen on the hill across the Anacostia River to the left (west). Here and below the mausoleum is the site of the Bladensburg Battlefield, which despite its name is not actually in Bladensburg proper. The Americans, from their positions, could see the dust on the horizon as the British marched northwest toward Bladensburg. Continue north 0.4 mile on 52nd Avenue to just before the intersection with Newton Street where, on the right (east) side, is the entrance to the Evergreen Cemetery. Buried here are Bladensburg residents who lived during the war, including Dr. David Ross, Jr.,

Tory Encounter

While the British rested at Addison Chapel, tradition claims that a local celebrity of Tory principles rode up upon a fine horse to greet them. The Tory's horse looked like an aristocrat beside the British horses, dusty and tired from the long journey over rough roads. The British bade the Tory to dismount, which he did. Then, to his dismay, they took his horse and gave him, in return, a worn-out hack. The Tory rode disgustedly away, no longer pro-British, but an ardent rebel.

who tended to the wounded. Some British troops continued north on 52nd Street while other troops turned left (west) on Quincy Street and then right (north) on 48th Street (then known as Spring Street). In this fashion, the British approached Bladensburg in a pincer-like movement. Follow Quincy Street. At the corner of Quincy and 48th Street is Bostwick House (*see the next tour,* Bladensburg Battlefield). Continue north on 48th Street to the intersection with Annapolis Road (Route 450, then called West Street) and turn left (west). Just after the railroad overpass over Annapolis Road on the left (south) is the entrance to the Bladensburg Waterfront Park. Stop and park here.

This concludes the British Invasion Tour. The Bladensburg Battlefield Tour begins here.

Battle of Bladensburg Tour

Particulars The Bladensburg battlefield suffers from development that has destroyed much of the historic integrity of the site. Some historic fragments remain, however, that make a visit worthwhile. The best way to visit the battlefield is by a combination of vehicle and foot. A walk from the Bladensburg Waterfront Park to the American third line (over a mile uphill one way) and back and then to Bostwick and Lowdnes Hill totals between 3 and 4 miles. Bicycles can be used with caution but are not recommended on Baltimore Avenue (Alternate U.S. Route 1), Bladensburg Road, or Kenilworth Avenue because of the heavy traffic. There are several fast food options along Bladensburg Road. For more upscale dinning and lodging, go to the New Carrollton area, east of Bladensburg. (*For information about the British landing at Benedict and march to Bladensburg see the previous tour,* British Invasion.)

Historical Background One of America's greatest defeats in the war occurred here on August 24, 1814, at the Battle of Bladensburg. Over 4,000 British forces, many veterans of the Napoleonic Wars under the command of Maj. Gen. Robert Ross, routed the American forc-

This detail of an 1806 pencil watercolor depicts the bridge over the Eastern Branch (now Anacostia) from the northwest looking southeast. The buildings in the center and to the left show the western edge of the village of Bladensburg. The sails and mast illustrate the port of Bladensburg. The bridge in this sketch is probably little changed from the bridge that the British crossed to attack the American defenders. (Benjamin H. Latrobe, *Sketch of Bladensburg, looking Northward* [southeastward?]; courtesy of The Maryland Historical Society)

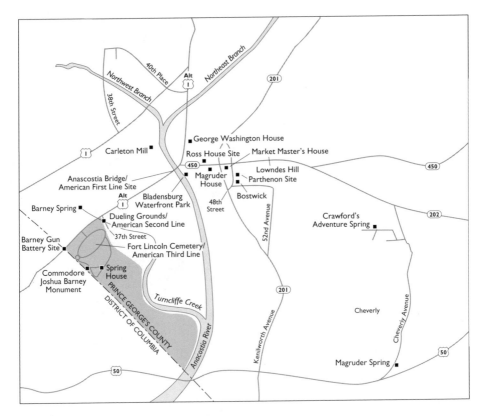

Bladensburg

es under the command of Brig. Gen. William Henry Winder. The American army consisted of approximately 6,000 largely raw militia, 1,000 regulars, 500 sailors from the Chesapeake Flotilla, and 114 U.S. Marines. The battle took place at Bladensburg because it provided the nearest fordable point across the Eastern Branch of the Potomac River, now called the Anacostia River. Here British forces could march on Washington without crossing a bridge. The Americans had destroyed Stoddert's Bridge and Eastern Branch Bridge, both farther downriver in the deeper section of the Anacostia. Brig. Gen. Tobias Stansbury and his troops from Baltimore had been en route to the Washington Navy Yard when he learned the British were marching to Bladensburg. He reversed course and reached the bridge at Bladensburg, but instead of burning it, he placed his artillery and men at a position west or behind the bridge. Soon thereafter, on the morning of August 24, 1814, Winder and his troops arrived from Washington.

The American forces hastily set up three defensive lines (it can be argued only two lines were formed, the first line falling back to a secondary position where only a few troops were deployed) west of the river along the Bladensburg-Washington Road, where present-day Cottage City, Colmar Manor, and Fort Lincoln Cemetery are located. The American lines were too far apart to support one another or to provide cross-firing positions. The British forces arrived about noon and attacked at about 1 p.m. After a three-hour battle, fought

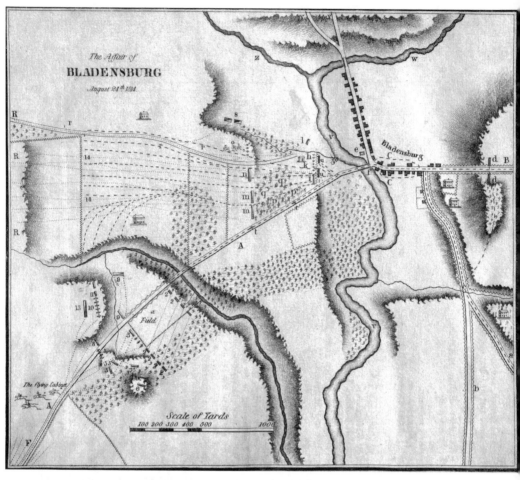

American 1816 map depicts the Battle of Bladensburg. Note detail of the president and his flying cabinet in the lower left corner. Key: a. Route of British from Long Old Fields. b. Road from the ferry to Bladensburg. c. British column divided here with contingent of troops ascending Lowndes Hill while a flanking detachment continued directly into Bladensburg. d. British troops formed here and halted for 20 to 30 minutes while Maj. Gen. Robert Ross observed the American positions. f. Bridge over Anacostia River. g. Mill later called Carleton's Mill. r r r. Road to Georgetown. v v. Eastern Branch (now Anacostia) of Potomac River. w. Northeast Branch. z. Northwest Branch. x. Turnpike road to Baltimore. y. Old road to Baltimore. A A. Turnpike to Washington City. B. Road to Governor's Bridge, Queen Anne, and Upper Marlboro by which the enemy retreated. C C. British advancing the attack. F. Retreat of the U.S. Marines, U.S. Chesapeake Flotillamen, District of Columbia and Maryland militiamen, and U.S. and militia dragoons. - - - March of the British. ••• Retreat of American troops. R R R. Retreat of Baltimore and other militia units. ("The Affair of Bladensburg August 24th, 1814," James Wilkinson 1816; Fort McHenry National Historic Monument collections; see *The War of 1812 in the Chesapeake: A Reference Guide to Historic Sites in Maryland, Virginia, and the District of Columbia,* by Ralph E. Eshelman, Scott S. Sheads, and Donald R. Hickey [Johns Hopkins University Press, 2010], p. 85, for a more detailed description of this map)

badly by both sides but especially by the Americans, the British outflanked and eventually routed the American first line, which collapsed into the second line, causing even greater confusion and leading to a general and disorganized retreat. Only the third line, manned by Com. Joshua Barney, his flotillamen, U.S. Marines, and militiamen, supported by five heavy naval guns, delayed the British advance by about thirty minutes before giving way. The British rested for two hours and then resumed their march on Washington, arriving about 8 p.m.

Dignitaries present during the early phases of the engagement included President James Madison, Secretary of State James Monroe, Secretary of Navy William Jones, Attorney General Richard Rush, and Secretary of War John Armstrong. For the first time in American history, the president as well as other high-ranking members of the government assumed an active role in the field in time of war. Some directed troop movements.

President James Madison wrote his wife, Dolley, from Bladensburg on August 24, 1814: *My dearest I have passed among the troops who are in high sprits and make a good appearance. The reports as to the enemy has varied from hour to hour, the last and probably best information is that they are not very strong and are without cavalry and artillery and of course they are not in a condition to strike at Washington.*

British Lt. George Robert Gleig's account of the American position was published in 1847: *They [Americans] were drawn up in three lines upon the brow of a hill, having their front and left flank covered by a branch of the Potomac, and their right resting upon a thick wood and a deep ravine. This river . . . flowed between the heights occupied by the American forces, and the little town of Bladensburg.—Across it was thrown a narrow bridge, extending from the chief street in that town to the continuation of the road, which passed through the very center of their position; and its right bank (the bank above which they were drawn up) was covered with a narrow stripe of willows and larch trees, whilst the left was altogether bare, low, and exposed. Such was the general aspect of their position as at the first glance it presented itself.*

African American Charles Ball's account of the battle was published in 1836: *If the militia regiments, that lay upon our right and left, could have been brought to charge the British, in close fight, as they crossed the bridge, we should have killed or taken the whole of them in a short time; but the militia ran like sheep chased by dogs.*

British Rear Adm. George Cockburn reported to Vice Adm. Alexander Cochrane on August 27, 1814: [Maj. Gen. Robert] *Ross, however, did not hesitate in immediately advancing to attack [the Americans], although our troops were almost exhausted with the fatigue of the march they had just made, and but a small proportion of our little army had yet got up . . . in spite of the galling fire of the enemy, our troops advanced steadily on both flanks, and in his front; and as soon as they arrived on even ground with him, he fled in every direction, leaving behind him ten pieces of cannon, and a considerable number of killed and wounded; amongst the later Commodore [Joshua] Barney, and several other officers; some other prisoners were also taken, though not many owing to the swiftness with which the enemy went off, and the fatigue our army had previously undergone . . . that the Enemy, Eight thousand Strong, on Ground he had chosen as best adapted for him to defend, where he had time to erect his Batteries, and concert all his measures, was dislodged as Soon as reached, and a Victory gained over him by a Division of the British Army, not amounting to more than Fifteen hundred men.*

On December 10, 1814, the Annapolis *Maryland Republican* printed an extract of a report by Congressman Richard M. Johnson from the committee appointed to enquire into the causes of the capture of Washington: [Brig. Gen. William Henry Winder] *harassed and exposed the troops he had actually under his command to such an extent, as to incapacitate them from being as efficient as they otherwise would have been . . . arranged and commanded them with such miserable skill as to be beaten ... that although some of the men did not act with bravery, but disorderly, there was a sufficient force on the ground, if it had been well arranged to have beaten the enemy; that the general is unfit for any important command, and that to him, principally, the enemy is indebted for his success of that day's.*

The American rout, derided as the "Bladensburg Races," has sometimes been called "America's Darkest Hour." Capt. Joseph Hopper Nicholson wrote to Secretary of Navy William Jones on August 28, 1814: *Good God! How have we been disgraced? Our cursed militia have been coming in one, two, and three at a time, and all speak highly of their gallantry.*

Begin your tour of the battlefield at **BLADENSBURG WATERFRONT PARK.** Use the Bladensburg map to help plan your visit.

BLADENSBURG WATERFRONT PARK. Address: 4601 Annapolis Road. **Parking:** free. **Hours:** grounds open 7 a.m. to sunset; visitor center open 9 a.m. to 4 p.m. **Facilities:** restrooms, picnic tables. **Contacts:** 301-779-0371; www.pgparks.com/places/nature/bladensburg.html. **Comment:** since there is no parking on Bladensburg Road, visitors should park here and walk across the pedestrian bridge to the opposite side of the river where the battlefield is located. The American first line was located at the west end of the Bladensburg Road Bridge. A second, shorter option is to continue by vehicle west on Bladensburg Road across the bridge and make a right (north) on 43rd Avenue and then right (east) on Bunker Hill Road. There is street parking at the end of the road, and the west end of the bridge is only a short walk away. Parking at Bladensburg Waterfront Park is the preferred option as it includes views of the British river crossing site. Bicycles may be used to access many of the Bladensburg sites but it is recommended to avoid Bladensburg and Annapolis roads.

Bladensburg Waterfront Park is located along the Anacostia River and provides a good view of the site where the British crossed a bridge and attacked the first line of the American defenses. Three War of 1812–related panels interpret the site. Walk west across the pedestrian bridge over the Anacostia River (or drive to Bunker Hill Road). Follow the riverside walk north under the Bladensburg Road Bridge and then west to view the site of the American first line (total distance approximately 0.3 mile).

The deployment of the American first line can be imagined from near the west end of the Bladensburg Road Bridge. The forks of the Northwest and Northeast branches of the Anacostia can be seen upriver. This fork or V is mentioned in many of the contemporary accounts of the battle. Bladensburg Road continues southwest toward Washington. At a diagonal to the west (slightly off to the right as you face the battlefield) one can see a berm built by the U.S. Corps of Engineers in the 1950s to control floods. Just to the left of the berm is Bunker Hill Road, then called Georgetown Pike. Most of the militiamen used this road as they retreated from the British advance.

Georgetown Pike intersected what today is Rhode Island Avenue, but the road is now blocked by a railroad line. An American gun battery was located behind earthworks hastily dug by citizens of Washington between this road and Bladensburg Road, approximately where a brick commercial building now stands. The actual bridge that crossed the river near this spot was a narrow wooden structure capable of accommodating only three persons standing side by side. To view the Carleton Mill (*see sidebar*) site, walk approximately 0.2 mile northwest to the intersection of Bunker Hill Road and 43rd Avenue. The mill was

Grist Mill

Carleton Mill was located near the north end of 43rd Avenue and Bunker Hill Road, Carleton Park, Cottage City. The grist mill, possibly used as a field hospital by the British, is mentioned in many of the official reports written after the battle. It was built in 1727 and owned by the family of Col. William Dudley Digges in 1814, although it has long since been named for Henry L. Carleton, who purchased it in 1857. In ruins by the 1950s, the mill was demolished by the Army Corps of Engineers during construction of flood-control measures. Two mill stones from Carleton Mill were incorporated into the private walkway at 3718 42nd Avenue, at the intersection with Bunker Hill Road, but since then they have been moved to the Market Master's House. Stones forming the wall at the 42nd Avenue property are said to be from the mill foundation. Please respect private property and do not trespass.

Carleton Mill as depicted in the 1850s with Bladensburg in the background. (Lossing, *Pictorial Field-Book of the War of 1812*)

located on the north side of Bunker Hill Road in a clump of trees in the park. Return to Bladensburg Waterfront Park and either walk to other sites such as Bostwick or continue your tour by vehicle to the American third line at Fort Lincoln Cemetery.

The **AMERICAN SECOND LINE** stretched on both sides of Bladensburg Road. The east side of the line was located roughly at a popular dueling grounds. Most of the battle took place on the northwest side of Bladensburg Road. It can be argued that the second line more correctly is where the first line repositioned after falling back from its first position.

AMERICAN SECOND LINE. Location: The American second line is poorly defined; it was concentrated on the north side of Bladensburg Road (Alternate U.S. Route 1) but shifted to the south side during the battle. The dueling grounds located at 37th Avenue are often said to be the location of the second line, but this is only a generalization. The area is heavily developed. **Parking:** parking can be found near the recreational ballfields on 38th Avenue. **Facilities:** none. **Comment:** there is little to see at this site as the original historic integrity has been greatly altered. Since there is no convenient parking and it is a bit of a hike (0.7 mile) from the Bladensburg Waterfront Park, it is recommended this site be skipped. Go directly to the American third line from which one can see the relative relationship to the American second line.

The American troops weren't interested in the dueling grounds per say, they were interested in the slight elevation just before Turncliffe Creek and the ravine formed by the creek. This provided a topographical advantage for the troops positioned there. But that advantage was lost when the first line panicked into the second line causing them to hastily retreat as well.

The **AMERICAN THIRD LINE** was located essentially along the District of Columbia–Maryland line with its center at Bladensburg Road.

AMERICAN THIRD LINE. Address: Fort Lincoln Cemetery, 3401 Bladensburg Road (Alternate U.S. Route 1), just northeast of Washington, D.C. / Maryland boundary. **Parking:** limited, at the mausoleum. **Hours:** 6:30 a.m. to dusk. **Facilities:** none. **Comment:** this is a private cemetery; visitors should show respect for the purposes of the property and not interfere with any funeral processions. The cemetery entrance is approximately 1 mile west from the Bladensburg Waterfront Park. The Barney monument near the mausoleum is about another 0.5 mile by road inside the cemetery. The Barney battery site on Bladensburg Road, at the District of Columbia line, is 0.2 mile north from the cemetery entrance.

The right flank of the American third line stood on what today is Fort Lincoln Cemetery, incorporated in 1912 and embracing 178 acres. Maj. George Peter's Georgetown Artillery was located on the northwest side of Bladensburg Road while the Chesapeake Flotillamen and U.S. Marines formed the center of the line near Bladensburg Road. These U.S. troops (not militia) offered the only effective American resistance during the battle. Com. Joshua Barney, commander of the flotilla, had been stationed on the Eastern Branch of the Potomac River in what is now known as Barney Circle, Pennsylvania Avenue, Southeast, Washington, D.C. (west side of John Phillip Sousa Bridge). Upon learning of the British approach at Bladensburg, Barney persuaded his superiors to grant him permission to join the fight. He and his men made a quick march to a position on Bladensburg Pike (now Bladensburg Road) at the District line. After displaying much courage, these troops were outflanked. Barney, by then wounded, ordered his men to retreat. Shortly after, Barney was taken prisoner and paroled on the spot by the British officers in acknowledgment of his bravery. Capt. Samuel Miller, in command of the U.S. Marines, was also wounded, al-

Dueling Grounds

Tradition claims that over fifty duels took place here, although only twenty-six are documented. One duel was held during the war on March 12, 1814, between Lieutenants Hall and Hopkins.

> The Baltimore *Patriot & Evening Advertiser* reported the duel on March 15, 1814: *We understand that a duel was fought on Saturday last, near Bladensburg, between lieut. [?] Hall and lieut. [?] Hopkins, both of col. [Henry] Carberry's regiment. At the second fire, lieut. Hopkins received the ball from his antagonist's pistol, in the breast, and expired immediately.*

Another duel, which took place on March 22, 1822, grew out of the *Chesapeake–Leopard* affair in 1807, an event that helped fuel the war. Com. James Barron commanded the U.S. frigate *Chesapeake* that surrendered to H.M. frigate *Leopard* off the Virginia Capes. Barron was court-martialed and suspended during hearings presided over by Com. Stephen Decatur. After years of exchanging rancorous letters, Barron challenged Decatur, who was mortally wounded in the duel. Gen. John Jackson, congressman from Virginia and brother-in-law of Dolley Payne Madison, was seriously wounded, but recovered, after a duel here in December 1809 with Joseph Pearson, a Federalist congressman from North Carolina. Also, Daniel Key, son of Francis Scott Key, was killed here in a duel in 1836.

Circa 1904 photograph of area of American Second Line entitled "Ravine at Bladensburg, Md., famed for fatal duels, near scene of British Victory, 1814." (From stereo-pair in collection of author)

though he managed to withdraw. Miller lost the use of an arm for the rest of his life. All of Barney's cannons were captured and destroyed.

Com. Joshua Barney wrote to Secretary of Navy William Jones on August 29, 1814: *I was informed the enemy was within a mile of Bladensburgh we hurried on, The day was hot, and my men much crippled from the severe marches we had experienced the preceding days. I preceded the men, and when I arrived at the line which separates the District from Maryland, the Battle began, I sent an officer back to hasten on my men, they came up in a trot, we took our position on the rising ground, . . . and waited the approach of the Enemy, during this period the engagement continued the enemy advancing, —our own Army retreating before them apparently in much disorder, at length the enemy made his appearance on the main road, in force, and in front of my Battery, and on seeing us made a halt, I reserved our fire, in a few minutes the enemy again advanced, when I ordered an 18 lb. to be fired, which completely cleared the road, shortly after a second and a third attempt was made by the enemy to come forward but all were destroyed, The enemy then crossed over into an Open field and attempted to flank our right, he was there met by three 12 pounders, the Marines under Capt. [Samuel] Miller and my men acting as Infantry, and again was totally cut up, by this time not a Vestige of the American Army remained except a body of 5 or 600 posted on a height on my right from whom I expected much support, from their fine situation, The Enemy from this point never appeared in force in front of us, they pushed forward their sharp shooters, one of which shot my horse under me, who fell dead between two of my Guns; The enemy who had been kept in check by our fire for nearly half an hour now began to out flank us on the right, our guns were turned that way, he pushed up the Hill, about 2 or 300 towards the Corps of Americans station'd as above described, who, to my great mortification made no resistance, giving a fire or two and retired, in this situation we had the whole army of the Enemy to contend with; Our Ammunition was expended, and unfortunately the drivers of my Ammunition Waggons had gone off in the General Panic, at this time I received a severe wound in my thigh . . . Finding the enemy now completely in our rear and no means of defense I gave orders to my officers and men to retire.*

L. O. Minear, former owner and president of Fort Lincoln Cemetery, established a tabular monument to Commodore Barney located just east of the cemetery mausoleum. A historic marker is near this monument. Both contain errors. The actual site of Barney's gun battery was farther to the northeast on Bladensburg Road at the District of Columbia line. That location has been called the brightest spot on the Bladensburg Battlefield. The monument has the U.S. Marine Corps insignia on its front and states "Barney and His Marines." Although Miller's marines were placed directly under the command of Barney during the engagement, Barney was also with his flotillamen, and he was a U.S. naval officer, not a marine. The marker claims Barney was in command of 500 men. Barney commanded about 500 flotillamen and 114 marines. The marker claims the battle lasted four hours and "the overpowering numerical odds won out." The battle lasted only about three hours, and although Barney and his men were outnumbered, the total American force was about 6,000, well over a thousand more than the British force.

The circa 1765 spring house northeast of the Barney Monument is said to be the only structure surviving from the original farm located on this portion of the battlefield. Tradition claims Barney was initially treated here for his wounds, but the actual spring where he was treated was probably located near the head of Turncliffe Creek, near the intersection of Oak and Otis streets on the north side of Bladensburg Road. Near the cemetery spring house remains a section of an 1862 earthwork known as Battery Jameson, built during the Civil War to support nearby Fort Lincoln, within the District of Columbia. These earthworks are not from the War of 1812.

For an even better view over the battlefield, Bladensburg, and the Anacostia River valley, continue south on Bladensburg Road into the District of Columbia. Turn left (southeast) on Eastern Avenue, which becomes Pine View Court. Follow it uphill across Com. Joshua Barney Drive, where it becomes Fort Lincoln Drive. Continue south just past Fort Lincoln Elementary School to a recreation area on left (east). Excellent vistas can be found from the viewing platform in the park.

The enthusiast with extra time may enjoy visiting the following War of 1812–related sites in or near Bladensburg: Bostwick, Lowndes Hill, George Washington House, Magruder House, Ross House site, and Riversdale House.

BOSTWICK. NRHP. Address: 3901 48th Street. **Parking:** limited, street. **Tours:** upon request. **Contact:** 301-927-7048. **Comment:** Bostwick can be viewed from 48th Street; it is about a 0.5 mile walk from the Bladensburg Waterfront Park, but made circuitous by a railroad line (*see map*). Future plans call for the restoration and opening of the house to the public. The marble steps up the terraced front lawn were recycled from the east front of the U.S. Capitol.

Col. Thomas Barclay, British prisoner-of-war agent during the war, resided at Bostwick, built in 1746. He warmly welcomed the British. British Maj. Gen. Robert Ross wrote to Secretary of State for War and the Colonies Henry Bathurst, 3rd Earl Bathurst on August 30,

The front facade of Bostwick is altered architecturally from its 1814 appearance by the addition of the porch and walled terrace. The British posted guards on the front steps and used the house as an office. (John O. Borstrup 1936 photograph; HABS, Library of Congress)

1814: *The Agent for British Prisoners of War* [Col. Thomas Barclay] *very fortunately residing at Bladensburg I have recommended the wounded Officers and Men to his particular attention and trust to his being able to effect their Exchange when sufficiently recovered.*

Annapolis Road (Route 450) descends **LOWNDES HILL.** The Americans began digging earthworks on Lowndes Hill on August 22, 1814, to defend Bladensburg on the main road leading from Upper Marlboro. These works were quickly abandoned when the troops withdrew to the west side of the Anacostia. American Maj. William Pinkney wrote on November 16, 1814: "a cloud of dust announced the advance of a body of troops [British] upon the upper road, and they soon showed themselves upon Lowndes' Hill, which they descended rapidly." American Capt. Henry Thompson wrote to Brig. Gen. John Stricker on August 24, 1814: "I . . . had scarcely crossed the Bridge [Bladensburg], before the British were descending Lowndes Hill."

Near the **GEORGE WASHINGTON HOUSE** (NRHR), located at 4302 Baltimore Avenue (Alternate U.S. Route 1) and completed in 1765, was located the British artillery position consisting of one 6 pounder, two small 3 pounder cannon, and Congreve rockets. The George Washington House is reputed to have cannonballs embedded in its walls from action during the battle but none are visible.

British troops marched past the **MAGRUDER HOUSE** (NRHP), located at 4703 Annapolis Road (Route 450), on their way to engage the enemy across the bridge at Bladensburg. Local tradition claims the only American civilian resistance at Bladensburg came from this house. This claim is doubtful as the building was not burned in retaliation and a contemporary map indicates the resistance came from a house no longer standing, nearer the bridge.

Ross House was used as a temporary hospital after the Battle of Bladensburg. (Phillip Huntington Clark circa 1890 photograph "The Old hospital Bladensburg"; courtesy of Joseph S. Rogers)

The **ROSS HOUSE** was located across the road from Magruder House at the corner of 46th Street and Annapolis Road (Route 450), now occupied by the Ernest Maier Building. Dr. David Ross, Jr., bought the circa 1749 Ross House in 1793. It served as a hospital for treating wounded after the Battle of Bladensburg. It is here that Com. Joshua Barney is believed to have been taken by the British for medical treatment after his initial treatment at the spring mentioned above. At least eighteen wounded British officers were treated here.

British Graves

The remains of six British soldiers are said to be buried in unmarked graves in Ross's former yard. Leonard C. Crewe, Jr., former chairman of the Maryland Historical Society, dismantled Ross House in 1957 and moved it to the Western Run Valley, Cockeysville, Baltimore County, where it was rebuilt using as much original material as possible and named Preservation Hill.

British Lt. George Robert Gleig's memory of the house was published in 1847:

I strolled up to a house which had been converted into an hospital, and paid a hasty visit to the wounded. I found them in great pain, and some of them deeply affected at the thought of being abandoned by their comrades, and left to the mercy of their enemies. Yet, in their apprehension of the evil treatment from the Americans, the event proved that they had done injustice to that people; who were found to possess at least one generous trait in their character, namely, that of behaving kindly and attentively to their prisoners.

Optional Side Trip **RIVERSDALE HOUSE.** Located about 3.5 miles from Fort Lincoln Cemetery and Bladensburg Waterfront Park, Riversdale House is well worth a visit if time permits.

RIVERSDALE HOUSE MUSEUM. NHL. Address: 4811 Riverdale Road, Riverdale Park. **Parking:** free. **Visitor Center Hours:** 9 a.m. to 5 p.m., Monday through Friday, and Sunday afternoon. **House Tours:** Friday and Sunday afternoons. **Fees:** $3 adults, $2 seniors/groups, $1 children 5 to 18, children under 5 free. **Facilities:** exhibits, restrooms. **Comment:** the history of the site during the War of 1812 is the subject of one interpretive panel in the visitor center. **Contacts:** 301-864-0420; www.pgparks.com/Things_To_Do/History/Riversdale_House_Museum.htm.

Baron Henri Joseph Stier built Riversdale, a stucco-covered five-part brick mansion, between 1801 and 1807. Rosalie Stier Calvert, "Mistress of Riversdale" and daughter of Stier, wrote in a letter in 1814, "We have been in a state of continual alarm." Mrs. Calvert's husband, George, with slaves from the plantation, helped bury the dead after the battle. She and her husband became friends with some of the wounded British officers left behind at Bladensburg. Henry Clay, a War of 1812 War Hawk, was a frequent visitor to Riversdale.

Rosalie Stier Calvert wrote to Charles J. Stier on December 27, 1814: *Among the wounded in our village* [Bladensburg] *there were* [Lt.] *Colonel* [William] *Wood, and a Major* [Francis F.?] *Brown, who stayed here two or three months and whose acquaintance we made.*

Rosalie Stier Calvert wrote to Charles J. Stier on March 20, 1815: *Of the 100 hogsheads of tobacco that I bought for you in 1810, seven were in one of the warehouses which the British*

1827 lithograph showing the south facade second-story windows on right from which the mistress of Riversdale, Rosalie Stier Calvert, observed "several cannonballs with my own eyes" during the Battle of Bladensburg. The battle was fought about 2 miles from the mansion. Rosalie probably saw Congreve rockets, which would have been more easily visible because of their smoky trails. (B. King from watercolor by Anthony St. John Baker; reproduced by permission of The Huntington Library, San Marino, California)

partially looted; they took five and left two. I hope the price we can get for the remainder will compensate you for this loss.

Rosalie Stier Calvert wrote to Isabel van Havre on May 6, 1815: *The burning of the public building in Washington is the best thing that has happened in a long time, as far as we are concerned, since this has finally settled the question of whether the seat of government would stay here. In the future they will no longer keep trying to change it, and as long as the union of states stands, the government will remain in Washington, despite the jealousy of Philadelphia, New York, and Baltimore. They are busy rebuilding the Capitol and all the buildings which were destroyed. I was quite calm during the Battle of Bladensburg because the only thing I feared was foragers, but we hardly suffered at all.*

British Route to Washington The British continued their march approximately 5 miles to Washington after a two-hour rest, leaving about 6 p.m. and reaching Capitol Hill about 8 p.m. The British followed Bladensburg Road (U.S. Alternate Route 1), which becomes Maryland Avenue. At the "old circus grounds," near Maryland Avenue and 15th Street NW, about 1.5 miles from the capitol, a large detachment of the British troops were left as a reserve guard.

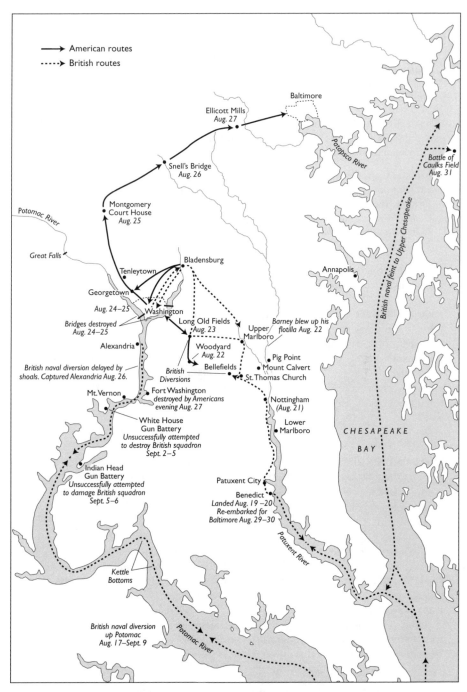

Map showing British routes to and from Washington and American routes to engage and withdraw from Bladensburg to Baltimore, August–September 1814 (updated, corrected, and redrawn from *The West Point Atlas of American Wars,* vol. 1)

British Lt. George Robert Gleig remembered that evening in the memoir he published in 1821: *General Ross . . . did not march the troops immediately into the city, but halted them upon a plain in its immediate vicinity . . . [then later] having advanced as far as the plain, where the reserve had previously paused, the first and second brigades halted; and, forming into close column, passed the night in bivouack.*

As the British advanced on Washington at sunset, they could see a red glow to the south-east of the city, where the Washington Navy Yard had already been torched by the American Navy to keep its ships and supplies out of British hands.

British Lt. George Robert Gleig wrote down his memories of that evening published in 1821: *It would be difficult to conceive a finer spectacle than that which presented itself as they [British troops] approached the town. The sky was brilliantly illuminated by the different conflagrations; and a dark red light was thrown upon the road, sufficient to permit each man to view distinctly his comrade's face. Except the burning of St. Sebastian's, I do not recollect to have witnessed at any period of my life a scene more striking or more sublime.*

To follow the British march and the burning of many public buildings in Washington, *see* the District of Columbia, Washington Tour *in part 2.*

American Retreat Route to Rockville and Then to Baltimore Brig. Gen. William Henry Winder and parts of his exhausted and scattered army rendezvoused about midnight, August 25, 1814, at Tenleytown, the community around the intersection of Nebraska and Wisconsin avenues, 3.0 miles north-northwest of Georgetown in northwest Washington, D.C. Seeing the red glare of the burning of many public buildings in Washington, Winder pressed his men on to Montgomery Court House (present-day Rockville), approximately 15 miles northwest of downtown Washington, where they camped around the **BEALL-DAWSON HOUSE.**

BEALL-DAWSON HISTORIC PARK. NRHP. Address: 111 West Montgomery Avenue. **Parking:** free lot off Middle Lane. **Hours:** Monday through Friday, 9 a.m. to 5 p.m. **Fees:** $3 for adults, $2 for seniors and children. **Facilities:** restrooms and gift shop. **Contacts:** 301-340-2825; www.montgomeryhistory.org/museum_beall_dawson.

Timbers stacked for use in the construction of the house were reportedly taken by the militia and used to fuel their campfires. Winder had expected to find food, tents, and other supplies sent by a quartermaster's wagon train, but the train had gone off to Virginia instead. Winder and his troops left at approximately noon, marching out the Baltimore Road east toward Baltimore, believed to be the next British target.

Some Maryland militia camped at Gaithersburg on August 26, 1814, on their way toward Baltimore. The exact location of the encampment is unknown but is believed to have been near a large oak tree that once grew near 5 North Frederick Street where the Verizon switching station is now located.

Col. William Dent Beall reported on November 22, 1814: *we encamped at Gaither's heights [Gaithersburg] , thence to Ellicott's Mills, thence . . . towards Baltimore.*

The main concentration of American troops camped the night of August 26 at Snell's Bridge, the Clarksville Pike span over the Patuxent River. The pike was then a major road between Montgomery Court House and Ellicott City.

Brig. Gen. William Henry Winder wrote: *When the forces arrived at Snell's bridge, on the upper branch of the Patuxent, I had concluded that, if the enemy was, as we had still reason to believe, proceeding to Baltimore, that it would be most advisable for me to proceed directly thither.*

British Withdrawal Route to Benedict The victorious British army withdrew from Washington, marching on the very streets they had traveled on their way into the city. The exhausted soldiers began passing through Bladensburg about midnight on August 26, 1814. Some stragglers did not pass until noon that day. About forty horses, ten or twelve carts and wagons, one ox cart, one coach, and several gigs were requisitioned to carry the wounded. This ragtag column was preceded by sixty or seventy cattle. About ninety British wounded were left behind.

British Lt. George Robert Gleig remembered the British withdrawal in a memoir published in 1833: *It was about eight o'clock at night when a staff-officer, arriving upon the ground, gave direction for the corps to form in marching order. Preparatory to this step, large quantities of fresh fuel were heaped upon the fires, while from every company a few men were selected who should remain beside them till the pickets withdrew, and move from time to time about, so as their figures might be seen by the light of the blaze. After this, the troops stole to the rear of the fires by twos and threes; when far enough removed to avoid observation, they took their place, and in profound silence, began their march.*

British Lt. Col. Harry Smith wrote in his autobiography published in approximately 1824: *The barrels of flour* [taken from Washington] *were arranged in the streets, the heads knocked in, and every soldier told to take some. Soldiers are greedy fellows, and many filled their haversacks. During a tedious night's march through woods as dark as chaos, they found the flour far from agreeable to carry and threw it away by degrees. If it had not been for the flour thus marking the track, the whole column would have lost its road.*

At Bladensburg, Lieutenant Gleig wrote the following vivid account, published in 1847: *When we reached the ground where yesterday's battle had been fought, the moon rose, and exhibited a spectacle by no means enlivening. The dead were still unburied, and lay about in every direction completely naked. They had been stripped even of their shirts, and having been exposed in this state to the violent rain in the morning, they appeared to be bleached to a most unnatural degree of whiteness. The heat and rain together had likewise affected them in a different manner; and the smell which rose upon the night air was horrible.*

The British followed essentially the same route back to Benedict with one major difference. Instead of following Addison Road, they took what today is Landover Road (Route 202) southeast to White House Road, west to Brown Station Road, south to Old Marlboro Pike, and east to Upper Marlboro.

Crawford's Adventure Spring is located just east of Bladensburg, next to a large beech tree in Cheverly Nature Park near the east side of the intersection with Baltimore-Washington Parkway (Route 295). Here British troops replenished their canteens. There is a plaque commemorating this spring but it is located high above the actual spring in the residential area of Cheverly. To access this marker, follow Crest Avenue south off Landover Road to the intersection with Lockwood Road. The spring monument is located near the northwest corner of the intersection. This is a residential area; please respect private property.

The exhausted British troops were finally able to rest near or at **NORTHAMPTON PLANTA-TION** in what today is Largo.

NORTHAMPTON PLANTATION SITE. Address: 10700 Lake Overlook Drive, off Lake Arbor Way, about 1.0 mile east of Landover Road (Route 202), near Largo, Prince George's County. **Parking:** free. **Hours:** daylight hours. **Fees:** none. **Facilities:** some archeological interpretation but no 1812 interpretation. **Contacts:** 301-627-1286; www.pgparks.com/ Things_To_Do/History/Northhampton_Plantation_Slave_Quarters.htm. **Comment:** only the foundation of a slave house remains visible today.

Lt. George Robert Gleig wrote about this event in a memoir published in 1821: *By seven o'clock in the morning* [August 26, 1814], *it was therefore absolutely necessary to pause, because numbers had already fallen behind, and numbers more were ready to follow their example; when throwing ourselves upon the ground, almost in the same order in which we had marched, in less than five minutes there was not a single unclosed eye throughout the whole brigade. Piquets were of course stationed, and centinels placed, to whom no rest was granted, but except these, the entire army resembled a heap of dead bodies on a field of battle, rather than living men.*

From the Largo area the British troops continued their return march to Upper Marlboro where some stragglers were arrested by local inhabitants. (*See sidebar in* British Invasion Tour, *in part 1, for details of this event.*) From Upper Marlboro the British apparently marched south along Chew Road to Duval Road (roads that no longer connect) to Fenno

Northampton was the home of Samuel Sprigg. (Circa 1895 photograph by unknown photographer; HABS, Library of Congress)

State Records at Mount Lubentia

Ironically, some state and Prince George's County records were moved to this Federal-style brick home, located at Largo, about 6 miles from Upper Marlboro, for safekeeping. No one could have imagined the British return route would take them so close to this location. Mount Lubentia is privately owned and not visible from public roads.

Mount Lubentia served as a temporary seat of government and housed documents for the county and state when the Prince George's County seat of government at Upper Marlboro was threatened by British attack. (Circa 1883–1888 photograph; HABS, Library of Congress)

These government document fragments were recovered from the attic of Mount Lubentia during restoration in the 1980s and 1990s. (Ralph Eshelman 2000 photograph)

Road and then to Nottingham. From Nottingham, the British apparently did not take the same route they used to march north. At least some took a more westerly route on what today is called Baden Naylor Road to Aquasco Road then back to Brandywine Road to Benedict. It is unclear why they would have taken this route, which is farther from the support of their naval vessels shadowing them along the Patuxent River, except possibly to protect the main column from an attack from the west. By taking this route, they passed **ST. PAUL'S PARISH CHAPEL.**

ST. PAUL'S PARISH CHAPEL, also called St. Paul's Episcopal Church. NRHP. **Location:** northwest of Baden-Naylor and Horsehead roads, just east of Brandywine Road [Route 381], Baden, Prince George's County). **Comment:** St. Paul's Parish Chapel dates from 1733–35, with alterations made in 1769, 1793, 1857, 1882, and 1921. Local tradition claims the marble baptismal font, sent from England in 1752, was knocked over and damaged by the British. It was repaired with copper bands.

The invading army successfully boarded their ships at Benedict after a twelve-day campaign and march of approximately 113 miles, not including diversions, patrols, or details beyond Capitol Hill.

This ends the Battle of Bladensburg Tour.

Saving the Declaration of Independence Tour

Particulars This approximately 36-mile-long tour is recommended only for the keenest of historical travelers. Nearly all the sites are privately owned and no onsite visits are possible, with the exception of the Patterson Mill site and the National Archives. The most important site, Rokeby Mansion, cannot even be seen from public roads. Furthermore, the intense development of the area has destroyed much of the historic integrity of the southern half of the route. Please respect privacy and do not trespass. Many of the actual documents saved from almost certain destruction can be seen today at the National Archives (*see visitor information below*).

Historical Background When the British threatened the nation's capital on August 23, 1814, State Department clerk Stephen Pleasonton led a contingent of twenty-two carts loaded with our nation's most important documents, including the Declaration of Independence, much of George Washington's correspondence, treaties, laws, many congressional and State Department records, probably the Constitution, the Articles of Confederation, and the Bill of Rights. The documents, packed in coarse linen bags, were first taken from Washington to Edgar Patterson's abandoned gristmill, located on Pimmit Run on the Virginia side of the Potomac River near Chain Bridge. Because this location was too near the Columbian Foundry (then called Foxall's Foundry) where cannon and munitions were manufactured, a likely British target located on the Maryland side of the river, the documents were next moved to Rokeby Mansion just outside Leesburg.

While scouting British movements at Bellefields, Maryland (*see* British Invasion Tour *in part 1*), Secretary of State James Monroe sent a message by courier to President James Madison about 9 a.m., August 22, 1814, stating "you had better remove the records." Many of the most important documents were housed at the Executive Office Building, also called the Southwest Executive Building, located where the Eisenhower Executive Office Building now stands. Here were the offices of the Secretary of State James Monroe and Secretary of War John Armstrong as well as the office of James Madison's brother-in-law Richard Cutts, superintendent general of military supplies. The building was burned about 8 a.m. on August 25, 1814.

Begin your tour at the **EXECUTIVE OFFICE BUILDING** site.

EXECUTIVE OFFICE BUILDING SITE. Location: northwest quadrant on south side of Pennsylvania Avenue and 17th Street. **Parking:** parking garages. **Comment:** this structure was nearly a duplicate of the original Treasury Department building on the east side of the quadrant. The State, War and Navy Building, now known as the Eisenhower Executive Office Building, was constructed on this site between 1871 and 1888. Because the original building no longer exists, it is suggested this be a pass by only.

Once the documents were packed at the Executive Office Building, the carts traveled approximately 4 miles to Chain Bridge. The exact route is unclear but they probably traveled northwest on Pennsylvania Avenue to Falls or Bridge Street (M Street today) to Georgetown to Chain Bridge. The abandoned **PATTERSON MILL** was located on the west side of the bridge.

PATTERSON MILL SITE. Location: Virginia side of Chain Bridge, which carries Chain Bridge Road (Route 123) over the Potomac River, Arlington County. **Parking:** a small parking area is located on the east side of 41st Street at the intersection with North Glebe Road. **Hours:** daylight hours. **Facilities:** none. **Comment:** the short trail is steep and rough in places. The trail along Pimmit Run is located on the west side of North Glebe Road just to the north of the parking area. The trail runs under Chain Bridge to the confluence of Pimmit Run with the Potomac River. There are several foundation ruins some of which may be from Patterson Mill.

There were three mill complexes in the area at the time, two owned by the Adams family. Patterson Mill is believed to be located closest to Chain Bridge. Barges from the Washington Navy Yard were brought near here in the hopes of saving them and their contents from British destruction. Dolley Madison crossed Chain Bridge on her way to Rokeby Farm (*see* First Family Flight Tour *in part 1*) escaping the advancing British army.

When it was realized the nearby Columbian Foundry, on the Maryland side of the bridge, could be a likely British target, Stephen Pleasonton obtained wagons from local farms and

Chain Bridge, built in 1811, the fourth bridge to span this section of the Potomac River, was used by Dolley Madison when she made her escape from Washington to Virginia. State Department records were stored in the abandoned Patterson Mill, possibly the very mill depicted in this 1839 published image. (*Potomac River, Chain Bridge at Little Falls,* wash painting by Augustus Kollner; Library of Congress)

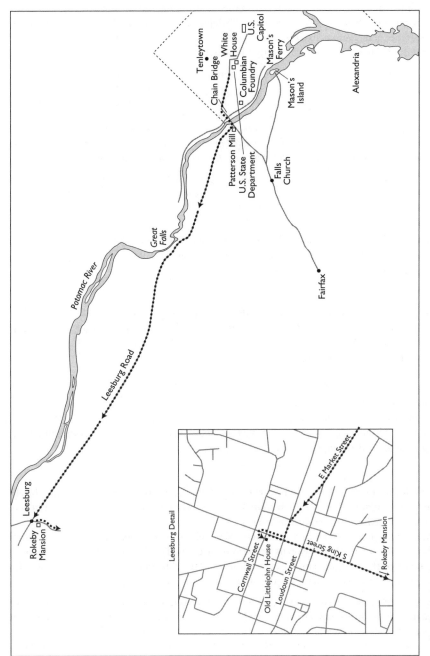

Saving the Declaration of Independence Route

moved the records a second time to the relative safety of Leesburg, approximately 30 miles to the northwest. It was here that Rev. John Littlejohn, a clergyman, sheriff, and former collector of internal revenue, lived. The wagons traveled west along Georgetown Pike (present-day Route 193) to present-day Leesburg Pike (Route 7) to Leesburg.

Although Leesburg, Loudoun County, Virginia, is 35 miles from Washington, citizens there observed a shimmering red light over the city during the British occupation. Rumors circulated that the British had burned every building in the capital. Pvt. John Leadley Dagg wrote in his autobiography: *news reached us, that British vessels were ascending the Potomac . . . I was therefore compelled . . . to become a soldier. With hasty preparation I joined the march; and, the first night, lodged in a hay loft near Leesburg. From this point we saw the light of the burning capitol, which the British had fired the day before.*

The wagon train, heaped with important federal records, stopped at the **OLD LITTLEJOHN HOUSE.**

OLD LITTLEJOHN HOUSE. NRHP. **Address:** 11 West Cornwall Street. **Comment:** this house is privately owned and only exterior views of the house are possible. Please respect private property and do not disturb occupants.

Pleasonton discussed the situation with Reverend Littlejohn who suggested the records be taken to the abandoned **ROKEBY MANSION,** fortuitously containing a brick storage vault in the basement. After locking the documents at Rokeby Mansion, Pleasonton gave the keys to Littlejohn for safekeeping.

ROKEBY MANSION. NRHP. **Location:** private drive on west side of Cleedsville Road (Route 650), 1 mile south of the intersection with King Street (U.S. Route 15), south of Leesburg. **Comment:** this house cannot be seen from the public road. Please respect private property and do not enter driveway or disturb the occupants.

Charles Binns probably stored court records here in a fireproof brick-walled and brick-arched basement room (*see illustration*). Here the federal records were stored until it was deemed safe to return them to Washington.

Much of the original Georgian character of Rokeby Mansion was changed in 1836, when Benjamin Shreve, Jr., then the owner, removed the clipped gables, remodeled the windows, and replaced the interior trim. The manor was enlarged in 1886 with a rear addition. The house was restored close to its original appearance in 1958.

Stephen Pleasonton wrote to Brig. Gen. William H. Winder on August 27, 1814: *I proceeded with them [documents] to the town of Leesburg, a distance of 35 miles, at which place an empty house was procured, in which the papers were safely placed, the doors locked, and the keys given to the Rev. Mr. [John] Littlejohn, who was then, or had been, one of the collectors of the internal revenue.*

Thanks to the efforts of Pleasonton and those who assisted him, the Declaration of Independence as well as many other important national documents were saved from pos-

The State Department records were stored at Rokeby Mansion, built in 1757 by Charles Binns II, first clerk of the circuit court of Loudoun County. (Ralph Eshelman 2001 photograph)

This brick arched storage chamber in the basement of Rokeby Mansion is where some of the federal documents were ultimately housed until it was deemed safe to return them to Washington. (Ralph Eshelman 2001 photograph)

Rescue of Other Public Records

In addition to safeguarding the portrait of George Washington, which was taken to a farm in Maryland, Dolley Madison also ordered important Cabinet papers, among other things, to be deposited in the Bank of Maryland.

Twenty-four-year-old clerk Lewis H. Machen and the office messenger, Tobias, transported the executive proceedings of the U.S. Senate by wagon to the Brookeville Academy (*see* President Madison's Flight *in the* First Family Flight Tour *in part 1*), Brookeville, Maryland, 18 miles from Washington, to keep them safe from the invading British Army.

U.S. House of Representatives clerks John Frost and Samuel Burch moved some records to an unknown location outside of the city of Washington. Frost also moved some committee records and claims and pensions records to a rental house near the Capitol but, unfortunately, the house caught fire during the British occupation and the documents burned.

Benjamin Homans and other clerks at the Washington Navy Yard ferried documents, maps, charts, plans, books, trophies, instruments, paintings, etc. up the Potomac River above Little Falls through the Little Falls Skirting Canal. Some records and books from the Executive Office Building were loaded on flour boats and sent up the Potomac River to the entrance of the canal. Homans served as caretaker of these items.

The papers and books of the U.S. Post Office were moved to the cellar of a farmhouse, somewhere outside the city and entrusted to a nineteen-year-old employee named Brown.

Dr. William Thornton moved the papers of the U.S. Patent Office to his farm located at what today is Bethesda. He also successfully persuaded the British to spare the Patent Office, housing the patent models, claiming they were works of art.

Also largely unknown is the effort of Elias Boudinot Caldwell, clerk of the Supreme Court, who moved the court's library into his house, saving the books from the same fate that befell the Library of Congress.

sible destruction. The Declaration of Independence was transferred from the State Department to the Library of Congress in 1921 and finally to the National Archives in 1952. During WW II, the Declaration of Independence and many other important national documents were temporarily stored at Fort Knox, Kentucky, for safekeeping. Few visitors, upon viewing these significant national treasures at the **NATIONAL ARCHIVES,** realize how close this nation came to losing them during the War of 1812.

NATIONAL ARCHIVES. Location: general public entrance at Constitution Avenue and 9th Street, NW. **Hours:** March 15 through Labor Day, 10 a.m. to 7 p.m.; day after Labor Day to March 14, 10 a.m. to 5:30 p.m. **Fees:** none. **Facilities:** exhibits, archives, shop, café, restrooms. **Contacts:** 202-357-5450; www.archives.gov. **Comment:** the Declaration of Independence and other significant documents are displayed in the Rotunda for Charters of Freedom; allow at least ninety minutes for tour.

This ends the Saving the Declaration of Independence Tour.

First Family Flight Tour

Particulars This tour is recommended only for the keenest of historical travelers. Most of the sites along the route are privately owned and no onsite visits are possible. Salona cannot be seen from public roads and Wren's and Wiley's taverns are no longer extant—in fact, the precise location of Wiley's Tavern in unknown. Furthermore, the intense development of the area has destroyed much of the historic integrity of the route. Please respect privacy and do not trespass.

This tour is actually two routes that took place nearly simultaneously. President Madison's Flight Tour is approximately 41 miles long (President's House to Brookeville plus another 18 miles for the return to Washington). The First Lady's Flight Tour is approximately 29 miles long (President's House to Minor's Hill plus another 6 miles for her return to Washington via Mason's Ferry).

Historical Background When it became clear that the American forces had failed to stop the British at the Battle of Bladensburg (*see* Battle of Bladensburg Tour *in part 1*), the President and the First Lady hastily fled the capital. James and Dolley Madison took separate routes to the relative safety of Virginia, with plans to meet at Wiley's Tavern. Their attempted rendezvous, however, was beset by near misses, misinformation, and constant fear of being captured along with concern about the future of their country.

President Madison's Flight

President James Madison, accompanied by U.S. commissioner for prisoners Brig. Gen. John T. Mason, Attorney General Richard Rush, and other aides, returned by horseback from the Bladensburg Battlefield (*see* Battle of Bladensburg Tour *in part 1*) to the President's House about 4 p.m. only to find that Dolley had already fled. He had sent her a message earlier advising her to have her carriage ready at a moment's notice in case the American forces failed to stop the invading army. Madison sent a message to Secretary of Navy William Jones, who was with his wife and Dolley at Charles Carroll's home called Bellevue (now Dumbarton House; *see* First Lady's Flight, *below, for details*) in Georgetown, requesting that they rendezvous at Columbian Foundry. But Madison thought better of that idea. He sent Tench Ringgold to Carroll's home with a second message instructing Dolley to meet him instead at Wiley's Tavern the next day.

As Madison, again by horseback, rode out toward Falls Church, Virginia, during the late afternoon on August 24, 1814, one can only imagine his thoughts then and during the days to come. Would the capital city be destroyed? Would the American army escape and be able to fight another day? Would the United States survive as an independent country? Would Dolley safely make it to Wiley's Tavern? Would Madison himself escape capture from the invading enemy? Rumors were rampant. Some reports suggested that the British were in hot pursuit, eager to capture the president of a country that dared to declare war on England. Madison could not have known at the time that no attempt was being made to follow and capture him. The British were more concerned about destroying public buildings

65

James Madison. (Circa 1828 Pendleton lithograph after painting by Gilbert Stuart; Library of Congress)

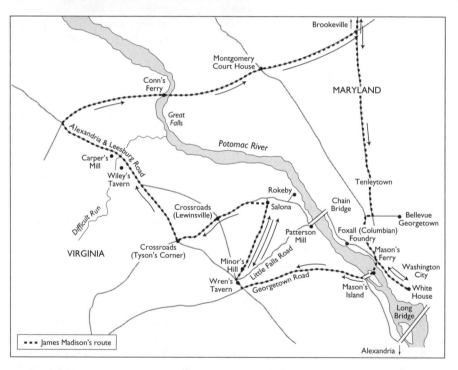

First Family Flight: James Madison's Route (revised and redrawn from *August 24, 1814: Washington in Flames,* by Carole L. Herrick, original map drawn by Charles Herrick)

British satirical cartoon in 1814 speculates that President Madison has fled to Elba to join Napoleon to the amusement of the Federalists he abandoned. (S.W. Fores, "The Fall of Washington or Maddy in full flight"; Library of Congress)

and war-related structures, supplies, and equipment in the capital city. The British officers were also concerned about a possible American counterattack. Once the goal of their destruction was complete, the British made a hasty withdrawal to the safety of their ships. But many Americans blamed Madison for the war and the humiliating American defeat at Bladensburg followed by the British capture of the capital.

President Madison was again accompanied by Richard Rush and Brig. Gen. John T. Mason. The exact route used is not entirely clear. From the President's House, Madison probably rode northwest out Pennsylvania Avenue and then west on what today is called K Street, across Rock Creek to Mason's Ferry (near present-day Key Bridge, about 1.6 miles), then by ferry across the Potomac River to Mason's Island and over the causeway into Virginia. Madison and his companions then traveled first to **WREN'S TAVERN** at Falls Church via Georgetown Road (essentially Lee Highway, U.S. Route 29) and then northwest on Leesburg Pike (Route 7) to Broad Street, approximately 6.5 miles.

WREN'S TAVERN SITE. Address: 400 East Broad Street, Falls Church. **Parking:** street. **Facilities:** none: **Comment:** tavern no longer extant; site marked by interpretive sign only.

Washington Navy Yard clerk Mordecai Booth arrived at Wren's Tavern about midnight, August 24, 1814. A traveler at the tavern claimed President Madison was less than a mile away. Another report said Madison was at Minor's Hill, at the intersection of Rockingham and Powhatan streets (*see* First Lady's Flight *for details*) approximately 1.5 miles to the north. Still other reports claimed the President was at **SALONA**. All of these sightings could have been accurate because the places mentioned were on the route taken by the President, although there is no authoritative account of the President's precise movements that night. President Madison did briefly stop at Wren's Tavern, then at Minor's Hill, but soon left for Salona, following in part what today is called Virginia Avenue, looking for his wife, Dolley.

SALONA. NRHP. **Address:** private driveway at 1214 Buchanan Street, south off Dolley Madison Boulevard (Route 123). **Comment:** this property cannot be seen from the public road. Please respect private property and do not enter driveway or disturb the occupants.

The President spent the night of August 24, 1814, at Salona, built circa 1804 for Rev. William Maffitt. (Ralph Eshelman 2001 photograph)

It is not clear exactly what route President Madison used to get to Salona, located approximately 2 miles north. He may have taken Old Falls Road (Route 694) or Old Dominion Drive (Route 309) north to Falls Road (parts of which are now named Chain Bridge Road and Dolley Madison Boulevard, Route 123), a circuitous approximately 4-mile route. He may have found a guide to take him to Salona along a shorter route using back roads. While the President was at Salona, Dolley was only about 2 miles east off Falls Road at Rokeby Farm (*see* First Lady's Flight). The next morning both parties set out for their planned rendezvous at **WILEY'S TAVERN**. President Madison returned to Falls Church hoping to receive word on the whereabouts of his wife, news about the enemy attack on Washington, and the location of the American army. At Wren's Tavern, the President was somewhat relieved when Capt. George Graham, commander of the Fairfax Dragoons, provided him with two armed cavalrymen, the first armed escorts to protect the President during his escape. Receiving word that Dolley might be at Salona, Madison retraced his steps only to learn that she had briefly stopped there but had already de-

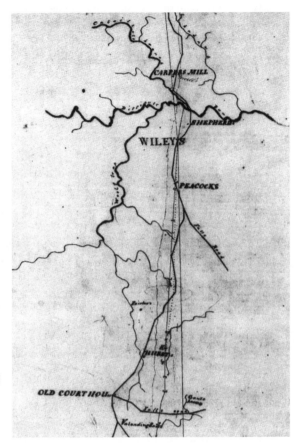

The location of Wiley's Tavern is shown on this 1827 road survey. Solid lines represent the then-existing roads and the dotted and narrower solid lines represent the proposed Leesburg Turnpike, which is essentially Leesburg Pike or Route 7 today. (A. Sommers 1827 "Plat of the contemplated Turn-pike Road from Alexandria to Difficult run by Wileys")

parted. William Jones, who accompanied Dolley and her companions, left word that the entourage was headed for Wiley's Tavern, further inland and presumed safe from possible British reprisals.

WILEY'S TAVERN SITE. Location: the precise location of the tavern site is unclear but is believed to lie east of the 9800 block of Leesburg Pike (Route 7), south of Difficult Run. **Comment:** no access.

Wiley's Tavern, about 8 miles northwest of Salona, was located along a now-abandoned eighteenth-century road that ran from the Shenandoah Valley to Alexandria. Colvin Run Road (north of Difficult Run) and Locust Hill Drive (south of Difficult Run) are remnants of this road. President Madison probably followed Falls Road (Chain Bridge Road) west to Great Falls Road (Lewinsville Road, Route 694), west to Leesburg Pike (Route 7) and then northwest, to Wiley's Tavern, a total of about 8 miles.

While en route to the tavern, President Madison, Richard Rush, and the two dragoons sought sanctuary from a severe storm at a crossroads. It is unclear at which crossroads this occurred; either the junction of Falls Road and Leesburg Pike (now Tyson's Corner) or the junction of Falls Road and Great Falls Road (now Lewinsville). Brigadier General Mason had left the party for unknown reasons but rejoined them later at Wiley's Tavern. Madison and his entourage made it to Wiley's Tavern just before sunset. There the President was relieved to finally be reunited with his wife. Comforted in knowing she was safe, but with rumors of nearby British troops, President Madison left the security of the inn about midnight accompanied by Jones, Rush, Mason, state department clerk John Graham, servants, and the two dragoons. They traveled to **CONN'S FERRY** in order to cross the Potomac River into Maryland, hopefully to join the American troops at Montgomery Court House. It is unclear what route the party took to the ferry, a Potomac crossing located about 5 miles to the northeast of the tavern. They may have taken what is now called Walker Road (Route 681) north and then traveled east on Arnon Chapel Road (Route 682), a total of about 4.5 miles.

CONN'S FERRY SITE. Location: Riverbend Park near the east end of Potomac Hills Street, east off Jeffery Road (Route 1268), east off River Bend Road (Route 603), Fairfax County. **Parking:** free. **Hours:** park: 7 a.m. to 8:30 p.m. daily; visitor center: Wednesday through Monday, 9 a.m. to 5 p.m., except January and February, when it opens at 11 a.m. **Fees:** none. **Facilities:** restrooms, picnic grounds, hiking, fishing, canoeing, kayaking, small boating, snack bar, gift shop, and nature center: **Contacts:** 703-759-3211; www.fairfaxcounty.gov/parks/riverbend.

Conn's Ferry was established by 1790 and provided a crossing of the Potomac River above Great Falls. The exact location of the ferry crossing is unclear, but it was probably near the boat ramp in today's park. Due to the construction of an aqueduct dam downstream, however, the river is wider and deeper today than it was normally in 1814. Once the President and his party reached the river crossing, they found that it was too dangerous to cross because the river was swollen as a result of the severe storm the previous evening. While the party sought shelter, possibly at the ferryman's home, Secretary of the Navy Jones returned to the inn, collected his family, and took them out of harm's way to Fredericksburg before rejoining the troops.

By the afternoon of August 26, the river level had dropped and President Madison and his entourage were able to cross the Potomac River into Maryland, then traveling about 8 miles, probably along Falls Road (Route 189) to Montgomery Court House (present-day Rockville), about 16 miles from the capital. The party was unaware that the British had by this time evacuated Washington. They arrived about 6 p.m., expecting to find Brig. Gen. William Henry Winder. (*see* Beall-Dawson House Site *in* Battle of Bladensburg Tour *for detail of the American encampment here.*) But, with limited success in regrouping the scattered American troops, Winder and his army had already left at approximately noon for Brookeville. The exhausted President and his party pushed on about another 11 miles to Brookeville.

Today there is no ferry or bridge at this spot across the Potomac River, so to continue the tour backtrack to Georgetown Pike (Route 193) east to the beltway (I-495) north to I-270 to Rockville.

To follow the President's route to Brookeville, start at the Courthouse Square in downtown Rockville, at the intersection of Jefferson and Washington streets, the main crossroads in town in 1814, and travel east on Jefferson Street, which becomes Veirs Mill Road (Route 586), then northeast on Norbeck Road (Route 28), and finally north on Georgia Avenue (Route 97) to **BROOKEVILLE.** President Madison would have actually traveled north on First Street and then east on Baltimore Road to Norbeck Road, but these connections are no longer possible because of railroad and new road construction.

BROOKEVILLE. NHD. Location: Georgia Avenue (Route 97). **Parking:** limited street. **Facilities:** none. **Comment:** this is a private residential area, please respect private property; none of the historic sites are open to the public. Do not disturb occupants.

Brookeville is a quaint little town of narrow streets and older homes within a National Historic District. In 1814, the town consisted of at least fourteen houses, two mills, a hide-tanning yard, a blacksmith, a post office (Madison House), and a private boy's school known as Brookeville Academy. President James Madison and members of his cabinet spent the night and part of the next day at Madison House. Brookeville therefore calls itself the "United States Capital for a Day," although in actuality it was occupied for less than twenty-four hours over parts of two days, from about 9 p.m., August 26, until about noon, August 27, 1814.

The Brookeville Academy is on the east side of High Street (Georgia Avenue extended) and south of the intersection with Market Street. A clerk and office messenger had moved the executive proceedings of the U.S. Senate by wagon from Washington to Brookeville Academy in order to keep them safe from the invading British Army (*see sidebar in* Saving the U.S. Constitution Tour *in part 1*). Many of the wall stones of the academy, established in 1808, contain graffiti, presumably carved by the students. The academy's original appearance was altered in 1848 with the addition of a second story.

The circa 1800 Federal brick **MADISON HOUSE,** also called the Caleb Bentley House and located at 205 Market Street, served as the temporary Executive Mansion. President James Madison, Attorney General Richard Rush, Brig. Gen. John T. Mason, State Department Chief Clerk John Graham, their servants, and a guard of twenty dragoons occupied the house and grounds. Quaker storekeeper and postmaster Caleb Bentley and his wife, Henrietta, owned the house, which took on its current name after Madison stayed here. Henrietta's granddaughter claimed that Henrietta Bentley allowed the President to take refuge at their home even though it was against their Quaker principles to have anything to do with war. Mrs. Bentley gave her room to the President and slept on the floor with her little daughter. Beds were spread in the parlor and the house was overflowing with the President's party. Her strongest impression of the experience was that the sentinels tramped around the dwelling all night ruining rose bushes and vegetables. The President sat up late sending and receiving dispatches. The next morning, on August 27, 1814, Secretary of State James Monroe met Madison at Brookeville. Learning that the British had abandoned Washington, Madison ordered his cabinet to return to the city. The Windsor chair Madison used while writing dispatches has been known since as "the Madison Chair." It is part of the White House collection. Henrietta Bentley was apparently a friend of Dolley Madison's and may have visited her at the President's House.

The Madison House served as a refuge for President James Madison during the British occupation of Washington. (Postcard postmarked 1906; courtesy of Montgomery County Historical Society)

While at the Bentley House, President Madison wrote to his wife, Dolley: *My dearest: Finding that our army had left [Rockville] we pushed on to this place with a view to join it, or proceed to the City as further information might prescribe. I have just received a line from Col. [James] Monroe saying that the enemy is out of Washington & on retreat to their ships, and advising immediate return to Washington. We shall accordingly set out thither immediately. I know not where we are in the first instance to hide our head but shall look for a place on our arrival.*

Margaret Bayard Smith, wife of Samuel Harrison Smith, president of the Bank of Washington and Commissioner of Revenue in the Treasury Department, also fled to Brookeville with her two daughters. She described Brookeville, on the Wednesday before the President arrived, in a letter to her sister: *We received a most kind reception from Mrs. [Henrietta] Bentley, and excellent accommodation. The appearance of this village is romantic and beautiful, it is situated in a little valley totally embosom'd in woody hill, with a stream flowing at the bottom on which are mills. In this secluded spot one might hope the noise, or rumor of war would never reach. Here all seemed security and peace! . . . This morning [Thursday] on awakening we were greeted with the sad news, that our city was taken, the bridges and public buildings burnt, our troops flying in every direction. Our little army totally dispersed . . . Every hour the poor wearied and terrified creatures are passing by the door. Mrs. Bentley kindly invites them into rest and refresh. Major [Charles S.?] Ridgely's troop of horse all breakfasted in town.*

Friday morning, Mrs. Smith visited Anna Maria Mason, a sick friend, about a mile away. That night she wrote: *The streets of this quiet village, which never before witnessed confusion, [are] now filled with carriages bringing out citizens, and Baggage wagons and troops. Mrs. Bentley's house is now crowded, she had been the whole evening sitting at the supper table, giving refreshment to soldiers and travellers. I suppose every house in the village is equally full. I never saw more benevolent people . . . The whole settlement are quakers. The table is just spread for the 4th or 5th time, more wanderers having just enter'd.*

Mrs. Smith apparently was not present at the Bentley House during the President's stay, but she wrote: *Just at bed time the Presd. had arrived and all hands went to work to prepare supper and lodging for him, his companions and guards,—beds were spread in the parlor, the house was filled and guards placed round the house during the night. A large troop of horse likewise arrived and encamp'd for the night, beside the mill-wall in a beautiful little plain . . . The tents were scattered along the riverlet and the fires they kindled on the ground and the lights within the tents had a beautiful appearance. All the villagers, gentlemen and ladies, young and old, throng'd to see the President. He was tranquil as usual, and tho much distressed by the dreadful event, which had taken place not dispirited.*

The President and his party traveled approximately 18 miles south to Washington, probably via Georgia Avenue (Route 97), arriving about 5 p.m. on August 27. Madison stayed at the home of his brother-in-law, Richard Cutts, on F Street, NW. Guards were posted around the house to protect the President, who was blamed by some for the failure of the government to stop the British invasion. But only about an hour after his arrival, Madison was met with another concern. The distant rumble of cannon fire, followed by an explosion about 7 or 8 p.m., announced the destruction of Fort Washington about 11 miles down the Potomac River. A British squadron was heading upriver toward Alexandria and Washington and there was fear once again that the British would attack the capital. (*see* Alexandria Tour *in part 2 for details.*) Some citizens urged the President to surrender Washington to the British. James Madison wrote his wife, believing she was still in Virginia, pleading that she remain there. But Dolley was already on her way to the capital.

First Lady's Flight

Hoping for the best but concerned about the future, Dolley Madison frantically waited at the President's House for her husband's return from the Bladensburg battlefield (*see* Washington, D.C., Tour *in part 2 for details*). When she received a hastily written note from President Madison, informing her that she should arrange her carriage for a possible speedy getaway, she immediately began packing trunks with important Cabinet papers. A wagon was loaded with these trunks and some personal belongings such as a clock, silver plate, books, and crimson velvet curtains from the oval drawing room. She also ordered that Gilbert Stuart's portrait of George Washington, purchased by Congress for the President's House in 1800 and hanging on the west wall of the dining room, either be saved

Dolley Madison. (Engraving made between 1804 and 1855 based on original painting by Gilbert Stuart; Library of Congress)

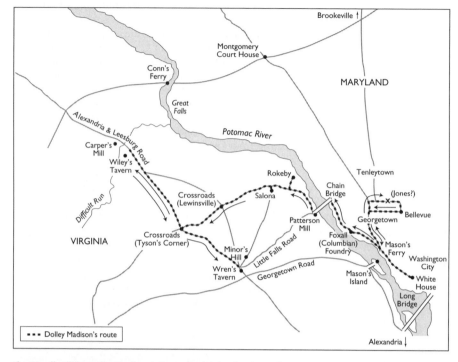

First Family Flight: Dolley Madison's Route (revised and redrawn from *August 24, 1814: Washington in Flames,* by Carole L. Herrick, original map drawn by Charles Herrick)

The full-length portrait of George Washington is the third in a series of four painted by Gilbert Stuart; the first done from life in 1796. Stuart painted only the head and shoulders of the White House portrait; William Winstanley completed the painting. Congress paid $800 for the eight by five foot painting in 1800. It was saved from burning in 1814 and hangs today in the East Room of the White House. (Photographic image of painting; Library of Congress)

or destroyed to keep it out of British hands. While writing a note to her younger sister Lucy, family friend Charles Carroll pleaded with her to leave immediately.

Dolley Payne Madison wrote (an after-the-fact recreation of her original letter) to her sister Lucy Payne Todd of an event that took place after 3 p.m., August 24, 1814: *Our kind friend, Mr.* [Charles] *Carroll, has come to hasten my departure* [from the President's House] *, and is in a very bad humour with me because I insist on waiting until the large picture of Gen.* [George] *Washington is secured.*

Dolley, along with her personal maid Sukey, her older sister Anna, and Anna's three children, rode by carriage toward Georgetown. They probably took Pennsylvania Avenue northwest and then headed north to Georgetown Heights, approximately 1.5 miles; first to the home of Secretary of Navy William Jones (exact location unknown) to pick up him and his family, then to the home of Charles Carroll known as **BELLEVUE**. There the entourage joined Anne Sprigg Carroll and waited.

BELLEVUE, now Dumbarton House. NRHP. **Address:** 2715 Q Street, NW, Georgetown. **Parking:** limited parking off 27th Street. **Hours:** Tuesday through Saturday, 10 a.m. to 1 p.m. **Fees:** $5. **Facilities:** house tours, restrooms. **Contacts:** 202-337-2288; www.dumbartonhouse. org. **Comment:** visit to house by tour only. This house was moved 100 feet from its original location in 1915 and the name changed from Bellevue to Dumbarton House in 1928.

Bellevue, now known as Dumbarton House, was built in 1805 by Charles Carroll, a wealthy landowner. (Charles E. Peterson 1942 photograph; HABS, Library of Congress)

President Madison sent a message to Secretary of Navy William Jones, instructing the waiting band to meet at the Columbian Foundry along the Potomac River northwest of Georgetown. Because of the panic and crush of fleeing Washingtonians, Madison sent a second message instructing Dolley to meet him the next day on the Virginia side of the river at Wiley's Tavern near Great Falls, about 16 miles northwest of Georgetown. Dolley, her servant Sukey, her sister Anna, and Anna's three children, Mrs. Jones, Mrs. Carroll, their children and servants, U.S. Navy clerk Edward Duvall, and William Jones traveled by carriage probably south on 28th Street to Falls or Bridge Street (M Street today), and west to Chain Bridge over the Potomac River, a distance of about 5 miles. In the relative safety of Virginia, they traveled northwest on Falls Road (now Chain Bridge Road, Route 123) about 1.5 miles to **ROKEBY FARM,** where they spent the night.

ROKEBY FARM SITE. Location: the farm house was located down Savile Lane northeast off Dolley Madison Boulevard (Route 123), McLean. **Facilities:** none. **Comment:** site not visible from public roads; no standing structure. Private property; not open to general public. Please do not trespass; respect privacy. The property known as Rokeby Farms Stables is not the property where Rokeby Farm was located.

The original Rokeby Farm house was completed in 1813 but apparently burned shortly after and was rebuilt circa 1820. Secretary of State James Monroe briefly stopped at Rokeby Farm while looking for the President, staying only long enough to have a quick meal. From a window of the farmhouse, Dolley could see a red sky from the fires set by the Americans at the Navy Yard and by the British on Capitol Hill. Ironically, the Rokeby Farm was owned by Richard and Matilda Lee Love, daughter of Federalist Ludwell Lee, a scion of the Virginia Lee family and a political opponent of James Madison's. Matilda was a niece of Henry "Light Horse Harry" Lee. Rokeby Farm was named by Matilda after a poem by Sir Walter Scott.

The next morning, Dolley and company left Rokeby Farm and traveled to Salona and then on to Wiley's Tavern (Dolley is believed to have taken Ballantrae Lane. A trace of this road can be seen from 1171–1173 Dolley Madison Boulevard to 1288 Ballantrae Farm Road; *see also* President Madison's Flight, *above*) to meet her husband as he had requested. Dolley continued northwest on Falls Road (now Chain Bridge Road), which forks west at the intersection with Georgetown Pike. This section of Chain Bridge Road is now called Dolley Madison Boulevard (Route 123), although it has been straightened, leaving behind a loop on the south side that still bears the name Chain Bridge Road. Dolley probably took Great Falls Road (now Lewinsville Road, Route 694) to Leesburg Pike (Route 7) to Wiley's Tavern, a distance of approximately 9 miles. She reached the tavern on the evening of August 25, 1814, just before a great storm passed through.

Tradition claims that the wife of the tavern owner was infuriated to learn that the wife of the President was in her home while her own husband was out fighting the enemy. She reportedly shrieked at the First Lady, demanding that she leave. It was only through the efforts of a friend that Dolley was permitted to remain. The President arrived after the storm, just before sunset. Dolley was finally united with her husband but their reunion was short. The President left about midnight to try to reach the American army in Maryland. Dolley proceeded the next morning, not west to the relative safety of inland Virginia, but toward Fall Church. She, her servant Sukey, her sister Anna, and Anna's children retraced their

Minor's Hill, situated on the highest elevation in the area, was named for the Col. George Minor family, who lived here. (Ralph Eshelman 2009 photograph)

route back down Leesburg Pike to Great Falls Road (now Lewinsville Road and Great Falls Street, Route 694) to Falls Church. From Falls Church, they probably traveled east on West Street to Williamsburg Boulevard to **MINOR'S HILL,** a total distance from Wiley's Tavern of approximately 10 miles.

MINOR'S HILL SITE. Location: geographically this hill is located near the intersection of Rockingham and Powhatan streets, just across the Fairfax County line in Arlington County. **Parking:** street. **Facilities:** none. **Comment:** historic marker. The house is located several blocks away in Fairfax County at the intersection of North Nottingham Street and Virginia Avenue. This house is privately owned; please respect privacy and do not trespass; pass by view only, no parking.

Dolley Madison and her entourage spent the nights of August 26 and 27 at Minor's Hill before returning to Washington on August 28. It is unclear whether they returned via Chain Bridge, which was damaged in the great storm, or the shorter route via Mason's Ferry, about 6 miles to the east. Dolley surely knew that the Long Bridge between Alexandria and Washington had been burned.

With the President's House in ruins, Dolley met her husband at the home of her brother-in-law Richard Cutts on F Street, NW. The first couple later moved into the Octagon House (*see* Washington, D.C., Tour *in part 2*) where the Treaty of Ghent was signed, officially ending the war. After her husband's death in 1836, Dolley lived in what today is sometimes referred to as the Dolley Madison House, located at 21 Madison Place, NW.

This ends the First Family Flight Tour.

Battle of North Point Tour

Particulars Parts of southeastern North Point Road (Route 20) are still relatively rural and give a feel of how the countryside might have appeared in 1814. Cows can be seen on a farm adjacent to the Todd House. This approximately 8-mile-long tour is best conducted by vehicle, although bicycles can be used with caution on the southern portion of the route. Be careful as there is no shoulder on the narrow North Point Road and North Point Boulevard can be congested from near the intersection with I-695 northward.

Begin your tour at North Point and follow the British route north to the battlefield site. The State of Maryland recently acquired an undeveloped nine-acre tract where part of the battle took place. This park, still in the planning stage, will eventually interpret the battle. Battle Acre, also on part of the battlefield, is nearby. There are several interesting tales related to the British march on Baltimore. These are provided as sidebars below. Restaurants become more numerous as one travels north, closer to Baltimore. Consider bringing a picnic lunch and stopping at North Point State Park, Fort Howard Park, Bear Creek Park, or Charlesmont Park. Several sites lack safe offroad parking, so please use caution.

Historical Background North Point is formed by the confluence of the Patapsco River and Back River. The British landed at this point to begin their pincer movement on Baltimore. The land force approached from the south and then east, and a naval force approached from the south. The land prong was met by an American force at what was then called Godley Wood. The battle was initially, and appropriately, called the Battle of Patapsco Neck. Over the years, it became known as the Battle of North Point, even though the action was 7.5 miles from North Point.

North Point is named for Capt. Robert North, who established a trading company on the tip of this peninsula in 1793. In preparation for their unsuccessful land assault on Baltimore, the British fleet anchored in Old Roads Bay, just off the point, on the evening of September 11, 1814. Approximately 4,500 troops began debarking about 3 a.m., September 12, 1814. At about 7 a.m., the advance elements began the 15-mile march to Baltimore followed by the main column about an hour later. Each man carried three days' provisions and 80 rounds of ammunition, 20 cartridges more than normal. Instead of the usual supply of clothing, the soldiers were allowed to take only one blanket, a spare shirt, and an extra pair of shoes. Hair brushes and other personal articles were to be shared.

British Commander Maj. Gen. Robert Ross was mortally wounded in a skirmish on North Point Road just south of Godley Wood prior to the Battle of North Point. The naval attack on Fort McHenry failed. By September 15 and 16, 1814, the British troops had withdrawn from the outskirts of Baltimore and were re-embarking on their ships.

Begin your tour at the **FORT HOWARD VETERANS HOSPITAL** grounds. Just inside the gate is a large green area that was the fort's parade ground. The fort was established in 1896 to defend Baltimore in anticipation of the Spanish-American War. Part of the fort grounds were turned over to the Veterans Administration in 1940. Follow Gettysburg Avenue 0.3 mile south to the waterfront.

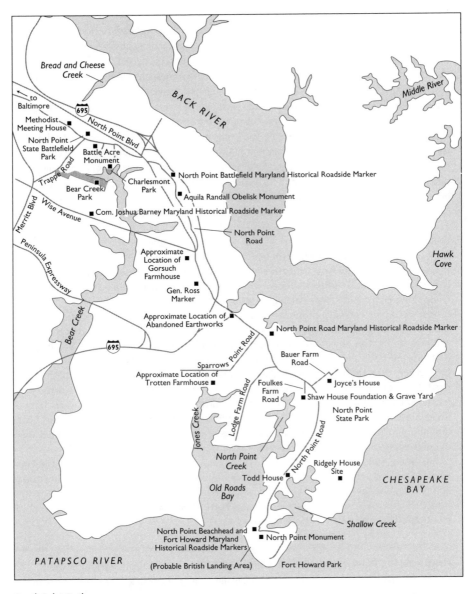

North Point Region

FORT HOWARD VETERANS HOSPITAL. Address: 9600 North Point Road. **Parking:** free. **Hours:** daylight hours. **Facilities:** none. **Comment:** this facility is pending redevelopment so the future is unclear. Presently a VA outpatient facility operates here during weekdays, but the hospital is closed. Access varies from time to time—sometimes open and other times restricted to VA patients only. Recently the grounds have been gated on weekends. A small undesignated parking area is located on the west side of North Point Road north of the gate. If vehicle access is restricted park and walk to the waterfront. If total access to the hospital grounds is denied go to Fort Howard Park, 0.6 mile beyond the hospital entrance. Park and walk south along the hospital property fence. The actual British landing site is not visible through the fence but the area where the British fleet anchored is visible offshore. For a better view, continue south past the Nicholson Battery to the waterfront. The landing beach area is around the bend in the shoreline to the right (west).

British troops came ashore during a moonless night. Visualize the formidable British fleet anchored offshore. Think of the panic that must have been felt by the citizens living in this rural area at the time. Imagine the thoughts of the British troops who had recently conducted a similar landing at Benedict (*see* British Invasion Tour *in part 1*). Could these troops have envisaged defeat after successfully taking Washington?

Just inside the entrance to the hospital grounds is the "North Point Beachhead" Maryland Historical Roadside Marker that claims Major General Ross was killed at the Battle of North Point. Actually, Ross was killed in a skirmish prior to the Battle of North Point. A plaque on the south side of the main hospital building claims "seven thousand troops" landed here from their fleet. The total number of British troops was closer to forty-five hundred. These troops actually withdrew from the outskirts of Baltimore, not the North Point battlefield as claimed on the plaque. The text on the "Fort Howard" Maryland Historical Roadside Marker, near the waterfront on Gettysburg Avenue, gives the first name of Lieutenant Colonel Harris as "Davis" but his name was actually David. Please note that because of redevelopment here these markers may be temporarily removed or relocated.

Assuming you gained access to the VA property, return to the main gate of the Fort Howard Veterans Hospital, and continue east (follow the signs) 0.6 mile to Fort Howard, a Spanish-American War–era fort (1898). Each September during the Defenders Day Celebration, the Battle of North Point is re-enacted at **FORT HOWARD PARK.** This park also provides picnic facilities and views of the Patapsco River.

FORT HOWARD PARK, NORTH POINT. Address: 9500 North Point Road. **Parking:** free. **Hours:** 8 a.m. to 7:30 p.m. in summer and normally 9 a.m. to dusk in winter but because of budgetary cutbacks the park may be closed in winter. **Facilities:** restrooms, picnic tables. **Contacts:** 410-887-7259; www.baltimorecountymd.gov/Agencies/recreation/countyparks/historicalsites.html. **Comment:** Fort Howard Veterans Hospital was built on part of the fort property in 1940.

Five of the six batteries at the fort are named for War of 1812 veterans. Battery Clagett is named for Lt. Levi Clagett, killed in the defense of Fort McHenry. Battery Harris is named for Lt. Col. David Harris, commander of a regiment of Baltimore artillery. Battery Key is named for Francis Scott Key, author of the lyrics that became "The Star-Spangled Banner." Battery Nicholson is named for Capt. Joseph Hopper Nicholson, captain of the Baltimore Fencibles, U.S. Volunteers. Battery Stricker is named for Brig. Gen. John Stricker, commander of the 3rd Brigade, Maryland militia.

Return to North Point Road and travel north following the route used by the British in their attempt to take Baltimore. On the right (east) side of the road can be seen glimpses of Shallow Creek. Ridgely House, an American lookout station, was located on the opposite side of Shallow Creek (*see sidebar*).

Ridgely House

The former Ridgely House was located near the end of Bay Shore Road. Ridgely House belonged to the Ridgely family, owners of Hampton Mansion and ironmasters of the Northampton Foundry that made cannons during the American Revolution and the War of 1812. An existing sketch of the house shows that, like Hampton Mansion, it had a cupola, which would have been an advantageous platform for observing the movement of enemy ships on the Bay. This cupola was used as a lookout station in 1813 and 1814.

A blue jack (flag) signaled that the British were standing down the Bay, while a white jack signaled the enemy was coming up the Bay. A white jack was raised on Sunday morning, September 11, 1814, serving notice that the British fleet was approaching Baltimore. When the signal was received in Baltimore that afternoon, three cannon shots were fired from Federal Hill to notify the citizens of a possible attack.

The Ridgely House cupola was used as a lookout and signal station. (Photograph of painting from *Old Baltimore,* 1931; courtesy Dundalk Patapsco Neck Historical Society)

Continue north on North Point Road 0.7 mile from the Fort Howard Hospital gate to **TODD HOUSE.**

TODD HOUSE. NRHP. Address: 9000 North Point Road. **Parking:** free. **Hours:** daylight. **Facilities:** no access to the interior of the house; the immediate grounds around the house are fenced but good views of the house are available during daylight hours; interpretive panel. **Contact:** 443-803-0517. **Comment:** Todd House is undergoing restoration and it is planned to open as a museum in the future. The cemetery contains gravestones that date from the War of 1812 era.

The Bernard Todd House, also called Todd's Inheritance, served as the headquarters for Lt. Col. William McDonald, who commanded troops assigned to prevent British raiding parties from landing along Patapsco Neck during the spring and summer of 1813. The house was also used as a signal house and horse courier station to report British movements in 1813 and 1814. A member of the Todd family reportedly served as one of the couriers. Three mounted videttes were stationed at the house on September 11, 1814. In retaliation for these military activities, the British burned the house and some outbuildings, forcing the Todd family to live in a granary for two years while the present house was built on the original house foundation. In 1853, Bernard Todd's heirs received $4,315, the appraised value of the burned property, from the U.S. government. A spyglass said to have belonged to Pvt. Bernard Todd, 1st Baltimore Hussars, is exhibited at the Flag House and Star-Spangled Banner Museum in Baltimore (*see* Baltimore Tour *in part 2*).

The Maryland Historical Roadside Marker "Todd's Inheritance" claims the house was burned as the British withdrew from their unsuccessful assault on Baltimore. The congressional claims records, used to determine compensation to the family for the destruction of the house, state it was burned during the British march on Baltimore.

Maj. William Barney wrote to Brig. Gen. John Stricker on March 23, 1813: *from this* [Todd] *House there is a tolerable river view of the Bay, from the Bodkin* [Point, Hancock's Resolution] *nearly across to Swan Point; Todds is a commodious two story frame house, with a large stable capable of accommodating in it and under its sheds at least thirty horses.*

Continue north 0.9 mile on North Point Road to the entrance of **NORTH POINT STATE PARK.** This park is a good place to stretch your legs, take a bike ride, or have a picnic.

NORTH POINT STATE PARK. Address: 900 North Point Road. **Parking:** free. **Hours:** grounds: 8 a.m. to sunset; visitor center: Wednesday through Sunday, 11 a.m. to 4 p.m. **Fees:** $3 per vehicle. **Facilities:** picnic, restrooms, hiking, biking trails. **Contacts:** 410-477-0757; www. northpointstatepark.homestead.com.; www.baygateways.net/general.cfm?id=91.

Continue north 0.4 mile on North Point Road to the unmarked Foulkes Farm Road on the left (south). As you pass Bauers Farm Road on the right (northeast), you may see a brick cream-colored stuccoed house, believed to date from before the war, in the distance. It may be what is referred to as "Joyce's" on an 1814 military map drawn by James Kearney.

The Shaw House Site and graveyard is down the unpaved Foulkes Farm Road 0.2 mile (*see sidebar for details*).

Shaw House

Shaw House Site and Graveyard, also called Foulkes Farmhouse, is located at the south end of Foulkes Farm Road, off North Point Road, near the intersection with Millers Island Road. Capt. Thomas Shaw built the house circa 1800. Maj. Gen. Robert Ross and a number of his men went to the Shaw House for some rest, ordered the family upstairs, and took possession of the first floor. Local tradition holds that a British lieutenant met Eleanor, a daughter of Mr. Shaw, on the stairs and tried to kiss her; but she broke away and jumped out from a second-story window. When Major General Ross heard of this incident, he supposedly punished the officer by sending him back to his ship.

Bethlehem Steel Corporation tore down the house in 1976, but the brick and stone foundation still survives. The graveyard is surrounded by a fence. The house site is located to the southwest of the graveyard, next to a residential trailer. Please respect the privacy of the occupants and do not enter the house site area—view the site from the graveyard only.

Shaw House as it appeared in the 1960s showing the upper windows, from one of which Eleanor Shaw reportedly jumped after the advances of a British lieutenant. This house was torn down about 1980. (Photographer unknown; courtesy Dundalk Patapsco Neck Historical Society)

Continue north 0.6 mile on North Point Road to the intersection of Lodge Farm Road on the left (southwest). The Lodge Farmhouse, where a British soldier reportedly used his bayonet to scratch the image of a Union Jack into the plaster wall above the mantelpiece, once stood near the end of this road, approximately one mile (*see sidebar for details*).

Continue north 0.1 mile on North Point Road to a Maryland Historical Roadside Marker on the right (east) side that merely proclaims the British marched along this road to attack Baltimore.

Lt. George Robert Gleig remembered the road in 1847: *In most of the woods they* [Americans] *had felled trees, and thrown them across the road; but as these abatis were without defenders, we experienced no other inconvenience than what arose from loss of time, being obliged to halt on all such occasions till the pioneers had removed the obstacle.*

Continue north 0.2 mile on North Point Road to the intersection of Sparrows Point Road on the left (southwest). Down this road, which existed in 1814, on Jones Creek, was the Trotten Farmhouse where the British reportedly demanded a cart to carry the body of Maj. Gen. Robert Ross (*see sidebar for details*).

Continue north 0.4 mile on North Point Road to the site of the abandoned and unfinished American defensive earthworks just north of the intersection with Delmar Avenue. Here the North Point peninsula narrowed to about a mile in width. Humphrey Creek, now filled in by Bethlehem Steel Corporation, penetrated in on the west and Greenhill Cove penetrated in on the east off Back River. The Americans abandoned these uncompleted earthworks to move to another choke point farther up the peninsula between the narrows of Bear Creek and Bread and Cheese Creek. The construction of North Point Boulevard and I-695 have destroyed the earthwork area.

Lodge Farmhouse

Located between Jones and North Point creeks, near the end of Lodge Farm Road, south off North Point Road, Lodge Farmhouse was owned by Sheppard Church Leakin. While building military earthworks overlooking the Philadelphia Road on the outskirts of Baltimore he nearly lost his life. A nearby tree that had been cut, fell and just missed him. The farmhouse burned circa 1960. No public access.

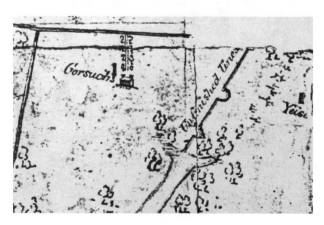

Map detail depicting Gorsuch House and unfinished entrenchments and gun emplacements. North Point Road is at the top and the head of Humphrey Creek is visible at the extreme south end of the earthworks. (From the James Kearney 1814 map "Sketch of Military Topography of Baltimore and its vicinity, and Patapsco Neck to North Point"; National Archives and Records Administration; copy at Fort McHenry National Historic Monument collections)

Sarah Trotten's Surprise

Trotten Farmhouse was owned by Dr. John Trotten and located inside what is now the Bethlehem Steel Corporation plant near Pennwood Road. Here a slave was reportedly forced to sample some wine to determine if it had been poisoned. After partaking of some wine, pickles, and preserves, one of the soldiers supposedly chalked on the front door, "We have found very good cheer with Mrs. Trotten and hope she will be at home when we return." Only a few hours later, the British did return, but this time to demand a horse, cart, and some blankets. To Sarah Trotten's surprise, the British did faithfully return the items. The Trottens later learned that the cart had been used to convey the body of Maj. Gen. Robert Ross to a small craft for conveyance to the fleet. The Trotten farmhouse was later used as the clubhouse for the Sparrows Point Country Club before burning down in 1954. Owing to the steel mill expansion the club moved north on Bear Creek.

Trotten Farmhouse. (Undated photograph by unknown photographer; courtesy Dundalk Patapsco Neck Historical Society)

Col. Arthur Brooke reported to Secretary of State for War and the Colonies Earl Bathurst, 3rd Earl Bathurst, on September 17, 1814: *Three miles* [actually over four miles] *from North point the enemy had entrenched himself quite across this neck of land . . . The enemy was actively employed in the completion of this work, deepening the ditch and strengthening it in front by a low Abbatis,—both which, however, he precipitately abandoned on the approach of our skirmishers, leaving in our hand some few dragoons, being part of his rear guard.*

Near here, British patrols captured a Mr. Nugent (probably Pvt. Neal Nugent) and two other dragoons (mounted militiamen) and took them to the Gorsuch House approximately 1.3 miles northwest off North Point Road (*see sidebar below*).

Due to the construction of I-695, the original North Point Road is truncated and replaced by North Point Boulevard (Route 151). A short section of the original North Point

Road dead-ends off to the right (north). Follow North Point Boulevard under the I-695 overpass. A second trace of the original North Point Road can be seen on the right (east). After traveling 0.6 mile north (approximately at 4630 North Point Boulevard, just past the DAP Inc. building on your right) you will pass a historic roadside marker on the left (west), partially hidden behind some recently planted trees. This marker cannot be read going in the north direction. It supposedly marks the location where Maj. Gen. Robert Ross died, about 1.5 miles northwest of where he was wounded. The marker, however, has been moved at least three times from its original location. The first, and presumably most accurate, location was on the east side of North Point Boulevard approximately 50 feet east of the road (approximately at the north end of where the DAP fence line is located today). Unfortunately, there is no safe place to pull off the road to read this sign so the text of the marker is repeated here:

AT THIS SPOT, ON SEPTEMBER 12, 1814, GENERAL ROBERT ROSS DIED. HE HAD BEEN MORTALLY WOUNDED IN CONFLICT APROXIMATELY 1-$\frac{1}{2}$ MILE NORTHWEST OF HERE, AT THE PRESENT SITE OF THE AQUILA RANDALL MONUMENT, AND CARRIED BY STRETCHER TO THIS POINT. HE WAS LATER INTERRED IN HALIFAX, NOVA SCOTIA.

Continue north 0.4 mile on North Point Boulevard to the intersection of Wise Avenue.

Christina Court and the North Point Industrial Center are just before this intersection on the left (west). The Gorsuch House (no longer standing) was located to the west of here (*see sidebar*).

Approximately 1.5 miles west on Wise Avenue, in front of the Patapsco High School on the right (north) side, is a Maryland Historical Roadside Marker dedicated to Joshua Barney who commanded the Chesapeake Flotilla and lived near here.

Continue north 0.2 mile on North Point Boulevard to the poorly marked intersection with North Point Road on the right (east). Turn right on North Point Road (Route 20). At this intersection, you can again see the North Point Road trace on the right (east) where the road originally intersected as a Y and not a T as today. Near here was a blacksmith shop, mentioned in several of the military reports at the time. You are now back on the British route. Travel 0.9 mile to the North Point Battlefield Maryland Historical Roadside Marker and **AQUILA RANDALL MONUMENT** on the right (northeast side) of North Point Road. It is just beyond the Old Battle Grove Road on the left (west) and the appropriately named Monument Industrial Building on the right (east).

AQUILA RANDALL MONUMENT. Location: near 3970 Old North Point Road. **Parking:** there is limited narrow shoulder parking just before the monument on the right-hand side of North Point Road. Use extreme caution. **Hours:** daylight hours. **Facilities:** none. **Comment:** the monument is surrounded by private property. Respect the privacy of the neighbors and the nearby commercial establishments.

The Aquila Randall Monument, originally erected by the First Mechanical Volunteers just south of here in July 1817, commemorates the loss of twenty-four-year-old Pvt. Aquila Randall, a member of the Mechanical Volunteers, 5th Regiment, Maryland militia, who fell during a skirmish preceding the Battle of North Point on September 12, 1814. Randall was the only member of this unit killed in the skirmish, as was also British commander Maj. Gen. Robert Ross. Some accounts claim Aquila Randall mortally wounded Major General Ross but others credit American sharpshooters Pvt. Daniel Wells and Pvt. Harry Mc-

Comas, both of whom also died in the conflict. The Wells and McComas Monument, in Baltimore (*see* Baltimore Tour *in part 2*), commemorates their sacrifice. The Aquila Randall Monument is among the first monuments ever erected on a battlefield in the United States. During the dedication, Benjamin C. Howard, the former commander of the Mechanical Volunteers, delivered a speech including the following lines: "It was here that the haughty General [Robert Ross] who declared he did not care if it rained militia atoned with his life for his opinion."

"I don't care if it rains militia"

Major General Ross and Vice Admiral Cockburn had breakfast at the Gorsuch Farmhouse on September 12, 1814. When Mr. Gorsuch sarcastically asked if they would be back for dinner, Ross supposedly boasted "I'll sup in Baltimore tonight—or in hell." British patrols brought in three captured dragoons after they had exchanged shots with them near the Americans' abandoned earthworks. During the interrogation the captives reported that twenty thousand men manned the Baltimore defenses. When it was determined that most were militia, Ross reportedly stated, "I don't care if it rains militia." Whether Ross ever made such statements will never be known, but he certainly could not have known his ultimate end was very near; he was killed soon after leaving the farm.

Gorsuch House. (Undated photograph by unknown photographer; courtesy Dundalk Patapsco Neck Historical Society)

This 1816 romanticized print depicts Maj. Gen. Ross falling into the arms of another officer while a Congreve rocket passes overhead. ("The Death of General Ross, near Baltimore—As soon as he perceived he was wounded he fell into the arms of a Brother Officer"; Library of Congress)

The Aquila Randall Monument as it appeared in the 1850s. (Lossing, *Pictorial Field-Book of the War of 1812*)

By 1944, the monument had suffered from neglect and the obelisk had fallen down. The monument was restored in 1945 by Eli Buniavas, a Croatian immigrant who acquired the property. He spent $7,000 on the restoration. The monument was mounted on a wedding cake–like pyramid of five steps on an elliptical lawn 90 by 20 feet and surrounded by an iron fence. When Buniavas died in 1962, the executor of his estate offered a 21 by 26 foot parcel called the Monument Lot to the State of Maryland, but the offer was declined. In 1977 the new owner, a Mr. McClees, offered the monument to the Baltimore County Department of Recreation and Parks, but this offer was also rejected. Because of road construction, the monument was moved in 1977 to its present location. A fence and 1945 pedestal were removed, giving the monument more of its 1817 appearance. The original location was within a circular curb visible just south near the intersection with Old Battle Grove Road. The monument is surrounded by private property without a designated caretaker. At some point, the monument was painted white with black letters.

Presidential Visit

On October 16, 1826, President John Quincy Adams visited the North Point battlefield. This was probably the first time a sitting president visited an American battlefield (other than when President James Madison was present briefly during the Battle of Bladensburg). Adams noted that there were no traces of the battle, although he was shown an oak tree in which it was said more than twenty of the enemy's musket balls had lodged. Adams picked up a dozen white oak acorns from under the tree to plant in Washington.

The monument includes the inscription "How beautiful is death, when earned by virtue." This quote is from Joseph Addison's drama *Cato: A Tragedy,* written in 1713 and popular during the Colonial period.

The historical marker next to the monument claims the British army consisted of seven thousand troops but the force was closer to forty-five hundred troops. Furthermore, based on contemporary reports, Maj. Gen. Robert Ross was probably mortally wounded on the high ground along the road further to the southeast, not here where the marker is located. This area was then known as Godley Wood. The name Old Battle Grove Road suggests a grove of trees. There are still some woods or thickets in the area. The Monument Inn was built at the intersection to accommodate travelers along North Point Road sometime after the battle.

Continue 0.2 mile north on North Point Road to the intersection with North Point Boulevard. The telephone poles on right (northwest) follow the original road trace. Turn right (north) on North Point Boulevard and immediately left to get back on North Point Road. You can see the original road trace again on the west side of North Point Boulevard, connecting to North Point Road. Continue north 0.5 mile on North Point Road to **BATTLE ACRE MONUMENT.** Notice how the road gains in elevation toward the American position, held on the high ground at a second narrowing of the peninsula.

BATTLE ACRE MONUMENT. Location: south side of 3100 block of North Point Road (Route 20), opposite intersection with Kimberly Road. **Parking:** street parking. **Hours:** daylight hours. **Facilities:** historic marker. **Comment:** there are plans to restore the park, which presently suffers from lack of maintenance.

Battle Acre Monument is believed to be in front of the main American line in the vicinity of a log house occupied by Capt. Philip Benjamin Sadtler's Baltimore Yagers (light infantry) at the beginning of the battle. Thus the historic marker is incorrect in stating that General Stricker's City Brigade was positioned here; they were actually located further to the west at the North Point State Battlefield site. It is an overstatement to proclaim the Americans "inflicted severe losses upon the main body of the British army," although the British loses were nearly twice that of the American loses.

A rough-hewn block of granite served as the cornerstone for the monument, which was laid on September 12, 1839, the twenty-fifth anniversary of the battle. To celebrate the occasion, the Fort McHenry garrison flag (the Star-Spangled Banner) was spread on the ground for all to see. Remains of entrenchments and a log hut bearing scares from cannonballs and musket balls were said to be visible. A flotilla of seven steamboats left Baltimore for Bear Creek carrying dignitaries, including two cabinet officers, two justices of the Supreme Court, the governor of Maryland, and at least three generals. Speeches and festivities were concluded with a national salute of artillery and infantry. The grand flag was then returned to Louisa Hughes Armistead at her residence in Mount Vernon, Baltimore (now the site of the Maryland Historical Society—*see* Baltimore Tour *in part 2*). Com. Joshua Barney's family is believed to have owned the property at or near where the park is now located.

Dr. Jacob Houck, Health Commissioner of Baltimore County, conveyed the deed for Battle Acre to the State of Maryland for the sum of one dollar on the day before the 1839 ceremony. Houck annually hosted a dinner for the North Point veterans at his nearby summer home called Houck's Pavilion. The monument, consisting of a square-shaped granite block with a bronze plaque (now missing) and a small cannon mounted on top, was not completed until the National Star-Spangled Centennial Celebration of 1914. Mrs. Reuben Ross Holloway was the driving force behind the effort to complete the monument. She also lobbied to get "The Star-Spangled Banner" designated our national anthem. The park was last restored in 1962.

The Baltimore *American* published an account of the monument dedication on September 12, 1839: *The procession having formed around the foundation of the Monument, the venerable Major General* [William M.?] *McDonald, aided by a soldier of the Revolution,* [Brigadier] *General T*[obias]. *E. Stansbury, Governor* [William] *Grason,* [Brigadier] *General* [Thomas Marsh] *Forman, and others proceeded to the cornerstone, in doing which in its cavity an official list of all the officers and privates who were in the Battle of North Point and Fort McHenry, lists of the present members of the military corps of the city, the newspaper of the day, coins &c. and a feu de joie* [firing of guns in celebration of a joyful event] *by the whole line of infantry.*

Continue north 0.2 mile on North Point Road to **NORTH POINT STATE BATTLEFIELD.**

NORTH POINT STATE BATTLEFIELD, ANNEX TO NORTH POINT STATE PARK. Location: northeast intersection of Trappe and North Point roads. **Parking:** no designated parking at site but limited parking can be found just north of the property and on surrounding streets. **Hours:** 8 a.m. to sunset. **Facilities:** none. **Contact:** 410-477-0757. **Comment:** the State of Maryland purchased this property, the last large undeveloped land in the area, to interpret the Battle of North Point. Parking and interpretive signage will be provided in the future. There is a pull off directly in front of this property on north side of North Point Road, but it is designated as a no parking area.

Engraving circa 1814 of the Battle of North Point depicting the American positions in the foreground and the British positions in the background. Key: I. British left flank. L. British artillery and rockets. M. British riflemen swarming American sharpshooters. O. Death of Major General Ross. ([Andrew Duluc], *First View of the Battle of Patapsco Neck*; courtesy of The Maryland Historical Society)

The North Point State Battlefield will interpret the engagement between the American and British forces that fought here. Brig. Gen. John Stricker, commanding a force of 3,200 men of the 3rd Brigade of the Maryland militia, faced the advancing British army. In the ensuing battle, the British sustained losses of 46 killed, 295 wounded, and 50 missing. The Americans, by contrast, lost only 24 killed, 139 wounded, and 50 captured. Although the American militia fought well, they were forced to withdraw in an orderly manner, unlike the panicked retreat at the Battle of Bladensburg. Instead of pursuing them, the tired British troops, up since at least 3 a.m. and now under the command of Col. Arthur Brooke, chose to camp for the night.

Stand on the north side of North Point Road, at the state battlefield property, and look southeast toward Battle Acre. It is hard to imagine that troops would have been lined up approximately a half mile across the choke point of the peninsula in front of you. You are essentially looking at the same view as provided in the contemporary illustrations above and on page 92. In that illustration North Point Road is clearly visible as well as the burning log

Battle of North Point viewed from behind the American line. (Lossing, *Pictorial Field-Book of the War of 1812,* see *The War of 1812 in the Chesapeake: A Reference Guide to Historic Sites in Maryland, Virginia, and the District of Columbia,* by Ralph E. Eshelman, Scott S. Sheads, and Donald R. Hickey, p. 158, for details of the units depicted in this print)

house believed to be where Battle Acre is now located. The head of Bear Creek, now largely filled in, was to the extreme right. The Baltimore Beltway, I-695, located beyond the trees on the left, approximates the end of the American left flank. In 1814, this battlefield was an open field with a tree line to the northeast stretching from Bread and Cheese Creek on the north to Bear Creek on the south. The American artillery consisting of six cannon was positioned across North Point Road at or near the intersection of Trappe Road. Haystacks were located on the field in front of the American line.

Visualize the Maryland militiamen lined up on each flank of the artillery, with riflemen stationed on the right flank stretching all the way to Bear Creek. The British, located among what are now the houses in the distance, moved a regiment forward against the American left flank. American Brig. Gen. John Stricker ordered two regiments from the rear, as well as two cannon on the road, to move to that flank to cover the British movement. Imagine the sound of cannon and musket fire and the smell of spent gunpowder in the air. Picture the men on both sides squinting through the thick smoke to ascertain their opponents' movement. Think of the fear and concern of the men as they saw some of their fellow soldiers fall and heard musket balls whistle by them. It all seems so impossible now with the sounds of automobile traffic and views of dense development. But the Battle of North Point took place here. Read Gleig's description of the battle to help visualize the scene.

British Lt. George Robert Gleig's account of the battle was published in 1833: *The British soldiers moved forward with their accustomed fearlessness, and the Americans, with much apparent coolness, stood to receive them. Now, however, when little more than a hundred paces divided the one line from the other, both parties made ready to bring matters more decided-*

ly to a personal struggle. The Americans were the first to use their small-arms. Having rent the air with a shout, they fired a volley, begun upon the right, and carried away regularly to the extreme left; and then loading again, kept up an unintermitted discharge, which soon in a great degree concealed them from observation. Nor were we backward in returning the salute. A hearty British cheer gave notice our willingness to meet them; and firing and running, we gradually closed upon them, with the design of bringing the bayonet into play . . . Volley upon volley having been given, we were now advanced within less than twenty yards of the American line; yet such was the denseness of the smoke, that it was only when a passing breeze swept away the cloud for a moment, that either force became visible to the other. It was not, therefore, at men's persons that the fire of our soldiers was directed. The flashes of the enemy's muskets alone served as an object to aim at, as, without, doubt, the flashes of our muskets alone guided the enemy.

For more pastoral views of the battlefield, visit Bear Creek and Charlesmont parks (see sidebars for details).

Continue 0.3 mile north on North Point Road to the **METHODIST MEETING HOUSE** site.

Bear Creek Battlefield Views

Those who wish to get a different perspective of the battlefield should visit Bear Creek Park and Charlesmont Park.

Bear Creek Park, located off Park Haven Road, north off Gray Haven Road, south off Lynch Road, east off Trappe Road, south off North Point Road (Route 20), provides a good view of the North Point battlefield. The British position is to the northeast and the American position to the northwest. The British withdrew their wounded by boat using Bear Creek.

> Maj. Gen. Samuel Smith wrote to Acting Secretary of War James Monroe on September 19, 1814: *on monday Brigadier General [John] Stricker took a good position at the junction of the two roads leading from this place to North Point, having his right flanked by Bear Creek and his left by a marsh. He here awaited the approach of the Enemy.*

Charlesmont Park, located at the south loop end of Charlesmont Road, south off North Point Road (Route 20), also located along Bear Creek, provides a good view of the North Point battlefield. On September 12, 1814, Brig. Gen. John Stricker placed his right flank at the head of Bear Creek near Charlesmont Park.

Methodist Meeting House, used by both the British and Americans as a field hospital, as it appeared in the 1890s. (Photographer unknown; courtesy Dundalk Patapsco Neck Historical Society)

METHODIST MEETING HOUSE site. **Address:** 2440 North Point Road, immediately north of Galilee Baptist Church. **Parking:** no designated street parking on North Point Road, use nearby street parking such as along Robinson Avenue. **Hours:** daylight hours. **Facilities:** none.

The Methodist Meeting House, also called Battle Ground Methodist Episcopal Church, and Bread and Cheese Creek Battle Monument are where Brig. Gen. John Stricker's 3rd Brigade of Maryland militia camped from about 9 p.m., September 11, until the morning of September 12, 1814. Stricker may have actually stayed in the church. On the night of September 12, 1814, following the battle, the British under the command of Col. Arthur Brooke, who replaced Maj. Gen. Robert Ross after his mortal wounding, also encamped here. The circa 1795 church served as a hospital after the engagement. When the church was remodeled in 1837, and again in 1858, hundreds of bullets were reportedly found in its frame. The church was demolished in 1921. A nearby log schoolhouse, demolished in 1927, also reportedly had numerous bullets lodged in its logs.

The Rev. Henry Smith, a Methodist circuit minister, visited the meeting house a few days after the engagement and remarked that the structure looked more like a slaughter-house than a house of worship. The meeting house became a place where veterans of the battle as well as other soldiers, politicians, and fraternal organizations gathered to commemorate the battle. A monument, placed by the Patriotic Order of Sons of America in Maryland to commemorate the Methodist Church and its role as a hospital in the Battle of North Point, was dedicated in 1914 by the Star-Spangled Banner Centennial Committee.

> British Rear Adm. George Cockburn wrote to Vice Adm. Alexander Cochrane on September 14, 1814: [the Americans] *gave way in every direction, and was chased by us a considerable distance with great Slaughter, abandoning his Post of the Meeting House situated in this Wood, and leaving all his Wounded and Two of his Field Guns in our possession.*

Dr. James Haines McCulloh, Jr., barely out of his teens, received his medical degree on July 17, 1814, and was appointed U.S. Army Garrison Surgeon at Hampstead Hill. He left Baltimore traveling to North Point in search of his father, who was among the militia. At the Methodist Meeting House on September 13, 1814, he attended to the wounded of both British and American soldiers.

> Dr. McCulloh, Jr., wrote to Gen. Samuel Smith on September 14, 1814: *I was shewn the meeting house in which some of our wounded men lay—along with a few British—on not finding my father here—I instantly requested permission to go over the field of battle—which was granted one of the [British] surgeons accompanying me—on reaching the field of action—the surgeon promised me the use of some litters to bring the wounded in . . . In the course of a few hours I had the wounded brought in which were 28 in number—2 of these died in the course of the night after I had dressed them and extracted their balls one of which was a grape [shot].*
>
> British Capt. James Scott remembered in 1834: *The meeting-house, a place of worship, the only building near the scene of battle, was converted into a temporary refuge for friends and foes. The temple of God—of peace and goodwill towards men—vibrated with the groans of the wounded and the dying. The accents of human woe floated upon the ear, and told a melancholy tale of ebbing tide of human life.*
>
> British Rear Adm. George Cockburn reported to Vice Adm. Alexander Cochrane on September 15, 1814: *The Night being fast approaching, and the Troops much fatigued, Colo-*

nel [Arthur] Brook determined on remaining for the Night on the Field of Battle, and on the morning of the 13th. leaving a small guard at the Meeting House to collect and protect the Wounded—We again moved forward towards Baltimore.

Some of the soldiers killed during the Battle of North Point are said to be buried in the Methodist Meeting House yard, but if grave markers were placed none survive. Tradition also claims some British soldiers were buried under what today is a landfill near the northeast end of Trappe Road. The American reserves were located at Cooks Tavern, approximately at the site of the Walmart near 1230 North Point Road, about 0.5 mile northwest of the intersection of Trappe Road with North Point Road.

The American forces withdrew to Baltimore while the British forces rested here at the Meeting House. The next morning the British continued their march to Baltimore.

This ends the Battle of North Point Tour, but for those who wish to follow the British route to what was then the outskirts of Baltimore, continue below.

British Route to Baltimore

Continue northwest 1.7 miles on North Point Road to the intersection of Eastern Avenue. North Point Road is disrupted by Eastern Avenue. (For those who may wish to skip this part of the British route which has little to see, go directly to the American defensive position on Hampstead Hill by turning left on Kane Street just beyond the railroad overpass, then right on East Lombard Street and follow it west under the I-95 and the I-895 overpasses until you come to the T at Linwood Avenue at Patterson Park. Rodgers's Bastion, the focal point for the area, is located at the northwest corner of the park at Baltimore Street and Patterson Park Avenue. [See Baltimore Tour *in part 2 for details on* Patterson Park *and* Rodgers's Bastion.])

The next section of the British route is now called Old North Point Road. It continues beyond Eastern Avenue before it becomes truncated by a railroad line. It is recommended not to take Old North Point Road but turn right (northeast) on Eastern Avenue and immediately exit to the right (south) on the cloverleaf to North Point Boulevard. Follow this road approximately 2 miles under I-95, under the railroad bridge, and over I-895 to Erdman Avenue. Immediately after passing over Pulaski Highway (U.S. Route 40), you will pass the Kell House site on the left (southwest).

The Kell House was located approximately at the athletic field southeast of Claremount School at 5301 Erdman Avenue. The topography of the Kell House site has been severely altered by road, railroad, and athletic field construction. The British reportedly used the Kell House as a headquarters on the evening of September 13 until the morning of September 14, 1814. Here, from a second-story window, Col. Arthur Brooke, commander of the British land forces, and his aides, reportedly observed the American forces strategically positioned on Hampstead Hill (*see* Patterson Park *under* Baltimore Tour *in part 2*). The heavily fortified earthworks constructed on these heights convinced Brooke to reconsider a direct attack on Baltimore from the east. He decided to reconnoiter the city's northern defenses beyond the American left flank of the earthworks.

A contingent of soldiers was sent to the north to reconnoiter the strength of the American left flank. They scouted as far as Furley Hall (*see sidebar*) about 1.7 miles north of the Sterett House (*see below*). Meanwhile parts of the British army spent the late afternoon and evening encamped approximately between the Joseph Sterett House and Murray's Tavern (*see sidebar*) a distance of about 0.5 mile with the main body essentially around the Herring Run area.

"British Troops Rest Near Tavern
While Officers Drink Wine"

Murray's Tavern was located approximately 0.7 mile west of Patterson Park near the intersection of Haven Street and Pulaski Highway. The British occupied positions near this tavern during the afternoon and evening of September 13, 1814.

Furley Hall, also called Bowley House, was approximately located on the south side of Bowleys Lane, 150 feet east of Plainfield Avenue, near Herring Run Park. British soldiers occupied Furley Hall during their northward-flanking maneuver. British officers reportedly helped themselves to William Bowley's wine. This site marks roughly the northernmost position of the British troops during the Battle for Baltimore. The house was damaged by fire in 1906 and demolished in 1953.

Furley Hall. (Circa 1895 photograph; courtesy Historical Marker Database Hmdb .org)

Continue 0.6 mile north on Erdman Avenue and turn right (east) on Federal Street 0.2 mile and right (south) to Wilbur Avenue where the **JOSEPH STERETT HOUSE** is located.

JOSEPH STERETT HOUSE. Address: 4901 Wilbur Avenue. **Parking:** street. **Hours:** daylight hours. **Facilities:** none. **Comment:** this house has several names including Surrey Farm, Sterett's Mansion, and Fox Mansion. The house has been severely altered by numerous additions and covered with stucco siding. It retains little if any resemblance to its 1814 appearance.

Here lived Lt. Col. Joseph Sterett who served as a colonel in the Baltimore City militia in 1812 and captain in the Independent Company of militia during the defense of Fort McHenry in 1814. An American courier from Todd House reported the landing and advance of the British troops at North Point here to Lieutenant Colonel Sterett. The north end of the British line occupied this position on the afternoon and evening of September 13, 1814. British troops supposedly broke into Sterett's wine cellar and, after enjoying his wine and food, thanked him with a note. The once-impressive Sterett House occupied a beautiful terraced slope overlooking the old Philadelphia Road (now Erdman Avenue).

The strength of the American defenses and the failure of a nocturnal British naval flanking maneuver against Fort McHenry ultimately persuaded Col. Arthur Brooke not to attack Baltimore. The colonel and his troops withdrew to their ships at North Point. Brooke later wrote to Secretary of State for War and the Colonies Henry Bathurst on September 17, 1814: "the capture of the town [Baltimore] would not have been sufficient to the loss which might probably be sustained in storming the heights [Hampstead Hill at Patterson Park]."

Continue to Rodgers' Bastion at Patterson Park (*see* Baltimore Tour *in part 2 for details*). This ends the British advance route to Baltimore.

PART 2 | Historic City, Town, and Regional Tours

MARYLAND

Annapolis and U.S. Naval Academy Tour

Particulars Annapolis is a historic, charming, walkable town. Most of downtown Annapolis is designated a National Historic District and the Maryland Statehouse and U.S. Naval Academy are designated National Historic Landmarks. Street parking is very limited and metered. Parking garages are recommended. The U.S. Naval Academy Stadium parking lot on Rowe Boulevard provides inexpensive parking with free shuttle service to the downtown area and U.S. Naval Academy Gate 1 (www.pinnacleparking.com/public_parking .htm). Bicycles are not recommended downtown as the streets are normally very busy. Excursion cruises are available from the waterfront (*see* appendix D).

In addition to the War of 1812 sites outlined below, enjoy the ambience of eighteenth- and nineteenth-century buildings alongside brick sidewalks. There are many historic homes, some open to the public, and numerous fine restaurants for all tastes, ranging in cost from reasonable to expensive. There are also hotels downtown, and generally less expensive lodging is available in the surrounding area. The scenic waterfront area serves as the focal point for tourists. This War of 1812 tour centers on the Maryland Statehouse, used as an observation post during the war, and the U.S. Naval Academy, where numerous naval war relics are on display. Highlights include the U.S. Naval Academy Museum and Tripoli Monument. Visitors may plan their tour to suit their own interests and time constraints.

Historical Background Annapolis became a military camp and served as the legislative center for the state government where issues relating to the defense of Maryland were debated.

> The Annapolis *Maryland Republican* reported on June 20, 1812: *The respective infantry companies of this city, are requested to meet at the state-house this morning at 9 o'clock, for the purpose of receiving their arms from the armory.*

Annapolis was the best-fortified city in Maryland, if not in the Chesapeake (Norfolk, Virginia, was protected by four forts). At the beginning of the war, the city was defended by no fewer than four forts. Fort Severn occupied the south side of the Severn River, where the U.S. Naval Academy is now located. Forts Madison and Nonsense (NRHP) were located on the north side of the Severn River, and a gun battery was located at Horn Point on the south side of Spa Creek. Fort Bieman, built during the Revolutionary War and located nearly opposite Fort Severn on the north side of the Severn River, may also have been used in the War of 1812. None of these forts are extant today with the exception of Fort Nonsense, located on military property and not accessible to the public.

The British fleet blockaded Annapolis in April and again in July of 1813. Because of the threat of a British attack, the public records were moved from the state capital on April 19, 1813, to the relative safety of Upper Marlboro, approximately 30 miles to the southwest in Prince George's County. No one could have foreseen that the British would never occupy Annapolis and that British forces would march through the hamlet of Upper Marlboro in August of 1814 on their way to capture Washington.

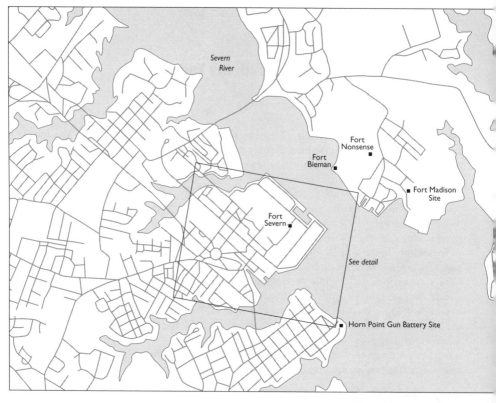

Annapolis Region

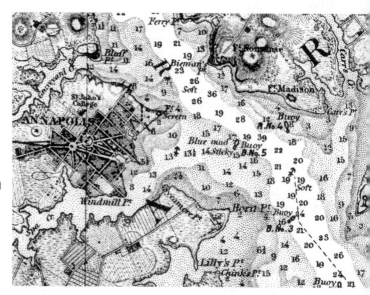

Detail of Annapolis and Severn River showing fortification locations. (George M. Bache and F. H. Gerdes, *The Harbor of Annapolis*, 1846, Maryland State Archives)

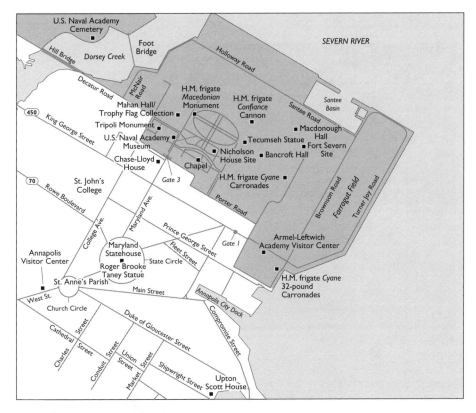

Annapolis Detail and U.S. Naval Academy

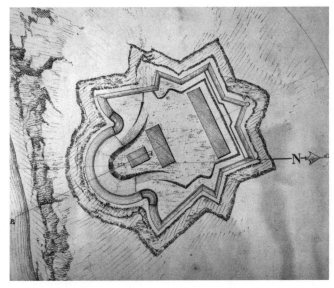

Fort Madison no longer exists but this 1819 plan illustrates the complexity of the fortification. (National Archives and Records Administration, Cartographic Section)

Sheet 10.

Fort Severn was built in 1808 and had changed little from this 1845 plan, the year it was demolished. (National Archives and Records Administration, Cartographic Section)

The Annapolis *Maryland Gazette and Political Intelligencer* reported on April 15, 1813: *Our city was alarmed at an early hour on Friday morning last by the discharge of several cannon from the fort* [Fort Severn], *and drums beating to arms—The alarm was caused by the arrival of several privateers, who reported that they had been pursued some considerable distance up the Bay by a part of the* [British] *blockading squadron.*

The Annapolis *Maryland Republican* reported on August 14, 1813: THE ENEMY . . . *One frigate said to be* [Rear] *Admiral* [George] *Cockburn's is opposite the harbor* [Annapolis], *within about six miles of the city. We have expected an attack for several nights past, and the most strict precautions are taken to prevent a surprise, guards are posted in every direction, and the troops are on their posts from 2 till 6 o'clock every morning. A schooner* [British] *has been sounding the harbor for two days past.*

Annapolis was threatened a second time in late August 1814 by a Royal naval squadron sailing up the Chesapeake. With the British occupation of Washington and the capitulation of Alexandria fresh on his mind, Judge Jeremiah T. Chase, chairman of the Annapolis Committee of Safety, endorsed a resolution to surrender the town if threatened by the British. The resolution did not pass.

When an even-larger British fleet sailed up the Chesapeake Bay to attack Baltimore in the second week of September 1814, people in Annapolis, again fearing an attack, fled the city in wagons loaded with their possessions.

Midshipman Robert J. Barrett, who served aboard one of those British vessels, wrote in 1841: *As we ascended the bay, alarm guns were fired in all directions; thus testifying the terror which the inhabitants of the surrounding country felt at the approach of the British arms . . . As we passed the picturesque town of Annapolis . . . we could plainly perceive the inhabitants flying in all directions.*

When the news of peace with England reached the Chesapeake on February 13, 1815, the citizens of Annapolis celebrated by brilliantly illuminating the Statehouse and other buildings with candles in the windows. They also fired cannons, rang bells, and built grand bonfires.

A good place to begin your tour is the Annapolis Visitor Center, where brochures, maps, and other information are available.

ANNAPOLIS VISITOR CENTER: Address: 26 West Street; also booth at City Dock, April through early October. **Hours:** 9 a.m. to 5 p.m. daily. **Parking:** city parking garages or stadium parking suggested (see www.visitannapolis.org/visitor-info/visitors-center/index. aspx). **Accessibility:** wheelchair accessible. **Contacts:** 1-888-302-2852; www.visitannapolis. org/visitor-info/visitors-center/index.aspx.

From the visitor center it is only a short walk (0.2 mile) to the **MARYLAND STATEHOUSE.**

MARYLAND STATEHOUSE. NHL. Address: 91 State Circle. **Hours:** 8:30 a.m. to 5 p.m., Monday through Friday, and 10 a.m. to 4 p.m. on weekends. **Fees:** none. **Facilities:** exhibits, tours, restrooms, visitor information. **Tours:** free upon request. **Accessibility:** wheelchair accessible. **Contacts:** 410-974-3400; www.msa.md.gov/msa/homepage/html/statehse.html. **Comment:** all visitors over 17 must present a photo ID.

The Statehouse, the third to occupy the site, was begun in 1772 and completed in 1779. It is the oldest functioning statehouse in the United States.

The Annapolis *Maryland Republican* reported on August 7, 1813: *For near a week past there has been from 20 to 25 sail of the blockading squadron in sight of this city* [Annapolis], *plainly perceptible from the dome of the state house.*

Public access to the dome is not allowed. The silver service, made by Samuel Kirk and Sons, Inc., of Baltimore on behalf of the citizens of Maryland, is displayed in the **MARYLAND SILVER ROOM.** This service was presented to the U.S. armored cruiser *Maryland* in 1906. The new U.S. battleship *Maryland* received the service in 1921. The State of Maryland received the service upon the decommissioning of the battleship after World War II. Each Maryland county and Baltimore City contributed a piece to the service, each with representative historic scenes and symbols. Examples of War of 1812 depictions include scenes of the bombardment of Fort McHenry and the birth of "The Star-Spangled Banner" found on the punch bowl.

Outside, near the front of the Maryland Statehouse, is the **ROGER BROOKE TANEY STATUE.** This statue is dedicated to Chief Justice of the Supreme Court Roger Taney, who practiced law in Annapolis from 1796 to 1799. Taney married Ann Phoebe Charlton Key, sister of Francis Scott Key. In 1856, Taney wrote an account of the writing of "The Star-Spangled Banner" that first appeared in print as the foreword to a volume of Key's poems. Since Key himself did not elaborate on the writing of the lyrics, Taney's account is a valuable contribution. The statue of Taney was sculpted by William Henry Rinehart (who also did the

The wooden dome of the Maryland Statehouse, the largest in the United States, served as an observation post for British movements on Chesapeake Bay. ("A Front View of the State-House &c. at Annapolis the Capitol of Maryland," *Columbian Magazine*, vol. 3, February, 1789)

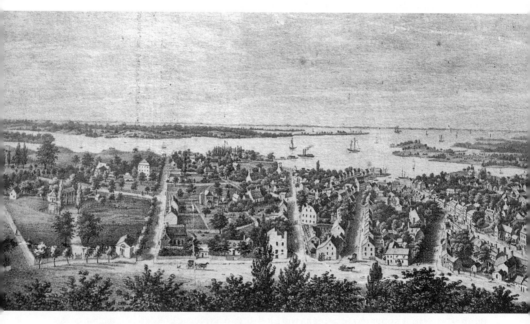

View from the dome of the Statehouse circa 1855 showing the mouth of the Severn River, Chesapeake Bay, Kent Island, and Eastern Shore beyond. (Lithograph by Edward Sachse circa 1855, *View of Annapolis;* courtesy of The Maryland Historical Society)

bronze doors to the U.S. Capitol) and dedicated December 10, 1872. It depicts Taney seated with his left hand resting on a book titled "THE CONSTITUTION."

The **U.S. NAVAL ACADEMY** is a short walk (0.3 mile) down (east) Maryland Avenue from the Statehouse. Take the time to peer into the right-hand lower parlor window or take a tour of the **CHASE-LLOYD HOUSE** (NHL, 22 Maryland Avenue; 410-269-1714; fee), built in 1769. In that room, Francis Scott Key married Mary Tayloe Lloyd on January 19, 1802.

U.S. NAVAL ACADEMY. NHL. **Hours:** open daylight hours; tours in summer: 9 a.m. to 5 p.m. daily; winter: 9 a.m. to 4 p.m. daily. **Parking:** none. **Fees:** none. **Tours:** adults $9, seniors $8, school children $7, preschool children free. Time of tours vary throughout year. **Tour Contact:** 410-293-TOUR (8687). **Accessibility:** wheelchair accessible. **Contacts:** 410-263-6933; www.usna.edu/visit.htm. **Comments:** There are two gates that may be used by visitors. The main gate (Gate 1), located at the end of King George Street, is recommended if you are interested in seeing the Armel-Leftwich Visitor Center and if you want to join a guided tour of the academy. If you prefer to visit on your own, you may enter through the closer Maryland Avenue gate (Gate 3). All visitors over 17 must present a photo ID. Civilian vehicles are not allowed on grounds.

MACDONOUGH HALL is named for Captain Thomas Macdonough (1783–1825) who, on September 11, 1814, commanded the American flotilla that won a major naval victory in Plattsburg Bay, Lake Champlain, New York.

Within **BANCROFT HALL** is **MEMORIAL HALL,** serving as a shrine to the academy's most-honored alumni. Here hangs a replica of the battle flag that contains the words "Dont Give Up the Ship" (proper punctuation would include an apostrophe in "don't," but no apostrophe appears on the flag). These words were supposedly uttered by the mortally wounded Capt. James Lawrence on June 1, 1813, when his ship, the U.S. frigate *Chesapeake,* fought the H.M. frigate *Shannon.* A banner with Lawrence's words was made at the order of Capt. Oliver Hazard Perry and used by him as a battle flag during his victorious action at Lake Erie aboard the U.S. brig *Niagara* on September 10, 1813. The original flag, exhibited at the U.S. Naval Academy since 1849, is on display at the U.S. Naval Academy Museum (*see below*).

Several relics from the War of 1812 are on the Academy grounds. The **H.M. FRIGATE *CON-FIANCE* 24 POUNDER CANNON** (north side of Bancroft Hall) is a war prize taken at the Battle of Lake Champlain on September 11, 1814. *Confiance* was struck no fewer than 105 times and 40 British sailors were killed and another 38 wounded. The cannon has a prominent dent on the muzzle from being struck by an American projectile during the battle.

The **H.M. FRIGATE *CYANE* 32 POUNDER CARRONADES** (a short cannon designed to throw a large projectile with small velocity) are war prizes captured off Madeira on February 20, 1815, by the U.S. frigate *Constitution*. One carronade is mounted on the east side of Bancroft Hall and two others on the east side of the Armel-Leftwich Visitor Center.

The **H.M. FRIGATE *MACEDONIAN* FIGUREHEAD MONUMENT** (northeast of Preble Hall and northwest of Bancroft Hall on west end of green) is a tribute to Capt. Stephen Decatur and the crew of U.S. frigate *United States.* On October 25, 1812, off the Canary Islands, the *United States* captured H.M. frigate *Macedonian.* The *Macedonian* was the only British frigate brought to America as a prize of war. The sculpture is a replica of the original figurehead, depicting Alexander the Great, taken from *Macedonian.* Four 18 pounder cannon taken

Congress awarded Capt. Charles Stewart, commander of U.S. frigate *Constitution*, a medal for his victories over H.M. frigate *Cyane* and H.M. sloop-of-war *Levant*. (Lossing, *Pictorial Field-Book of the War of 1812*)

from *Macedonian* complete the monument designed by Baltimore native Edward Berge. A plaque on the monument describes the action. The U.S. Navy Trophy Flag Collection includes the flag from *Macedonian,* which was reportedly laid at the feet of Dolley Madison during a ball in December 1812 to celebrate Congress's decision to enlarge the navy. This monument was located at the Gosport (Portsmouth) Navy Yard until 1875.

The **U.S. NAVY TROPHY FLAG COLLECTION** consists of naval flags captured during American wars. Thirty-four flags in the collection date from the War of 1812. Many of them are on display in the main hall and main stairwell in Mahan Hall (north end of Stribling Walk, opposite Bancroft Hall). Examples include the jack (a small flag flown at the bow of a ship, usually to indicate nationality) and a pendant from H.M. frigate *Guerriere,* captured August 19, 1812, by the U.S. frigate *Constitution* about 750 miles east of Boston. It was during this engagement that *Constitution* earned the nickname "Ironsides," which soon became "Old Ironsides." Also in the collection are the ensigns from H.M. frigate *Cyane,* H.M. frigate *Macedonian,* and H.M. frigate *Confiance.*

The **TECUMSEH STATUE** (Tecumseh Court, near southeast edge of the green in front of Bancroft Hall) is named for the Shawnee chief who, with his brother the Prophet in 1808, established a village called Prophet's Town near Lafayette, Indiana. Using this village as their base, the brothers headed a movement that encouraged their people to return to traditional Indian ways. Tecumseh formed a defensive confederacy of many American Indian tribes to hold their lands against the white man. While he was away, Indiana Territory Governor William Henry Harrison led an expedition on November 7, 1811, against Prophet's Town, destroying it after the fierce Battle of Tippecanoe. Tecumseh joined the British at the beginning of the War of 1812 and was killed on October 5, 1813, at the Battle of the Thames in Upper Canada. The Tecumseh Statue is the only known monument in the Chesapeake region that commemorates the role of American Indians in the War of 1812. Ironically, the "Tecumseh" monument is a bronze copy made in 1930 of the original circa 1817 wooden figurehead "Tamanend" from the U.S. ship-of-the-line *Delaware,* built at Gosport Shipyard, Portsmouth, Virginia. The bronze replica was presented by the Academy class of 1891. Tamanend was chief of the Delaware tribe. How it came to be known as the Tecumseh Statue is unclear. As a tribute to Tecumseh and in hope of good luck, it is painted with washable paint before every home football game, during the week that Navy plays Army, and whenever there is a commissioning ceremony for midshipmen. Pennies are also traditionally placed on the monument for good luck before exams.

The **TRIPOLI MONUMENT,** initially known as the Naval Monument (northwest side of Preble Hall), was originally erected at the Washington Navy Yard. It is the oldest military monument in the United States and the first to be approved by U.S. Officers of the American Naval Mediterranean Fleet. The officers donated $3,000 for the design and construction of the monument to eulogize five American naval officers and one midshipman who fell during the Tripolitan Wars in 1804. Largely through the efforts of Com. David Porter, Sr., it was erected in 1808 as Washington's first outdoor monument. The monument was reportedly mutilated by the British on August 25, 1814, although some accounts claim local citizens vandalized the monument in protest of the army's failure to protect the city. The monument, sculpted in 1806 by Giovanni C. Micali of Carrera Italian marble taken from the same quarry used by Michelangelo, was brought to the United States as ballast by the U.S. frigate *Constitution.* The monument consists of a rostral column crowned by a flying eagle.

The column shaft is decorated with the bows of corsair vessels and the faces of Barbary pirates. On one side of the base on which the shaft rests is a sculptured basso-rilievo of Tripoli, its fortresses in the distance and the American fleet in the foreground. Benjamin Henry Latrobe added inscriptions to the other three faces, including the names of the officers who fell in the battle. Against Latrobe's wishes but insisted upon by Porter, an anti-British inscription was added. The inscription, no longer present, blamed the British for the damage to the monument. At three corners of the base are half-life size marble allegorical figures representing History, Fame, and Commerce. (Some sources include Glory, which is represented by a lamp, not a figure.) Although the monument was restored after it was damaged in 1814, there is speculation that the figures are not in their original positions. The monument, built to be 15 feet high, was raised on a large block of stone when moved to the western portico of the U.S. Capitol in 1831. It was moved a second time to the Naval Academy in 1860. The **U.S. NAVAL ACADEMY MUSEUM** is located immediately south of the monument.

Lost Copy of Key's Manuscript

Near the bandstand on Chauvenet Walk is the Joseph Hopper Nicholson House site. Nicholson (1770–1817), Francis Scott Key's brother-in-law, occupied a home that stood on the south side of Scott Street, once parallel to Maryland Avenue, near where the chapel now stands. The original manuscript of Key's lyrics that eventually became "The Star-Spangled Banner" was kept here in a desk in Nicholson's house for many years. The plaque that marks this spot incorrectly claims the house belonged to Judge Joseph Hopper Nicholson. The house was owned by his son, who served as secretary of state of Maryland in 1838–39.

Peter Magruder, secretary of the Naval Academy, claimed that when Francis Scott Key had scribbled down the first draft of his lyrics that later became the words to the national anthem, he showed it to Nicholson, who suggested alterations. Having made the alterations on a new copy, Key tossed the original in a wastebasket. Nicholson supposedly retrieved the copy and placed it in a pigeonhole in a desk at his home. When expansion of the Naval Academy required the destruction of the house, the furniture was removed. In 1890, a daughter discovered the draft copy in the desk. The manuscript was passed on to Rebecca Lloyd Shippens, Nicholson's granddaughter. This copy of Key's draft is now exhibited at the Maryland Historical Society, in Baltimore.

Facsimile of Perry's blue battle flag with white letters "DONT GIVE UP THE SHIP." It is among the best known American naval battle flags. At one time all midshipmen who entered the Naval Academy stood beneath this flag to take their oath. (Lossing, *Pictorial Field-Book of the War of 1812*)

The Barbary War Tripoli Monument, originally located at the Washington Navy Yard, was reportedly vandalized by the British during the War of 1812. (Lossing, *Pictorial Field-Book of the War of 1812*)

U.S. NAVAL ACADEMY MUSEUM. Location: Preble Hall at northwest corner of Maryland Avenue and Decatur Road. **Hours:** Monday through Saturday, 9 a.m. to 5 p.m., and Sunday, 11 a.m. to 5 p.m. **Fees:** none. **Accessibility:** wheelchair accessible. **Contacts:** 410-293-2108; www.usna.edu/Museum.

The U.S. Naval Academy Museum contains prints, paintings, and artifacts relating to naval aspects of the War of 1812. The museum has recently undergone an extensive renovation of its exhibits with many interactive monitors and excellent animations of various naval engagements added. Among the War of 1812 exhibits is the original flag "Dont Give Up the Ship" used by Capt. Oliver Hazard Perry during his victorious engagement with the British on September 10, 1813, during the Battle of Lake Erie.

On the south side of historic Annapolis is the **DR. UPTON SCOTT HOUSE** (NRHP, 4 Shipwright Street; private, exterior views of house only), where Francis Scott Key stayed with his great-uncle while he attended St. John's College.

This ends the Annapolis Tour.

Baltimore Tour

Particulars Baltimore is a historic and popular tourist destination; especially the Inner Harbor area, which is easily walkable. There are numerous accommodations and eating establishments to suit every budget. There is bus, train, and water taxi service. Bicycles are not recommended on the congested downtown streets, but cycling is possible around Federal Hill and Fort McHenry. Parking is available at numerous garages and lots throughout the city. Visitors may plan their tour to suit their own interests and time constraints.

Historical Background Baltimore was a leading seaport and builder of Baltimore clippers (schooners). Known for their speed, these clippers, many constructed at Fells Point, were often used as privateers. Baltimore was also the site of deadly pro-war riots in 1812. After the American defeat at the Battle of Bladensburg and the British occupation of Washington, the British set their sights on Baltimore. This engagement produced one of America's foremost icons, a flag known as the Star-Spangled Banner, which inspired the lyrics that became our national anthem.

On April 16 and August 8, 1813, a Royal Navy squadron moved up the Patapsco River within sight of Baltimore. The British ships alarmed the citizens and caused the forts to be manned, but no attack followed. These threats induced Fort McHenry commander Maj. George Armistead to commission two flags, a storm flag 17 by 25 feet and a garrison flag 30 by 42 feet. The latter was the subject of Francis Scott Key's famous lyrics a year later.

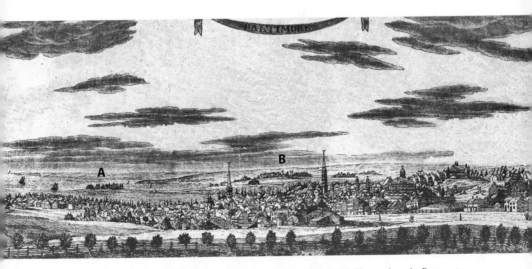

Baltimore was the third largest city in America during the War of 1812. This illustration, the first contemporary panorama of the city, was produced 1810 looking south. Key: A. Fort McHenry. B. Federal Hill with its flagstaff and observatory. ("Baltimore," Aquatint by J. L. Boqueta de Woiseri; courtesy of The Maryland Historical Society)

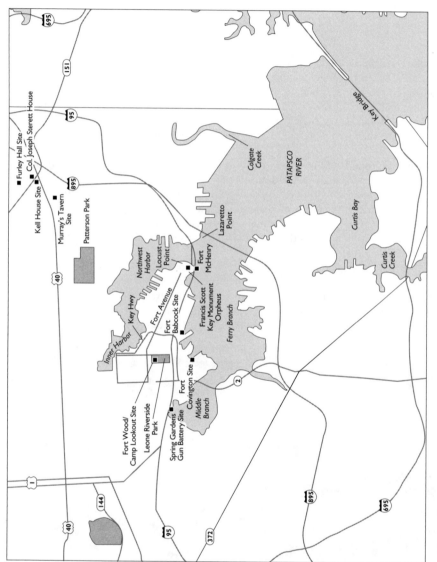

Baltimore City

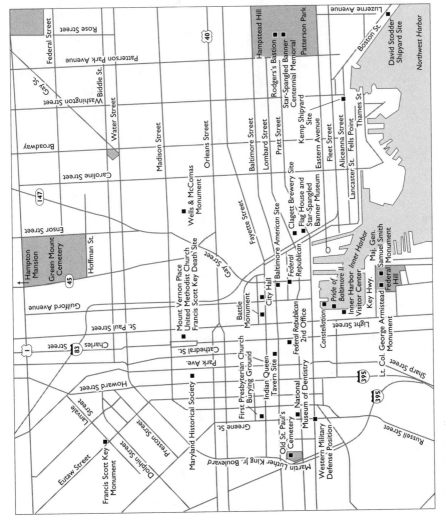

Baltimore City Detail

"The Conspiracy against Baltimore, or The War Dance at Montgomery Court House" is a Republican cartoon lampooning the Federalists. Alexander Contee Hanson, editor of the Baltimore *Federal Republican,* is depicted with devil horns overlooking his friend and legal advisor Robert Goodloe Harper, seated with a harp. To their right is Capt. Richard J. Crabb with a crab ornamenting his *chapeau de bras* (hat). Farther to the right is Charles J. Kilgour with a bull's head symbolizing the "bull-headed" insistence of continuing to publish antiwar editorials. To the left of the harp is a Federalist war dance with Gen. Henry "Light Horse Harry" Lee (center left) wearing a *chapeau de bras.* (1812 engraving; courtesy of The Maryland Historical Society)

After the British victory at the Battle of Bladensburg and occupation of the nation's capital in the fall of 1814, the threat to Baltimore increased. Volunteers and militiamen poured into Baltimore to assist in its defense. Among them was twenty-three-year-old James Buchanan, a militiaman from Pennsylvania who forty-two years later became the fifteenth president of the United States.

The Royal Navy entered the Patapsco River on September 11, 1814. From here the British began their unsuccessful land and sea attack on the city.

Baltimorean Deborah Cochrane wrote her friend Ruth Tobin of Elkton, Maryland, on September 15, 1814: *Our alarm guns were fired twenty minutes past twelve, since then the bells rang, drums beating, the houses generally lighted; we have all been up since that second. We know not the hour when we may be attacked.*

When the attack came, it was violent as reported by the Baltimore *Niles' Weekly Register* on October 1, 1814: *The houses in the city were shaken to their foundations; for never, perhaps from the time of the invention of cannon to the present day, were the same number of pieces fired with so rapid a succession.*

Pvt. George Douglas, one of the Baltimore defenders, wrote to a friend in Boston on September 30, 1814: *I give you joy, my dear friend; after a tremendous conflict we have got rid of the enemy for the present. Baltimore has maintained its honor. It has not only saved itself, but it must tend to save the country by showing Philadelphia, New York and other cities how to contend against the enemy with spirit, bravery and unanimity, all of which have been shown in the memorable days and nights of the 12th, 13th and 14th of September 1814.*

Sea Monsters and Dramas Provide
Diversion from War

Despite the threat of attack in 1814, Baltimoreans still found time for entertainment. The circus came to town with brilliant displays of horsemanship, including "The Mamaluke Manoeuvre." At Joseph Clarke's Market Space one could view the Mammoth Horse, said to be twenty hands high (about six feet six inches tall from hoof to shoulder), the largest horse ever produced in Europe or America. This horse and other animals could be seen for 25 cents. The Baltimore Museum (236 Market Street) had animals preserved through taxidermy, including a twenty-foot-long snake, a shark, an alligator, two sea monsters, sucking and flying fish, and a lamb with two heads and five legs. The Peale's Baltimore Museum and Gallery of Fine Arts (Holliday Street) offered "extra illuminations" (candles or torches) for Christmas and New Year's Eve. Dramas such as *The Robbers* and *The Exile* played at the theater.

Contemporary cartoon "John Bull and the Baltimoreans" satirizes the British retreat from Baltimore. Gen. Robert Ross's death is depicted in the distant center with a militiaman in the woods to the left stating "Now for this Chap on Horseback. There's a *Rifle Pill* for you—Thank a *quietus*." (1814 etching by William Charles; Library of Congress)

A Republican Boston newspaper was quoted in the Baltimore *Niles' Weekly Register* on October 1, 1814: *Rejoice, ye people of America! Inhabitants of Philadelphia, New York and Boston rejoice! Baltimore has nobly fought your battles! Thank God, and thank the people of Baltimore!*

When word of peace with England reached the city, Baltimore Mayor Edward Johnson issued a proclamation on February 15, 1815, announcing the restoration of peace. A general illumination of window candles and torches followed.

A mass gathering of the citizens of Baltimore was held on April 10, 1815. The Baltimore Republican Committee sent a congratulatory address to President James Madison, who replied on April 22: *In the varied scenes which have put to the test the constancy of the nation Baltimore ranks among the portion most distinguished for devotion to the public cause. It has the satisfaction to reflect that it boldly and promptly espoused the resort to arms when no other honorable choice remained; that it found in the courage of its citizens a rampart against the assaults of an enterprising force; that it never wavered nor temporized with the vicissitudes of the contest; and that it had an ample share in the exertions which have brought it to an honorable conclusion.*

Inner Harbor Area

The Inner Harbor of Baltimore is the center for Baltimore tourist attractions. Several War of 1812–related sites are within walking distance. The **INNER HARBOR VISITOR CENTER** is a good place to begin your tour of the downtown area.

INNER HARBOR VISITOR CENTER: Address: 401 Light Street. **Hours:** 9 a.m. to 6 p.m. daily. **Fees:** none. **Parking:** limited metered parking near visitor center, parking garage suggested. **Facilities:** brochures, maps, restrooms. **Accessibility:** handicap accessible. **Contacts:** 1-877-225-8466; www.baltimorecity.gov/Visitors.aspx. **Comment:** there is a water taxi service with several stops including Fort McHenry (April through September) and Fells Point (1-800-658-8947; www.thewatertaxi.com). Boat excursions are also available at the waterfront (*see* appendix D).

From the visitor center it is a 0.5 mile walk south to **FEDERAL HILL** (NHD, bounded by Key Highway, Covington Street, and Warren and Battery avenues), from which there is an excellent overlook of the Inner Harbor. Here, on this promontory, a "marine observatory" and flag signal station was established in 1795 to notify the city of ship arrivals. During the War of 1812, a military observation post, signal station, and one-gun battery occupied the heights. When the British threatened Baltimore in April of 1813, the battery fired its gun to warn the citizenry.

The Baltimore *Federal Gazette* reported on April 17, 1813: *The British squadron . . . now in sight of the town, and have been signaled from the Observatory* [Federal Hill].

The glow of the burning of Washington on August 24–25, 1814, could be seen from Federal Hill. On September 12, 1814, the battery reportedly fired three shots in quick succession to inform Baltimoreans that the British had landed on North Point.

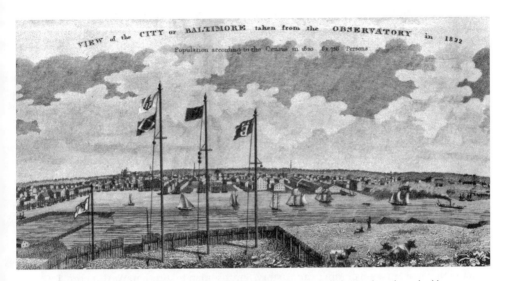

View of Baltimore looking north from Federal Hill. A bridge of scows built in 1814 (not shown in this 1822 view) between Fells Point (right opposite shore) and the shoreline at the east slope of Federal Hill (right near shore) provided a more direct line of communication and faster troop movement between Hampstead Hill, Ferry Point, and the Fort McHenry fortifications. (Detail from Thomas H. Poppleton, "Plan of the City of Baltimore" 1822 [1852]; courtesy of Enoch Pratt Free Library, Central Library/State Library Resource Center, Baltimore, Maryland)

The Baltimore *American* reported on September 12, 1814: *Yesterday morning, the British fleet were plainly seen from Federal Hill, and towards the afternoon they seemed to be work-ing into the mouth of the Patapsco river . . . On firing alarm guns as signals of their approach, all the corps of every description turned out with alacrity.*

From here many citizens watched the bombardment of Fort McHenry on September 13–14, 1814.

A civilian account of the bombardment from Federal Hill was published in the Salem, Massachusetts *Gazette* on September 27, 1814: *The night of Tuesday* [13th] *and the morn-ing of Wednesday (til about 4 o'clock) presented the whole awful spectacle of shot and shells, and rockets, shooting and bursting through the air . . . As the darkness increased, the awful grandeur of the scene augmented. About one in the morning, the British passed several of their vessels above the Fort* [Wood] *and near to town, but providently they were met by the fire of . . . marine battery.*

Sailing Master Leonard Hall, a member of the crew of the U.S. sloop-of-war *Ontario*, manned the gun battery. The U.S. sloops-of-war *Ontario* and *Erie*, both built at Fells Point in 1813, within sight of Federal Hill, were anchored off Fells Point during the attack on Baltimore.

Captain Robert T. Spence reported to Secretary of Navy William Jones on October 3, 1814: *It is with deep regret that I inform you of the death of Sailing Master Leonard Hall of the On-tario who departed this life a few days since* [the 22nd], *after a short illness, occasioned by his excursions and nightly exposure, during the late preparation in the defense of Baltimore.*

Two monuments to Baltimore War of 1812 heroes are in the park that surmounts Federal Hill: Lt. Col. George Armistead, commanding officer at Fort McHenry during the Battle for Baltimore; and Maj. Gen. Samuel Smith, officer in charge of the defense of Baltimore. There is also a cannon, dredged from the harbor and believed to date from the War of 1812, that was mounted on Federal Hill in 1959.

The **LT. COL. GEORGE ARMISTEAD MONUMENT,** designed and sculpted by G. Metgerat, was first erected in 1827 by the City of Baltimore at City Spring on Saratoga Street. After years of neglect, the monument was dismantled in 1861 and placed in storage. In 1882 the marble cannons and flaming bomb were incorporated into a second monument located at Eutaw Place and dedicated on September 9, 1882. This monument was moved in 1886 to Federal Hill, where it was vandalized about 1966. Eight years later the monument was restored again.

The city of Baltimore presented Armistead with a punch bowl, ten silver cups, and an oval serving tray and ladle. The inscription reads as follows: "Presented by a number of citizens of Baltimore to Lt. Col. George Armistead for his gallant and successful defense of Fort McHenry during the bombardment by a large British force on the 12th and 13th of September when upwards of 1500 shells were thrown; 400 of which fell within the area of the Fort and some of them of the diameter of this vase." The Armistead bowl resides in the National Museum of American History, Smithsonian Institution, Washington, D.C (*see* Washington, D.C., Tour *in part 2*). A replica of this bowl is on exhibit at Fort McHenry. When Lieutenant Colonel Armistead died in 1818 at age thirty-eight, minute-guns (distress guns fired every minute to signal mourning or distress) were fired from Federal Hill to punctuate his funeral ceremonies.

The **MAJ. GEN. SAMUEL SMITH MONUMENT,** sculpted by Hans Schuler and erected by the National Star-Spangled Banner Centennial Commission, was originally dedicated on July 4, 1918, in Wyman Park. It was moved in 1953 to the Inner Harbor and then in 1971 to Federal Hill. Smith served as a captain in Gen. William Smallwood's Battalion of the Continental Line in 1776 and as a major and lieutenant colonel in the 4th Regiment from 1776 to 1777. He received a wound while serving at Fort Mifflin, Pennsylvania, on October 23, 1777, and resigned from the army in 1779. Smith commanded the American forces defending Baltimore during the War of 1812. Smith is buried at First Presbyterian Church Burying Ground in Baltimore.

On the opposite side of the Inner Harbor, 0.6 mile from the visitor center to the east, is the **FLAG HOUSE AND STAR-SPANGLED BANNER MUSEUM.**

Armistead's Brothers

Lt. Col. George Armistead had four brothers who also served in the War of 1812. Two died during the war. Capt. Lewis Gustavus Adolphos Armistead, 1st U.S. Rifles, was killed on September 17, 1814, during a sortie from Fort Erie, in Upper Canada. Capt. Addison Bowles Armistead, born 1768, died on February 10, 1813, in Savannah, Georgia, while in the service.

FLAG HOUSE AND STAR-SPANGLED BANNER MUSEUM. NHL. **Address:** 844 East Pratt and Albermarle streets. **Hours:** Tuesday through Saturday, 10 a.m. to 4 p.m. **Fees:** $7 adults, $6 seniors (55 or older), $6 military, $5 student (K–12), children under 6 free, group rates available; programs available. **Parking:** limited free parking on Albermarle Street, parking garage across from Pratt Street entrance. **Accessibility:** museum and first floor of Flag House wheelchair accessible. **Contacts:** 410-837-1793; www.flaghouse.org.

The George Armistead monument can be seen through the arched passageway to the left of the gazebo in its original setting at City Spring. (Lossing, *Pictorial Field-Book of the War of 1812*)

The George Armistead monument consisted of a marble tablet flanked by two marble cannons surmounted by a flaming bomb. (Lossing, *Pictorial Field-Book of the War of 1812*)

In 1816 the citizens of Baltimore presented to Lieutenant Colonel Armistead this silver punch bowl in the shape of a thirteen-inch British mortar bomb supported by four silver American eagles. (Lossing, *Pictorial Field-Book of the War of 1812*)

The Flag House is the former home of seamstress Mary Pickersgill and where she made the Star-Spangled Banner assisted by her thirteen-year-old daughter Caroline, her nieces, Margaret and Jane Young, her mother Rebecca Flower Young, and probably her servants.

Caroline Pickersgill Purdy, about 1876, wrote Georgiana Armistead Appleton, daughter of Lieutenant Colonel George Armistead, then owner of the flag: *the flag was made by my mother Mrs. Mary Pickersgill, and I assisted her . . . The flag being so very large, my mother was obliged to obtain permission from the proprietors of Claggett's brewery which was in our neighborhood to spread it out in their malt house.*

Both the 30 by 42 foot garrison flag, better know as the Star-Spangled Banner, and Fort McHenry's smaller 17 by 25 foot storm flag were made here. A plaque mounted on the house proclaims that the "Star Spangled Banner . . . floated over Ft. McHenry during the bombardment by the British September 13th and 14th 1814 and . . . inspired Francis Scott Key to write his immortal poem." The smaller flag, completed on August 13, 1813, is probably the flag that actually flew over Fort McHenry during most, if not all, of the stormy period during the bombardment. The practice at Fort McHenry to this day is to fly the smaller flag in inclement weather. The larger garrison flag was raised after the bombardment had ceased while the British fleet withdrew down the Patapsco River. The garrison flag cost $405.90.

Pickersgill lived in the house from 1807 until her death in 1857. She built an addition in 1820. The City of Baltimore purchased the building in 1929 and removed a storefront window to restore it to its original appearance. Other additions include a rear building added in 1953 and a museum addition in 2002. In the house and museum, artifacts include wool fragments of the Fort McHenry garrison flag, personal items belonging to Francis Scott Key, and military items from the War of 1812.

Because of its size, the American garrison flag for Fort McHenry was spread out by seamstress Mary Pickersgill in the malt house of Eli Clagett's brewery that once stood at 800 East Lombard Street, immediately west of the Flag House Star-Spangled Banner Museum. Eli Clagett served as a private in the Baltimore United Volunteers and was wounded at the Battle of North Point.

BATTLE MONUMENT is located 0.6 mile north of the Inner Harbor Visitor Center.

BATTLE MONUMENT. NRHP. Location: North Calvert between Fayette and Lexington streets. **Hours:** unlimited. **Fees:** none. **Parking:** none.

Battle Monument, located at the former courthouse green, is the first substantial war memorial built in the United States. The cornerstone of the 52-foot-tall monument, designed by J. Maximilian Godefroy, a French emigré, was laid September 12, 1815, on the first anniversary of the Battle of North Point. A year later construction began on the monument itself. A procession formed on Great York Street (now East Baltimore Street) and proceeded to Monument Square. The procession included a funeral car surmounted with a plan of the intended monument. Six white horses escorted by six men in military uniform led the car guarded by the Baltimore Independent Blues, 5th Regiment. The architect and his assistants, under the direction of Maj. Gen. Samuel Smith, Brig. Gen. John Stricker, Lt. Col. George Armistead, and Mayor Edward Johnson, laid the cornerstone of the cenotaph monument. Books containing the names of the subscribers who paid for the monument, the newspapers from the preceding day, United States gold, silver, and copper coins, and a copper plate on which was engraved the date and names of those who participated in the ceremony were deposited under the cornerstone. Upon the completion of the laying of the cornerstone, a detachment of artillery fired a federal salute. This was followed by the firing of minute-guns (distress guns fired every minute to signal mourning or distress during military funerals) and the ringing of the bells in nearby Christ Church. All business was suspended for the day.

Sculptor Antonio Capellano of Florence, Italy, executed the statue of Lady Baltimore, which was mounted in December 1925, on top of the monument. Lady Baltimore guides a ship's rudder, the sign of navigation, with her left hand and raises a laurel wreath of victory aloft in her right hand. She faces the field of battle. At her feet repose the National Eagle and a bomb symbolizing the attack on Fort McHenry.

Battle Monument was erected to commemorate those citizens who died while defending Baltimore. In 1827 the monument became the design for the official seal of the city. (Lossing, *Pictorial Field-Book of the War of 1812*)

Depicted in relief at the base of the column on the south and north sides are, respectively, the Battle of North Point, the death of Maj. Gen. Robert Ross, mortally wounded in a skirmish before the Battle of North Point, and the bombardment of Fort McHenry. On carved ribbons wrapped diagonally across the monument and spelled out in copper lettering are the names of the men who fell in battle. The monument base consists of eighteen layers representing the eighteen states in the Union in 1815. The three steps at the base of the monument represent the three years of the war. An eagle stands atop each of the four corners of the base. A column rises from the base depicting bundled rods representing strength in union.

For many years, this was the site of the main commemoration of Defenders Day. "Old Defenders," the survivors of the defense of Baltimore, were honored by military escorts and martial music. J. Maximilian M. Godefroy, the designer of Battle Monument, also redesigned the defensive entrenchments on Hampstead Hill after the battle to better defend the city in the event of a second British attack.

Other Baltimore Sites

The following sites are scattered around Baltimore and are too far apart for leisurely walking: Francis Scott Key Memorial, Maryland Historical Society, First Presbyterian Church Burying Ground, Patterson Park, Wells and McComas Monument, Fort McHenry, Fort Wood, and Hampton Mansion.

Pride of Baltimore II

While in the Inner Harbor area it is worth looking to see if the *Pride of Baltimore II* is in port (call 1-888-55-PRIDE for information). Because this vessel serves as a world ambassador to Baltimore, it is not always at its berth. The *Pride of Baltimore II,* built in 1988, illustrates a typical Baltimore schooner or clipper used as a privateer during the War of 1812. This replica is based on the *Chasseur,* constructed at the Thomas Kemp Shipyard in Fells Point and later made famous under the command of Capt. Thomas Boyle. Hezekiah Niles, editor of the Baltimore *Niles' Weekly Register,* on April 25, 1815, referred to the *Chasseur* as the "pride of Baltimore" because of its success as a privateer. Many former crew from the *Chasseur* served during the defense of Baltimore.

FRANCIS SCOTT KEY MONUMENT: Location: Eutaw Place and West Lanvale Street. **Hours:** daylight hours. **Fees:** none. **Parking:** limited street parking. **Accessibility:** wheelchair accessible.

The **FRANCIS SCOTT KEY MONUMENT** is an impressive sculpture that depicts Key returning from his British detainment standing in the bow of a small boat holding up his manuscript to an allegorical figure of Columbia on a four-columned marble canopy. Columbia proudly holds the Fort McHenry garrison flag. Gold-leafed tableaus on the base of the canopy depict the British bombardment of Fort McHenry on one side and the ramparts and cannons of Fort McHenry on the other. French sculptor Jean Marius Antonin Mercie, an 1868 recipient of the Prix de Rome, sculpted the monument, which was donated by tobacco importer Charles L. Marburg and erected in 1911. The monument originally had Key's birth date as 1779, but it has since been corrected to 1780. The monument was restored in 1998.

MARYLAND HISTORICAL SOCIETY: Address: 201 West Monument Street. **Hours:** Wednesday through Sunday, 10 a.m. to 5 p.m. **Fees:** $4 adults, $3 seniors, student with ID, and children 13 to 17, children under 13 free. **Parking:** free, lot entrance off West Monument Street. **Facilities:** exhibits, museum store, research library. **Contacts:** 410-685-3750; www.mdhs.org. **Accessibility:** wheelchair accessible.

The Maryland Historical Society possesses paintings, prints, and artifacts from the War of 1812, including the earliest known draft of Francis Scott Key's lyrics, probably written at Indian Queen Tavern the night after the bombardment from notes taken aboard the flag-of-truce boat on September 15, 1814. This draft was given to Joseph Hopper Nicholson, Jr., Key's sister's husband, who had it published. In the collections are Havre de Grace hero John O'Neill's presentation sword and his daughter Matilda O'Neill's snuff box, reportedly given to her by Rear Adm. George Cockburn (*see* Havre de Grace *under* Head of the Chesapeake Tour *in part 2 for more details about this hero*). Another presentation sword is that of John Adams Webster, a hero in the Battle for Baltimore. Also in the collections are portraits of Lt. Col. George Armistead, Maj. Gen. Samuel Smith, Brig. Gen. John Stricker, and Com. Joshua Barney, painted in 1816 by the celebrated Rembrandt Peale under a commission by the City of Baltimore. Other paintings include 1814 veteran Thomas Ruckle's *Troops Assembled on Hampstead Hill, Battle of North Point, near Baltimore, Sept. 12, 1814,* and Alfred Jacob Miller's *Bombardment of Fort McHenry Sept. 13–14, 1814,* based on sketches made at Fort Wood (*see below*). One of the more interesting artifacts is a tin cup used by Samuel Etting with the signatures of the officers who served with him during the bombardment of Fort McHenry. Ironically, the Maryland Historical Society demolished the house of Christopher Hughes Armistead and his mother Louisa, where the Star-Spangled Banner resided for many years in her care. The Society now occupies that site.

FIRST PRESBYTERIAN CHURCH BURYING GROUND: Location: West Fayette and Greene streets. **Hours:** 8 a.m. to dusk daily. **Fees:** none. **Tours:** first complete weekend of each month, Friday at 6 p.m. and Saturday at 10 a.m. **Parking:** limited street parking; public transportation recommended. **Contacts:** 410-706-2072; www.westminsterhall.org; click tours.

At least twenty-five individuals who played a role in the War of 1812 are buried at **FIRST PRESBYTERIAN CHURCH BURYING GROUND** (church is NRHP), also called Western Burying Ground, Westminster Burying Ground, or Old Westminster Cemetery. French emigré J. Maximilian M. Godefroy designed the Egyptian-style gateposts on the west side of the cemetery. Godefroy is most noted for his design of Battle Monument, but he also designed the tomb of Brig. Gen. Samuel Smith located here. Smith was in command of the defense of Baltimore. Godefroy assisted in planning some of the outerworks at Fort McHenry and other defenses of Baltimore in 1814.

PATTERSON PARK. NHD. Location: bounded by Baltimore Street, Eastern, Patterson Park, and Linwood avenues. **Hours:** daylight hours. **Fees:** none. **Parking:** street parking.

PATTERSON PARK occupies Hampstead Hill, one of the three natural promontories of high ground used to defend the eastern approaches to Baltimore. American troops, private citizens, and

Where Is Edgar Allan Poe?

David Poe, grandfather of poet Edgar Allan Poe, served as a quartermaster in the American Revolution and as a seventy-one-year-old served as a private during the Battle of North Point. The remains of Edgar Allan Poe originally rested with his grandfather at the back of the First Presbyterian Church Burying Ground churchyard (also called Western Burying Ground, Westminster Burying Ground or Old Westminster Cemetery), but in 1875 the poet's body was dug up and reinterred under a grand marble tomb. However, local tradition claims those digging up his body may have gone in the wrong direction and actually dug up the body of a militiaman who died of disease while serving on Hampstead Hill during the War of 1812. Whether this is true is unknown.

slaves built a line of earthworks on this high ground that reaches an elevation of 80 to 120 feet at its northern end, near where Johns Hopkins Hospital is now located, and 40 to 80 feet in height at the southwest corner of Patterson Park. The earthworks, designed by Robert Cary Long and William Stuart, extended about a mile, stretching north from Belair Road south to Harris Creek, near the harbor. Hampstead Hill formed the heart of these defenses. All of those exempt from military duty, including "free people of color," were requested to report to Hampstead Hill on Sunday morning, August 28, 1814, at 6 a.m. with "provision for the day" to assist the city in building defenses. Owners of slaves were requested to send them to work as well.

One of the defenders, Pvt. George Douglas, wrote the following to a friend in Boston on August 30, 1814: *Every American heart is bursting with shame and indignation at the catastrophe* [at Washington]. *All hearts and hands have cordially united in the common cause. Everyday, almost every hour, bodies of troops are marching in to our assistance. At this moment we cannot have less than 10,000 men under arms. The whole of the hills and rising grounds* [Hampstead Hill] *to the eastward of the city are covered with horse-foot and artillery exercises and training from morning until night.*

Just east of Hampstead Hill, the British marching from North Point (*see* Battle of North Point Tour *in part 1*), reached their farthest forward advance toward Baltimore on September 13, 1814.

American Maj. Gen. Samuel Smith wrote the following in his official report to Secretary of War James Monroe on September 19, 1814: *On Tuesday the enemy appeared in front of my intrenchments, at the distance of two miles, on the Philadelphia road, from whence he had a full view of our position. He manoeuvred during the morning towards our left, as if with the intention of making a circuitous march and coming down on the Harford or York roads. Gens.* [William H.] *Winder and* [John] *Stricker were ordered to adapt their movements to those of the enemy, so as to baffle this supposed intention . . . This movement induced the enemy to concentrate his forces . . . in my front, pushing his advance to within a mile of us, driving in our videttes and showing an intention of attacking us that evening. I immediately drew Gens. Winder and Stricker nearer to the left of my intrenchments and to the right of the enemy, with the intention of their falling on his right or rear should he attack me; or, if he declined it, of attacking him in the morning. To this movement and to the strength of my defenses . . . I am induced to attribute his retreat, which . . . he was so favored by the extreme darkness and a continued rain that we did not discover it until daylight.*

British Rear Adm. George Cockburn wrote to Vice Adm. Alexander F.I. Cochrane on September 15, 1814: *towards Baltimore, on approaching which, it was found to be defended by extremely Strong Works on every Side, and immediately in front of us by an extensive Hill on which was an entrenched Camp and great quantities of artillery, and the Information we collected added to what we observed, gave us to believe there were at least within their Works from 15 to 20,000 Men.*

American 1st. Lt. Jacob Crumbaker wrote on September 12–13, 1814: *That night about eight* [actually about four] *thousand of the enemy's land forces lay within a mile and a half of us. We could see them at their fires and could hear the hogs squeal as they killed them in their camp. But about three o'clock in the morning when they found they could not silence our fort they threw some rockets down the bay as a signal for the land forces to retreat which they did in great haste and left some of their stragglers behind wich were taken prisoners by our men next day.*

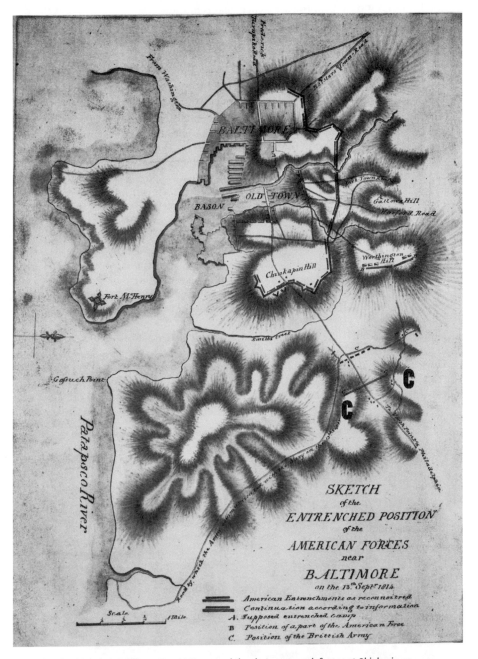

This colored British drawing shows Fort McHenry and the city's eastern defenses at Chinkapin or Hampstead Hill and Worthington Hill. A line marked "C" shows the British farthest advance to Baltimore. ("Sketch of the Entrenched Position of the American Forces near Baltimore on the 13th Sept. 1814," Puteney Malcolm Papers; William L. Clements Library, University of Michigan)

American Pvt. John Leadley Dagg wrote: *At the first dawn, every eye was directed towards the Fort, to see whether the American banner still waved there; and when the morning mists had sufficiently dispersed, we were filled with exultation at beholding the stars and stripes still floating in the breeze.*

RODGERS'S BASTION OR BASTION NO. 5, located on the highest ground along the northwest side of Patterson Park, east of Patterson Park Avenue between Baltimore and Gough streets, served as the center of the American defenses. It is occupied today by an 1891 pagoda built near the end of Pratt Street. Sparrows Point and the landscape over which the British marched to Baltimore can be seen from the battery site, but even better from the pagoda. The pond in the park was once part of Harris Creek, which has suffered from severe filling. The contours of the earthwork are still discernable today. The original armament consisted of two naval guns. Several cannon are also mounted on the site of Rodgers's Bastion, erected by the Society of the War of 1812 in 1906 and later refurbished as part of a Boy Scouts of America Eagle Scout Project. Reputed to have been used in the defense of Baltimore, they consist of 4 and 6 pounder cast iron guns, five mounted and a sixth buried in the ground with its barrel up. While these may be field cannon from the war, they are too small to be typical of the principal cannon used at this gun battery. The outline of **BASTION NO. 4,** at the Taurus Oval, is located near the northwest corner of the park. It was armed with seven cannon.

Near the Pagoda is the **STAR-SPANGLED BANNER CENTENNIAL MEMORIAL,** designed by J. Maxwell Miller, that fancifully depicts two children who found a scroll while on their way home from school. The scroll tells the story of how the national anthem came to be written. The sculpture served as the centerpiece of a float in the 1914 centennial parade before it was placed in Patterson Park to commemorate the centennial of the writing of "The Star-Spangled Banner." Pupils of the Baltimore City School System donated funds for the memorial.

Rodgers's Bastion was still intact in the 1850s as shown in this drawing. Key: A. Fort McHenry with its garrison flag. (Lossing, *Pictorial Field-Book of the War of 1812*)

WELLS AND McCOMAS MONUMENT:
Location: Ashland Square, Old Town Mall, East Monument and Aisquith streets. **Parking:** limited street parking. **Hours:** daylight hours. **Fees:** none. **Comment:** eleven blocks north of the Inner Harbor.

The **WELLS AND McCOMAS MONUMENT** commemorates Daniel Wells and Henry Gough McComas, both privates in Capt. Edward Aisquith's Sharpshooters, 1st Rifle Battalion, Maryland Militia. While serving as part of Gen. John Stricker's advance guard, both were killed on September 12, 1814, during a skirmish preceding the Battle of North Point. Legend holds that Wells, age nineteen, and McComas, age eighteen, shot British Maj. Gen. Robert Ross, but there is no documentary evidence to substantiate the story.

The 21-foot-tall Wells and McComas obelisk monument is decorated for the sesquicentennial. (Unknown photographer, circa 1880, courtesy of The Maryland Historical Society)

Nevertheless, they became known as the "boy heroes" of the War of 1812. Both were originally buried together in a cemetery near where Johns Hopkins Hospital now stands. Their remains were later moved to Green Mount Cemetery, where on September 10, 1858, they were exhumed for a second time and laid in state for three days at the Maryland Institute Building, Market Place. On the morning of September 12, 1858, on the anniversary of their death, their bodies were taken in a procession from Baltimore Street to Ashland Square and re-buried there. The base for their monument was not constructed until 1871 and the monument was not completed until May 18, 1873.

On the occasion of the final burial of the two boys, a local who described himself as "one who was a little boy at the time of the Battle for Baltimore" composed a song entitled "Wells and McComas Funeral and Monument Song," sung to the tune of "The Star-Spangled Banner." One year later, local playwright Clifton W. Tayleure wrote a play in honor of Wells and McComas called *The Boy Martyrs of Sept. 12, 1814, A Local Historical Drama in Three Acts.* The play was performed in Baltimore at the Holliday Street Theater in 1858 to commemorate the reburial in Ashland Square. *The Boy Martyrs of Sept. 12* is a fictionalized telling of their alleged shooting of Maj. Gen. Robert Ross.

FORT McHENRY NATIONAL MONUMENT AND HISTORIC SHRINE. NHL. **Location:** east end of Fort Avenue. **Parking:** free. **Hours:** 8 a.m. to 5 p.m.; summer, fort open until 6:30 p.m. **Fees:** $7 adults, children under 16 free. **Accessibility:** wheelchair accessible. **Facilities:** visitor

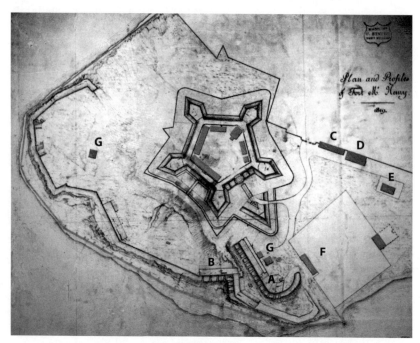

Plan of Fort McHenry showing its 1814 appearance. Note the brick-faced star fort and gun platforms along the Patapsco River outside the fort. Key: A. Upper Water Battery. B. Lower Water Battery. C. Gunhouse (1807). D. Storehouse (1807). E. Hospital (1814). F. Barracks and parade ground. G. Powder Magazines. Other than the fort, only the foundations survive. (1819 plan; National Archives and Records Administration)

center, restrooms, picnic, gift shop. **Contacts:** 410-962-4290; www.nps.gov/fomc. **Comment:** seasonal water taxi service is an option for those wishing to visit the fort from either the Inner Harbor or Fells Point.

FORT McHENRY NATIONAL MONUMENT AND HISTORIC SHRINE, operated by the National Park Service, is the site of the famous bombardment that inspired Francis Scott Key to write the lyrics that became our national anthem. Originally named Fort Whetstone in 1776 for the point it is located on, it was renamed in 1798 after James McHenry, then Secretary of War. The star-shaped fort controlled the entrances to both the Northwest Branch and the Ferry Branch of the Patapsco River and thus served as the cornerstone of the water defenses of Baltimore. The present fort configuration dates from the late 1830s, not 1814. Postwar changes include the removal of the water batteries in 1829 and 1836, the raising of the bastions and ramparts, the addition of a second-story to the barracks in 1829, and the removal of numerous pre-1814 structures located on the exterior of the fort. In addition, most of the guns date from after the 1814 conflict. The big Rodman cannons are Civil War-era artillery. A partial reconstruction of the 1814 water battery was completed in 2005-6 and features two period 1809 French 36 pounder cannons.

A defensive boom, consisting of ships' masts laid end to end and fastened together by chains, was stretched 600 yards across the narrows of the Northeast Branch from Fort McHenry to Lazaretto Point on the opposite side.

Maj. George Armistead, commander of Fort McHenry, reportedly wrote to Maj. Gen. Samuel Smith in 1813: *We, Sir, are ready at Fort McHenry to defend Baltimore against invading by the enemy. That is to say, we are ready except that we have no suitable ensign to display over the Star Fort, and it is my desire to have a flag so large that the British will have no difficulty in seeing it from a distance.*

That flag, made by Mary Pickersgill (*see* Flag House and Star-Spangled Banner Museum *above*) in Baltimore, was raised at the fort at 9 a.m., September 14, 1814, as the Royal Navy sailed out of the Patapsco River after failing to take the city. Because of the rainy inclement conditions during the bombardment, the fort's smaller storm flag probably flew during most of the action.

During the 25-hour bombardment, the British fired an estimated 1,800 explosive shells (bombs) while the fleet remained mostly outside the range of the fort's guns.

Prior to the Battle for Baltimore, Maj. George Armistead, commander of Fort McHenry, had made a request for two 10-inch mortars located at the Greenleaf Point Federal Arsenal, Washington, D.C. Although the mortars were sent, no shot, fuses, or carriages were included, rendering them unusable. Thus the fort did not have guns with sufficient range to match those of the British fleet.

Opposite page, bottom

Detail of Fort McHenry depicting trees within the fort, the water batteries below and left, sunken ships and moored gun barges at left. The bulkhead-like linear structure along the shore is floating masts chained together and positioned by piles to prevent amphibious landings. The small structure above the water batteries is a hot shot furnace. While this drawing is considered accurate for its detail, the fort's garrison flag depicts an anchor in a circular star field. (Detail from *An Eyewitness Sketch of the Bombardment of Fort McHenry*, date and artist unknown; courtesy of The Maryland Historical Society)

British Lt. George Robert Gleig wrote his memories of the bombardment in 1833: *To the fleet the fort on the water was accordingly left, which by bombardment would, it was presumed, reduce it to ruins in a few hours . . . At last, when midnight was close at hand, a solitary report, accompanied by the ascension of a small bright spark into the sky, gave notice that the bombardment had begun. Another and another followed in quick succession.*

More than any other site, Fort McHenry has come to symbolize the United States experience in the War of 1812. The bombardment of the fort could be heard all the way to Elkton, Maryland, approximately 48 miles northeast of Baltimore. On exhibit in the fort's visitor center is a British 32 pounder incendiary Congreve rocket. This weapon inspired the words the "rockets' red glare" in "The Star-Spangled Banner," written by Francis Scott Key. On or about September 17, 1814, every individual in the fort received a printed copy of Key's lyrics.

An American account of the raising of the garrison flag was written by Pvt. Isaac Munroe, who served at Fort McHenry, and published in the Boston *Yankee* on September 30, 1814: *At dawn . . . our morning gun was fired, the flag hoisted, Yankee Doodle played, and we all appeared in full view of the formidable and mortified enemy, who calculated upon our surrender in 20 minutes after the commencement of the action.*

British Midshipman Robert J. Barrett remembered the incident in 1841: *After bombarding the forts and harbor of Baltimore for twenty-four hours, the squadron of frigates weighed, without firing a shot, upon the forenoon of the 14th, and were immediately followed by the bombs [bomb-ships] and sloops of war. In truth, it was a galling spectacle for the British seaman to behold. And, as the last vessel spread her canvas to the wind, the Americans hoisted a splendid and superb ensign on their battery, and fired at the same time a gun of defiance.*

After first going to the visitor center, look for the nearby **GEORGE ARMISTEAD MONUMENT.** This memorial to Lt. Col. George Armistead, commander of Fort McHenry, was sculpted by Edward Berge, presented by the City of Baltimore Society of the War of 1812, and erected in September 1914. The inscription on the monument gives Armistead's year of birth as 1779, but it was actually 1780. Continue into the fort.

In the **HEADQUARTERS** office (bottom floor of barracks near the gunpowder house) is where Maj. George Armistead conducted the defense of Fort McHenry during the War of 1812. Here Armistead requisitioned the fort's garrison and storm flags made by seamstress Mary Pickersgill, both of which flew over the fort in September of 1814. A British mortar shell (bomb) is displayed here with another in the visitor center. Capt. Frederick Evans, U.S. Corps of Artillery, second in command at Fort McHenry, took the shell now on display in the visitor center to his home in Columbia, Pennsylvania, after it fell harmlessly at his feet and failed to explode. His family donated the shell to the park in 1937.

A rare 13-inch carcass shell, fired by the H.M. bomb-ship *Volcano* during the night of September 13, 1814, is in the Armistead office. It is one of four carcass shells known to be fired that night to light the American shore defenses and to signal the beginning of a British flanking attack on Fort McHenry.

Near the gate inside the fort stands an 89-foot high **FLAG STAFF** from which flies a replica of the Star-Spangled Banner. In 1958, seven feet below the surface, archeologists discovered oak timber cross-braces that supported the original 1814 flag staff. The replica flag staff was installed in 1959 and replaced in 1989. From this staff, a 30 by 42 foot replica garrison flag is flown, a tradition that continues to the present day, weather permitting. The original cross-braces are on display in the barracks. Visitors lucky enough to be present soon after the fort opens or before it closes are usually permitted to help hold the flag during raising and lowering.

This noncontemporary illustration shows how the thirty-two heavy cannon were mounted behind a defensive earthwork called the water battery. (Artist L. Kenneth Townson 2002; courtesy National Park Service)

Outside the fort, near the river shore, is the **WATER BATTERY REPLICA.** A small section of the demolished earthwork has been recreated to illustrate its 1814 appearance. An interpretive panel discusses the importance of the gun battery and the type of guns that were placed here.

West, toward the park gate, is the Fort McHenry **MEMORIAL TREE GROVE** (near the Francis Scott Key Orpheus Memorial). Between 1932 and 1933, thirty-five memorial markers and crab apple trees were placed in honor of heroes of the defense of Baltimore during the War of 1812. Each tree had a bronze marker dedicated to these war heroes, although a few have disappeared over the years. Several of the trees that had died were replaced in 2006.

West of the fort, near the park entrance, is the **FRANCIS SCOTT KEY ORPHEUS MONUMENT.** In 1914, Congress funded this 24-foot-tall statue, known as "Orpheus with the Awkward Foot," to mark the centennial of the writing of "The Star-Spangled Banner." Sculptor Charles H. Neithaus's design was selected from thirty-four submitted in a national competition. President Warren G. Harding delivered a speech during the unveiling ceremony on June 14, 1922, the first coast-to-coast radio broadcast by a president. Orpheus (the great musician and poet of Greek mythology) is depicted playing a lyre. The monument's marble base bears a medallion honoring Francis Scott Key, while the pedestal contains a time capsule filled with documents of patriotic and historical interest. In 1966 the statue was moved here from its original site near the fort's main entrance. Despite popular belief, the figure depicted does not bear any resemblance to F. S. Key.

There were several smaller forts and gun batteries erected to protect the flanks of Fort McHenry, but all of these have been destroyed over the years and are unaccessible with the exception of **FORT WOOD.**

LEONE RIVERSIDE PARK / FORT WOOD SITE: Location: Randall and Johnson streets. **Parking:** free. **Hours:** daylight hours. **Fees:** none. **Facilities:** 28-acre park with picnic and recreation facilities.

Located at what is now known as Leone Riverside Park, Fort Wood defended the right flank of Fort McHenry. It mounted seven 24 pounder naval guns although the fort was not completed prior to the British attack. The fort also served as a military camp. This battery played an active role in repulsing the British night flanking offensive on September 13–14, 1814. The camp site was long used as an observation post and was first known as Camp Lookout. After the bombardment of Fort McHenry, Camp Lookout became Fort Wood, named after Lt. Col. Eleazer Derby Wood, an artillery officer killed on September 17, 1814, leading a sortie from Fort Erie, Upper Canada. The federal government turned the property over to Baltimore City for use as a park in 1854.

A civilian eyewitness account of the action at Fort Wood as seen from Federal Hill was published in the Salem, Massachusetts, *Gazette* on September 27, 1814: *The well directed fire of the little fort* [Wood] . . . *checked the enemy on his approach, and probably saved the town from destruction in the dark hours of the night. The garrison was chiefly incommoded by the shells, which burst in and about the fort, whilst they had no bomb-proof shelter. As the darkness increased, the awful grandeur of the scene augmented. About one in the morning, the British passed several of their vessels above the Fort and near to town, but providently they were met by the fire of . . .* [the] *marine battery.*

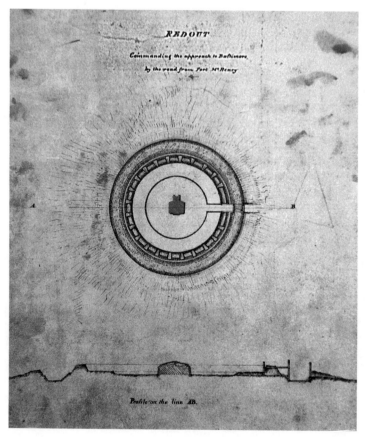

Fort Wood / Camp Lookout consisted of an earthen magazine enclosing an earthen circular redoubt, 180 feet in diameter, and an outer ditch and pine palisade. (1819 plan; National Archives and Records Administration, Cartographic Section)

Painter Alfred Jacob Miller (1810–74)

Best known for his paintings and sketches of the Indians and fur trappers of the Rocky Mountains, Miller painted at least two scenes depicting the bombardment of Fort McHenry. Alfred was only four years old at the time of the battle. His father, George Miller, served as a private in Capt. John Berry's Washington Artillery stationed at Fort McHenry during the bombardment. Prior to his western travels and fame, Alfred painted or sketched the view from Fort Wood in 1828–29. His noncontemporary paintings correctly show Forts Babcock and Covington. The site still offers a panorama of the harbor although it is now somewhat obstructed by buildings that were not there when Miller executed his paintings. Miller's painting, *Bombardment of Fort McHenry Sept. 13–14, 1814,* is exhibited at the Maryland Historical Society. A second painting, *The Battle of Fort McHenry,* is privately owned and reproduced here.

Detail of *The Battle of Fort McHenry.* (Oil painting by Alfred Jacob Miller; Christie's Images)

HAMPTON MANSION, a National Historic Site operated by the National Park Service, is considered one of the finest and largest surviving examples of Georgian architecture in the United States. Hampton is 3 miles north of the Baltimore City line.

HAMPTON MANSION. NHS. **Address:** 535 Hampton Estate Lane. **Parking:** free. **Accessibility:** wheel chair accessible. **Hours:** mansion, 9 a.m. to 4 p.m.; grounds, 9 a.m. to 5 p.m. **Fees:** none. **Facilities:** self-guided and led tours, restrooms, gift shop. **Contacts:** 410-823-1309; www.nps.gov/hamp.

Charles Carnan Ridgely (1790–1829), the second master (owner) of Hampton, also owned the nearby Northampton Foundry, which supplied cannon to Baltimore privateers during the War of 1812. Ridgely was commissioned a brigadier general in the Maryland militia in 1794 and served as a member of the Baltimore County Troop of Cavalry during the War of 1812. He also contributed a hundred barrels of flour worth $600 to Baltimore City to aid in the war effort. Two 13-inch British shells, one stamped with the British broad arrow, are located at the rear stair landing of the mansion. How these unexploded shells, almost certainly from the bombardment of Fort McHenry, ended up at Hampton is unknown. Ridgely is buried in the family vault at Hampton. The Ridgely family first lived at Ridgeley House, now demolished, at North Point, which served during the war as a signal station (*see* Ridgely House *sidebar in* Battle of North Point Tour *in part 1*).

This ends the Baltimore Tour.

Southern Maryland Tour

Particulars Southern Maryland sites not part of the British Invasion Tour or Bladensburg Battlefield Tour are included here. The quaint waterfront town of Solomons is a good place to seek lodging and food, although Lexington Park and Prince Frederick offer alternatives. Boat excursions on the lower Patuxent River are available from the Calvert Marine Museum (*see* appendix D). Canoeing, kayaking, and small boating opportunities also exist on the Patuxent River (*see* appendix C). Visitors may plan their tour to suit their own interests and time constraints.

Historical Background Bounded by Chesapeake Bay on the east, the Potomac River on the west, and penetrated by the Patuxent River in the middle, southern Maryland provided easy water access for British raiding parties. No other region of Maryland suffered more raids and skirmishes. Here the largest naval engagement on Maryland waters (Battle of St. Leonard Creek) took place. Here also the British landed a force of over four thousand troops who marched overland (*see* British Invasion Tour *in part 1*), defeated the Americans at the Battle of Bladensburg (*see* Battle of Bladensburg Tour *in part 1*), and captured Washington (*see* Washington, D.C., Tour *in part 2*). A British naval squadron on the Potomac forced the destruction of Fort Washington and the capitulation of Alexandria (*see* Alexandria Tour *in part 2*).

SOLOMONS VISITOR CENTER. Address: 14175 Solomons Island Road, directly opposite Calvert Marine Museum at foot of Governor Thomas Johnson Bridge. **Parking:** free. **Hours:** November through March, Thursday through Sunday, 9 a.m. to 5 p.m.; April through October, 9 a.m. to 5 p.m. daily. **Accessibility:** handicapped accessible. **Contacts:** 410-326-6027; www.baygateways.net/general.cfm?id'30. **Comment:** brochures and maps available.

CALVERT MARINE MUSEUM. Address: 14200 Solomons Island Road. **Parking:** free. **Hours:** 10 a.m. to 5 p.m. daily. **Fees:** $7 adults, $6 military and 55 or older, $2 children 5 to 12, children under 5 free. **Facilities:** exhibits, restrooms, gift shop, picnic facilities. **Contacts:** 410-326-2042; www.calvertmarinemuseum.com. **Comment:** this museum has three specialties: maritime history, fossil history of Calvert Cliffs, and the estuarine biology of the Patuxent River. Plan a minimum of two hours if you wish to see all the exhibits. Boat tours of the lower Patuxent River on a historic oyster buy-boat are available from the museum (*see* appendix D).

The **CALVERT MARINE MUSEUM** exhibits artifacts recovered from one of the vessels of the Chesapeake Flotilla scuttled on August 22, 1814, in the Patuxent River, as well as an animated map of the British invasion route up the river. Before leaving you may wish to drive

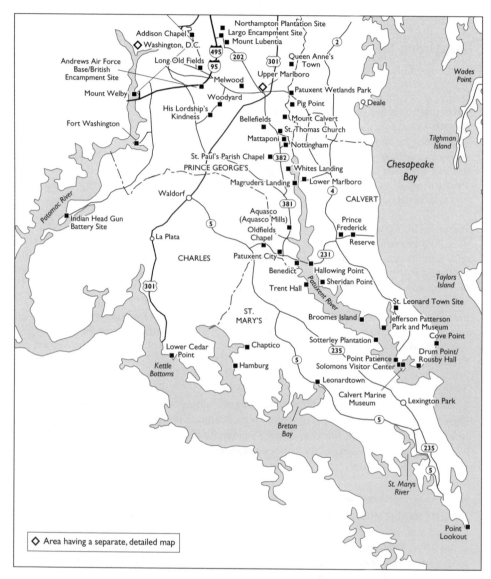

Southern Maryland

south down Solomons Island Road to view the mouth of the Patuxent River where the British carried out raids on both sides of the river and blockaded the river, trapping the Chesapeake Flotilla within the waterway. A Royal Navy fleet carrying over four thousand troops passed the island on its way to Benedict, where the invading force landed (*see* British Invasion Tour *in part 1*).

Optional Side Trip **SOTTERLEY** and **POINT LOOKOUT STATE PARK.** From Solomons, you may wish to drive over the Thomas Johnson Bridge to visit Sotterley (12 miles one way) and Point Lookout State Park (26 miles one way). Or you can head north to Jefferson Patterson Park and Museum (16 miles north).

POINT LOOKOUT STATE PARK. Location: south end of Point Lookout Road (Route 5), Scotland, St. Mary's County. **Parking:** free. **Hours:** 6 a.m. to sunset. **Fees:** weekends and holidays, $5 per person, $6 out-of-state; other times, $3 per vehicle. **Facilities:** restrooms, picnic facilities, canoeing, kayaking, and small boating (*see* appendix C). **Contacts:** 301-872-5688; www.dnr.state.md.us/publiclands/southern/pointlookout.html

---

Point Lookout is located at the confluence of Chesapeake Bay and the Potomac River, now Point Lookout State Park. On March 25, 1813, U.S. Postmaster General Gideon Granger established an observation post there to monitor British activity on Chesapeake Bay. Henry Weitz was appointed the first agent of the post, but he was replaced by Thomas Swann in June. In late spring of 1813, a British barge was sent to scuttle a grounded British ship off Point Lookout. Elwiley (Wily) Smith and a party of ten or twelve men armed with "squirrel guns" fired on the barge from behind a fence. The defenders claimed that four of the British sailors were hit and the barge retreated without completing its mission. On July 19, 1813, the U.S. Post Office began a daily express courier system between Point Lookout and Washington, D.C., keeping the capital informed of British fleet movements on the Bay. Point Lookout served as a staging area for the local militia in the early summer of 1813 until two thousand to three thousand British forces occupied the point between July 19 and July 27, 1813. The British used the point as a base for raids on St. Mary's County.

Capt. James Forrest's report of July 27, 1813, was printed in the Annapolis *Maryland Republican* on July 31, 1813: *Our situation is extremely critical. From two to three thousand of the enemy are in complete possession of the point of land below the Ridge, which is two and half miles from Point Look Out. They have been five or six miles higher up procuring stock; and have now in Mr. Armstrong's corn field about 200 head of cattle, &c. Several of our most respectable inhabitants have been taken by the enemy . . . Many negroes have also been taken, some of whom have escaped and returned to their masters. Seven of the enemy's regulars have deserted, and are now with us. The whole fleet is yet lying off Point Look Out. What will be their next movement I know not. They have landed 6 pieces of artillery, and it is ascertained that they have on board rockets in abundance.*

Early on August 17, 1814, Thomas Swann, the forward observer at Point Lookout, sent a courier named Carmichael to warn Washington that he had spotted the combined British invasion fleet moving up Chesapeake Bay. The Americans had also established an observation base at Smith Point, Virginia, on the opposite side of the entrance to the Potomac River. They had detected the fleet the evening before.

The Annapolis *Maryland Republican* reported on August 20, 1814: *Various rumors have been in circulation for two or three days past, relative to a large naval force which is said lately to have arrived in the bay. On Thursday last it was stated by an express from Point Look Out, that there were forty six sail in the bay, amongst which we understood there were several transports, bearing a large number of troops.*

Midshipman Robert J. Barrett recounted his memories of the event in 1840: *It was a glorious and imposing spectacle to behold these noble ships standing up the vast bay of the Chesapeake, into the very heart of America; manned, too, with eager souls, panting for fame . . . The flags of three British Admirals,* [Vice Adm. Alexander F.I.] *Cochrane,* [Rear Adm. George] *Cockburn, and* [Rear Adm.] *Poultney* [Pulteney] *Malcolm, were proudly flying at the mastheads of their respective vessels* [ships-of-the-line] , *the Tonnant, Albion, and Royal Oak.*

SOTTERLEY. NRHP. Location: east end of Sotterley Gate Road (Route 245), St. Mary's County. **Parking:** free. **Hours:** Tuesday through Saturday, 10 a.m. to 4 p.m., Sunday, noon to 4 p.m. **Fees:** self-guided tours, $3 per person; guided tours, $10 adults, $8 seniors, $5 children 6 to 12, children under 6 free. **Facilities:** historic house, outbuilding including slave quarters, restrooms, gift shop. **Contacts:** 301-373-2289; www.sotterley.org.

SOTTERLEY PLANTATION, built as early as 1717, was owned by George Plater V. Plater's uncle, Col. John Rousby Plater, served as his guardian since George was in his teens at the time. Militia crossed the Patuxent River to join other troops on June 10, 1814, during the Battle of St. Leonard Creek (*see* Jefferson Patterson Park and Museum *below*). The British landed near Sotterley and attacked an estimated three hundred militiamen who quickly fled.

British Capt. James Scott in his 1834 memoirs relates that an unnamed daughter of Col. John Rousby Plater stated: *How shall I express to you the feelings of shame that consume me, when I inform you the sight of a British barge alone is sufficient to put to flight every man in our neighbourhood? What, what must be the opinions of our enemies of such conduct! I blush for my countrymen!*

Captain Scott also wrote: *Colonel* [John Rousby] *Plater . . . told the* [Rear] *Admiral* [George Cockburn] *that he had done his utmost to bring forward his regiment (militia) to beat him back, but that they had deserted him, and he surrendered himself a prisoner, feeling he was entirely at his mercy. This candour at once gained the favour and protection of Admiral Cockburn, and the most rigid orders were issued, and sentinels placed around, to secure the premises from molestation or injury. The gallant Colonel himself remained at perfect liberty . . . For his conduct, Colonel Plater was held up by a democratic portion of the republican press as something akin to a traitor.*

Despite the reported assurance of protection proclaimed on June 14, 1814, by Rear Admiral Cockburn, the British burned a tobacco warehouse and a house formerly occupied by the militia. In addition, at least thirty-nine slaves from Sotterley escaped to British vessels.

The Annapolis *Maryland Republican* reported on June 18, 1814: *a flag of truce was sent to the St. Mary's side of the Patuxent* [opposite St. Leonard Creek near Sotterley] *to demand cattle, with a threat that they would destroy the houses if they were not furnished, the demand we understand was not complied with, & in the evening eleven barges were sent over, but no houses were destroyed; a few shot were fired onshore by the enemy, but it is uncertain what damage was done. By a gentleman who left St. Leonards . . . we learn that 17 barges went to the opposite side of the river that evening; that several shots were fired, and some houses destroyed; amongst others it was expected a warehouse near Col. Plater* [of Sotterley], *for the storage and inspection of tobacco was burnt.*

Capt. Joseph Nourse reported to Rear Adm. George Cockburn on July 23, 1814: *the people on either side of the Patuxent are in the greatest alarm and consternation many are moving entirely away from both Calvert & St. Marys, and I think in a short time they will be nearly deserted, those that remained at home all their Slaves have left them and come to us, last night 39 Men Women and Children came from Colonel Plater's.*

JEFFERSON PATTERSON PARK AND MUSEUM. NHD. **Location:** near south end of Mackall Road (Route 265), Mackall, Calvert County. **Parking:** free. **Hours:** April 16 to November 1, Wednesday through Sunday, 10 a.m. to 5 p.m. **Fees:** none. **Facilities:** exhibits, restrooms, picnic facilities, hiking trails. **Contacts:** 410-586-8501; www.jefpat.org. **Comment:** the park hosts an annual 1812 re-enactment in September.

JEFFERSON PATTERSON PARK AND MUSEUM is located at the confluence of St. Leonard Creek and Patuxent River. On this property, U.S. Army troops were mustered to support the Chesapeake Flotilla. Soldiers, U.S. Marines, and U.S. Navy flotillamen erected a gun battery during the Second Battle of St. Leonard Creek. James John Pattison, who owned

Battles of St. Leonard Creek
(June 8–10 and June 26, 1814)

Com. Joshua Barney commanded a flotilla of gun barges and gunboats known as the Chesapeake Flotilla. He encountered a superior British naval force on June 1 near the mouth of the Potomac River and, after a brief skirmish, retreated to the safety of the Patuxent River.

After moving upriver into St. Leonard Creek, Barney was attacked by the British on June 8, 9, and 10. Wave after wave of British gunboats, schooners, and barges attempted to destroy the American flotilla. In this series of engagements, known as the First Battle of St. Leonard Creek, Barney repulsed each attack. Casualties on both sides were light.

Next, in an attempt to draw Barney from his lair, the British began a campaign of destruction along the Patuxent. In response, the Americans launched a poorly coordinated pre-dawn attack on June 26. Shore batteries pounded the British ships at the mouth of the creek, followed shortly thereafter by a waterborne flotilla attack. This engagement, known as the Second Battle of St. Leonard Creek, ended in a draw, and again casualties on each side were light. The engagement, however, did enable Barney to slip out of the creek and move his flotilla up the Patuxent River.

Determined to destroy the flotilla, British boats moved up the Patuxent in August 1814. Just above where Maryland Route 4 now crosses the Patuxent, the British discovered the flotilla on August 22, only to watch it being blown up by the Americans to keep it out of enemy hands.

property here, lost two slaves, who fled to the British side. On March 26, 1814, John Stuart Skinner, who also owned property here, was commissioned purser of the flotilla. He made a Revere-like ride to warn the Americans in Washington of the approach of the British in August 1814 and served as agent for the exchange of prisoners. He accompanied Francis Scott Key to seek the release of Dr. William Beanes, whom the British had taken to their fleet in retaliation for his arrest of British stragglers. From their flag-of-truce boat, they witnessed the bombardment of Fort McHenry. On June 11, 1814, the British burned Skinner's St. Leonard property. They also burned his birthplace, The Reserve, during their July 19, 1814, raid on Prince Frederick. An exhibit about the war at this property is located in the barn just below the visitor center. A replica naval gun battery is located on a nearby hill and several War of 1812 interpretive panels are located throughout the park.

From Jefferson Patterson Park and Museum, continue on Mackall Road to Broomes Island Road (Route 264) to Solomons Island Road (Route 4) north to Upper Marlboro.

Optional Side Trip **LOWER MARLBORO.** If time permits, an optional side trip to Lower Marlboro, another site raided by the British, provides a nice view of the Patuxent River.

LOWER MARLBORO, a colonial town located on the Patuxent River, is located at the end of Lower Marlboro Road, approximately 4 miles west off Solomons Island Road (Route 4). Here a British force of about 160 Royal Marines and a detachment of 30 Colonial Marines (former slaves) took the village without resistance after the militia and most of the townsfolk had fled. The British occupied the town from about 6 p.m., June 15, to about 8 a.m., June 16, 1814. Tobacco warehouses, with 2,500 hogsheads of tobacco valued at more than $125,000, were burned, a small schooner captured, and a civilian named J. W. Reynolds taken. Reynolds was later offered in exchange for a Royal Marine the British believed had been captured at Benedict by the Americans on June 21, 1814.

A British account of the raid by Captain Robert Barrie was reported to Rear Admiral George Cockburn on June 19, 1814: *I pushed on towards* [Lower] *Marlborough where I understood there were several Stores of Tobacco and other property, and As Marlborough is near the Seat of Government* [Washington] *I thought an attack on this Town would be a sad Annoyance to the Enemy and oblige the Regulars and Militia to try their strength with us, but I was deceived as both Militia and Inhabitants made off to the woods and we were allowed to take quiet possession of a Town admirably situated for Defense, here we passed the night without molestation though only eighteen Miles from Washington, in the morning I loaded a small Schooner with Tobacco and having plentifully supplied ourselves with Stock, I burnt Tobacco Stores containing two thousand and five hundred Hogsheads of this valuable Article and then Embarked.*

The Broome Burning

Broomes Island, located on the Patuxent River at the south end of Broomes Island Road (Route 264), was the site of a British raid. On June 12, 1814, the home of John Broome VII was burned, possibly because he raised and maintained a militia company at his own expense.

An American account of the raid was published in the Baltimore *American & Commercial Daily Advertizer* on June 20, 1814: *They opened all the feather beds they could find, broke the doors and windows out and so tore the houses to pieces inside as to render them of very little value.*

A second American account by an unnamed merchant was published in the New York *Herald* on June 25, 1814: *I am sorry to inform you that the British have this forenoon BURNT the Tobacco Ware-Houses at lower Marlborough . . . they took a schooner (Capt. David's) and loaded her . . . near Lower Marlborough, they forced some negroes off with them— got some stock, poultry, &c.*

The Chesapeake Flotilla was briefly stationed at Lower Marlboro after its escape from St. Leonard Creek (*see* Jefferson Patterson Park and Museum *above*) in late June, 1814. Local tradition states a few British soldiers are buried here although there is no firm evidence supporting the claim. At the ferry/steamboat landing, an interpretive panel provides information about Lower Marlboro and the surrounding area during the War of 1812.

Rear Adm. George Cockburn reported to Vice Adm. Alexander F. I. Cochrane about his meeting with Maj. Gen. Robert Ross during their march toward Washington on August 22, 1814: *I endeavored to Keep with the Boats and Tenders as nearly as possible abreast of the Army under Major General Ross that I might communicate with him as occasions offered, according to the plan previously arranged, and about mid-day yesterday I accordingly anchored at the Ferry House opposite Lower Marlborough where I met the General [Ross] and where the Army halted for some hours.*

Night Raid

Prince Frederick, the county seat of Calvert County, suffered a night raid on July 19, 1814, after the British landed and marched 9 miles from their ships on the Patuxent River. With little resistance from the local militia, they burned the jail, a tobacco warehouse, and the courthouse, where sick and wounded from the Chesapeake Flotilla had been treated and some naval stores, including munitions, were deposited. During their return to their ships, the British also took twenty slaves from one plantation.

Other sites in the southern Maryland region include Chaptico Christ Episcopal Church, Fort Washington, and Mount Welby.

CHAPTICO CHRIST EPISCOPAL CHURCH. Location: intersection of Maddox (Route 238) and Budds Creek–Deep Falls roads (Route 234), St. Mary's County. **Parking:** free. **Hours:** daylight hours. **Fees:** none. **Facilities:** none. **Comment:** please respect the church and graveyard.

After landing at nearby Hamburg, on July 30, 1814, British forces under Rear Adm. George Cockburn marched to **CHAPTICO,** located at the head of Chaptico Bay, off the Wicomico River, where they conducted a raid. The landing here, as well as landings at Lower Cedar Point and Leonardtown, were part of Cockburn's assault along the Potomac. At Chaptico, many houses, as well as the wharf and tobacco sheds, were destroyed and the church was damaged. The British reportedly broke every pane of glass in the village. Christ Episcopal Church was built in 1736 under the supervision of Philip Key, grandfather of Francis Scott Key. Several members of the Key family are buried in the Key vault which is located immediately behind the church. The vault is identified only by "DEFAIS LE FOI." and the image of an eagle perched on a shield holding a key in its beak. During the British raid, the church suffered damage to its marble floors when horses were reportedly stabled there. A raised wooden floor now covers the original damaged floor. The church organ was also damaged and some grave vaults desecrated. The Maryland legislature approved a lottery in 1815 to repair the damage. Hence, most of the interior of the church dates from after 1814. The brick bell tower was added in 1913. The differences between the American and British accounts of this raid are striking.

One Slave's Saga

Charles Ball, a slave born in Calvert County about 1790, was owned by Levin Ballard of Lower Marlboro. At about the age of twenty, Ball was rented to a "man with epaulets on his shoulders" at the Washington Navy Yard. Ball worked as a cook under Com. Joshua Barney for the Chesapeake Flotilla during the First and Second Battles of St. Leonard Creek. Ball was also present during the Battle of Bladensburg, where he said the militia "ran like sheep being chased by dogs." After the war, Ball returned to Calvert County and was sold to a Georgia slave trader from whom he escaped. Returning to his family in Calvert County, Ball worked as a free black, saved money, and purchased a small farm near Baltimore. After ten years, he was re-enslaved by his former master. On his third attempt, he again escaped, and at great risk returned to Baltimore to seek his family members, but they had been kidnapped and sold south into slavery. Ball lived the rest of his life in Philadelphia as a free man. Charles Ball is probably a pseudonym. His real name is unknown.

Rear Adm. George Cockburn reported to Vice Adm. Alexander Cochrane about the raid on July 31, 1814: *passing the Night in the Boats I landed at daylight yesterday with the Marines about Three Miles below Chaptico, which Place we marched to and took Possession of without opposition. I remained all day quietly in Chaptico whilst the Boats shipped off the Tobacco which was found there in considerable quantity, and at Night I re-embarked without molestation. I visited many Houses in different parts of the County we passed through, the owners of which were living quietly with their Families and seeming to consider themselves and the whole Neighborhood as being entirely at my disposal, I caused no further Inconvenience to* [them], *than obliging them to furnish Supplies of Cattle and Stock for the use of the Forces under my orders.*

British Capt. Robert Rowley reported to his superiors about the raid in August 1814: *on 30th. We went 20 miles up the Wicomico River, there took possession of the Town of Chaptico—where some Ladies who had heard of our good behaviour at Leonards Town remained—and sang and played on the Piano. We took from thence 70 Hhds. of tobacco, some flour, & military stores but preserved their houses purchased from them stock and various articles of provisions. The men all fled, but the Ladies remained to see the wonderful* [Rear] *Admrl.* [George] *Cockburn and the British folks.*

Baltimore *Niles' Weekly Register* published an American account of the raid on August 14, 1814: *they* [British] *got about 30 hhds.* [hogsheads] *of tobacco and no other plunder, the inhabitants having moved all their property out of their grasp. Yet here they made a most furious attack on every window, door, and pane of glass in the village, not one was left in the whole . . . They picked their stolen geese in the church, dashed the pipes of the church organ on the pavement, opened a family vault in the churchyard, broke open the coffins, stirred the bones about with their hands in search of hidden treasure—all this in the presence of their worthy admiral. During all this havoc, not a man was in arms within fifteen miles of them, and they worked until ten o'clock at night, before they got the tobacco on board their vessels owing to the shallowness of the creek that leads up to Chaptico warehouse, they rolled more than half the tobacco one mile.* [Brigadier] *General* [Philip] *Stuart was encamped with the militia near sixteen miles from these free-booters; I presume he is waiting for a regular field action with the British. He has no confidence in our trees and bushes, as militia had in the revolutionary war.*

Former Maryland Governor Robert Wright wrote about the raid on October 19, 1814: *I passed through Chaptico shortly after the enemy left it, and I am sorry to say that their* [British] *conduct would have disgraced cannibals; the houses were torn to pieces, the well which afforded water for the inhabitants was filled up, and, what was still worse, the church and the ashes of the dead shared an equally bad or worse fate. Will you believe me when I tell you that the sunken graves were converted into barbacue holes? The remaining glass of the church windows broken, the communion table used as a dinner table, and then broken to pieces. Bad as the above may appear, it dwindles into insignificance, when compared with what follows: the vault was entered and the remains of the dead disturbed. Yes, my friend, the winding sheet was torn from the body of a lady of the first respectability, and the whole contents of the vault entirely deranged! The above facts were witnessed by hundreds as well as myself, and I am happy to say, that but one sentiment pervaded our army. I immediately showed it to general Philip Stuart, lately commanding the American troops at that place, who read and declared it strictly true; that Cockburn was at the head of it; that they destroyed the* [church] *organs; that judge Key's lady* [relative of Francis Scott Key] *, who had been last put into the vault, was the person alluded to; that her winding sheet was torn in pieces, and her person wantonly exposed; and that his men were exasperated to desperation by this conduct.*

FORT WASHINGTON PARK. NRHP. **Address:** 13551 Old Fort Road off Indian Head Highway (Route 210), Prince George's County. **Parking:** free. **Hours:** grounds, open 8 a.m. to sunset; fort, open 9 a.m. to 5 p.m. April through October and 9 a.m. to 4:30 p.m. rest of year. **Fees:** $5 per vehicle and $3 per walkers and bike riders. **Facilities:** exhibits, small gift shop, restrooms, picnic tables. **Contacts:** 301-763-4600; www.nps.gov/fowa. **Comment:** Fort Washington today has no resemblance to what the destroyed fort looked like in 1814. No vestiges remain of the 1814 fort. The park is operated by the National Park Service.

FORT WASHINGTON, originally named Fort Warburton after the estate on which it stood, was completed in 1809 and renamed to honor George Washington, who chose the defensive site in 1794. Both names were used during the War of 1812. Fort Washington, the earliest fortification built for the defense of Washington, offered a strategic location as the river channel narrows and swings close to the Maryland side, forcing ships to approach the fort bow on as they began to pass up the river and then stern on after they passed. Only when directly opposite could a passing warship (other than bomb-ships) effectively bring its guns to bear on the fort.

Lt. Theodore Maurice described the fort in 1815 as a small star-shaped earthwork with a circular gun battery in front. It mounted two 32 pounder, two 50 pounder, and nine 24 pounder guns. The fortification was based on the design of Fort Madison near Annapolis but altered to fit the four-acre parcel. The 1814 fort was built at the ravelin (detached fortification with two embankments projecting outward and forming a salient angle) adjacent to the 1898 Battery White that is located on the riverside, outside of the walls of the main fort. A water battery closer to the shore mounted 18 pounder naval guns while, behind the fort on the hill where the present stone fort is located, was a brick octagonal blockhouse with six 18 pounder Columbiade guns.

The British described the fort as a "most respectable defense," but an article in the Baltimore *Federal Republican* on July 23, 1813, had little good to say: *The mighty preparations made to resist this formidable over bearing force, is Fort Warburton, a mere pig pen with 13 guns mounted and a battery with seven guns more.*

Maj. Gen. James Wilkinson described the defense of the Potomac in 1816 as consisting

This 1958 aerial view of Fort Washington shows the 1824 walled fort in the center and the Spanish-American War–era batteries located in the right foreground. Key: A. Approximate location of the 1814 fort, which is no longer extant. (Abbie Rowe 1957 or 1958 photograph; HABS, Library of Congress)

of: *the sloop of war* Adams, *with a few small gunboats, and Fort Washington, a mere water battery of twelve or fifteen guns, bearing upon the channel in the ascent of the river, but useless the moment a vessel had passed. This work was seated at the foot of a steep acclivity, from the summit of which the garrison could have been driven out by musketry, but this height was protected by an octagonal Block house, built of brick, and of two stories altitude, which being calculated against musketry only, could have been knocked down by a twelve pounder.*

In 1814, Fort Washington had a garrison of only forty-nine men under the command of Capt. Samuel T. Dyson, U.S. Army. After a brief British bombardment by a squadron of six Royal Navy warships under the command of Capt. James Alexander Gordon, Dyson ordered the fort blown up and the cannons spiked about 7 or 8 p.m., August 27, 1814. Dyson's decision allowed the British to take the city of Alexandria without the fort firing a single shot.

Capt. James Alexander Gordon reported on the destruction of the fort on August 27, 1814: *Fort Washington appeared to our anxious eyes, and to our great satisfaction it was considered assailable. A little before sunset the squadron anchored just out of gunshot, the bomb vessels at once taking up their positions to cover the frigates in the projected attack at daylight next morning, and began throwing shells. The garrison to our great surprise, retreated from the fort and a short time afterward Fort Washington was blown up, which left the Capitol of America and the populous town of Alexandria open to the squadron without the loss of a man. It was too late to ascertain whether this catastrophe was occasioned by one of our shells or whether it had been blown up by the garrison, but the opinion was in favor of the latter. Still we are at a loss to account for such an extraordinary step. The position was good, and its capture would have cost us at least fifty men and more had it been properly defended.*

Capt. Samuel T. Dyson reported to Secretary of War John Armstrong on the destruction of the fort on August 29, 1814. His report was reprinted in the Annapolis *Maryland Republican* on September 3, 1814: *The orders received from Brig. Gen. [William H.] Winder through Major [Robert G.] Hite, verbally, on the 24th inst. were, in case I was oppressed, or heard of an enemy in my rear, to spike our guns and make my escape over the river. The enemy approached by water on the 27th, and we had learnt that day through several channels that the enemy had been reinforced at Benedict 6000 [actually 4,370] strong, and that they were on their march to cooperate wish [with] the fleet, in addition to the force which left the city. Under all these circumstances, the officers under my command were consulted, and agreed it was best to abandon the fort and effect a retreat. The force under my command was thought not equal to a defense of the place.*

Captain Dyson was placed under arrest and relieved of his command. He was afterwards court-martialed and found guilty of abandoning his post and destroying government property. As a result, he was dismissed from the service.

With Fort Washington destroyed, the Americans hastily erected batteries at White House, on the Virginia shore, and Indian Head, on the Maryland shore, to impede the British withdrawal back down the Potomac. Both of these sites are on military property: Indian Head is inaccessible and White House is currently accessible with photo ID. Near Fort Washington, the Americans unsuccessfully attempted to send fire-ships into the British squadron.

Annapolis *Maryland Republican* reported on the fire-ship attack on September 10, 1814: *The enemy's vessels dropt down the river from Alexandria on Friday night; and on Saturday com. [John] Rodgers has possession of the unfortunate town. On Saturday two or three fire-ships were sent down to the frigates then lying off [Fort] Warburton, but did not take effect on them. The river was immediately covered with barges, thirty or forty in number, and these dangerous objects were towed out of the way of the vessels. The scene was witnessed from the high grounds of the city, and was very interesting—the river being covered with vessels and boats of almost every description.*

MOUNT WELBY. NRHP. **Address:** 6411 Oxen Hill. **Parking:** free. **Hours:** 8 a.m. to 4:30 p.m. daily. **Fees:** none. **Facilities:** exhibits, restrooms and picnic facilities. **Contacts:** 301-839-1176; www.nps.gov/oxhi/index.htm. **Comment:** Mount Welby is located at Oxen Cove Park/Oxen Hill Farm operated by the National Park Service. From the house, there is a splendid view of the Potomac River and distant Washington, D.C.

The circa 1811 **MOUNT WELBY,** overlooking the Potomac River, was the home of Dr. Samuel DeButts. His wife, Mary Welby DeButts, wrote letters to her sister describing Capt. James Alexander Gordon's British squadron advance up the Potomac River, firing Congreve rockets, three of which landed near her home.

Mary Welby DeButts wrote to Millicent Welby Ridgehill on March 18, 1815: *I cannot express to you the distress it has occasioned at the Battle of Bladensburg we heard every fire (that place being not more 5 or 6 miles from us). Our House was shook repeatedly by the firing upon forts & Bridges, & illuminated by the fires in our Capitol. It was indeed a Day & night of horrors, the fleet debarkment from [Rear] Admiral [George] Cockburn's fleet lay directly before our House. The Capitulation of Alexandria & the result you must have seen in the Public papers. We left home for Loudoun (Virginia) while the British Vessels were in our River, passing in the ferry Boat close to them without being molested; you know not how it hurt me to think I was so near my Country men, & must look upon them as Enemy, whom I should have rejoiced to have shown every attention to; we found three Rockets on our Hill evidently pointed at our House but fortunately did not reach it.*

To protect the rear of nearby Fort Washington, Brig. Gen. Robert Young and 454 men were stationed at Mount Welby. These troops later joined the American forces defending the White House Gun Battery on the Virginia shore of the Potomac. From near here on September 4 and 5, 1814, Capt. John Rodgers of the U.S. Navy launched fire vessels against the British squadron.

The Annapolis *Maryland Republican* described the fire-boat attack on September 10, 1814: *A fireship was sent down on Monday afternoon by com. [John] Rodgers, which had very nearly encountered one of the frigates of the enemy, but was grappled and towed out of the way by his barges. A torpedo [mine] was sent down on Monday evening, after the British fleet passed [David] Porter's battery [White House Gun Battery], and exploded about 9 at night, with what effect is not yet known.*

Capt. John Rodgers reported to Secretary of Navy William Jones about the fire-boat attack on September 9, 1814. His report was reprinted in the Baltimore *Niles' Weekly Register* on October 1, 1814: *proceeded down the Potomac with three small fire vessels under the protection of four barges or cutters, manned with about sixty seamen, armed with muskets, destined against two of the enemy's frigates and a bomb-ship, which lay about 2 1-2 miles below Alexandria . . . I have no doubt, would have succeeded in destroying two at least of the enemy's ships, had not the wind failed them sometime before, and particularly after they had reached the uppermost ship, within the range of musket shot . . . Of the enemy's boats, some were employed in towing off the fire-vessels, and the rest in pursuit of our four cutters . . . On the 4th inst. I had another fire vessel prepared, but it being calm, I ordered . . . the four cutters, to proceed with one of the remaining lighters . . . to attack the bomb-ship, which in the anxiety of the enemy to get below the temporary forts [White House Gun Battery and Indian Head Gun Battery] . . . had been left exposed to attack.*

Capt. James Alexander Gordon reported to Vice Adm. Alexander F. I. Cochrane his account of fire-boat attack on September 9, 1814: *Contrary winds again occasioned us the laborious task of warping the Ships down the River in which a days delay early took place owing to the [H.M. bomb-vessel] Devastation grounding. The Enemy took advantage of this Circumstance to attempt her destruction by three fire vessels and attended by five row Boats.— But their object was defeated by the promptitude and gallantry of Captain [Thomas] Alexander who pushed off with his own Boats and being followed by those of the other Ships chased the boats of the Enemy up to the town of Alexandria.*

This ends the Southern Maryland Tour.

Maryland Eastern Shore Tour

Particulars The Eastern Shore of Maryland has many quaint, historic towns that attract numerous visitors. One of the most popular is St. Michaels, which also boasts several War of 1812–related sites. It is suggested you begin you tour here as there are excellent restaurants as well as places to stay in St. Michaels and nearby Easton. For those who choose to visit the upper Eastern Shore area, the Kitty Knight Inn, saved from burning during a British raid by the inn's namesake, located at Georgetown, is also a good place to stay. Visitors may plan their tour to suit their own interests and time constraints. For information on Fort Stokes, located on the North Fork of the Tred Avon River, Talbot County, *see* appendix C, as it can be seen only by boat.

Historical Background Maryland's Eastern Shore has a wealth of sites related to the War of 1812. The battles of Caulks Field and St. Michaels were the largest engagements, but there were also at least eleven skirmishes and sixteen raids on Maryland's Eastern Shore. This tour highlights some of these actions.

ST. MICHAELS. NHD. Location: Route 33, approximately 10 miles west of Easton, Talbot County. **Parking:** street and lot parking. **Facilities:** public restrooms. There are two museums, many excellent restaurants, and lodging ranging from B&Bs and motels to hotels. **Contacts:** 1-800-808-SMBA (7622); www.stmichaelsmd.org/about/history1.html. **Comment:** St. Michaels does not have a visitor center, but brochures can be obtained at the Chesapeake Bay Maritime Museum ticket office. St. Michaels is a charming historic town and a good place to walk, bicycle, or paddle (*see* appendixes A, B, *and* C). *See* appendix D *for boat excursions on the Miles River.*

ST. MICHAELS, a well-known shipbuilding center that produced privateers, was a prime target for British attack. Among the successful privateers built here were the *Surprise,* that captured forty-three prizes; the *Caroline,* that captured thirty; the *Lawrence,* that captured twenty-two; and the *Fairy,* that took four British prizes worth $67,500. Altogether, twenty-eight Talbot County vessels, many St. Michaels built, operated against British shipping during the war. Perry Spencer built at least eight barges for the Chesapeake Flotilla, but the exact location of his shipyard is unknown.

St. Michaels is one of only two towns in Maryland that twice successfully defended itself from British attacks. (The other was Elkton.) The first engagement, known as the "Battle of St. Michaels," took place at twilight on August 10, 1813. The village later become known as the "town that fooled the British," but see discussion below.

An American account of the engagement was published in the Annapolis *Maryland Gazette and Political Intelligencer* on August 19, 1813: *the enemy made an attack on that place* [St. Michaels] *with 10 or 12 barges. From the extreme darkness of the night they succeeded in*

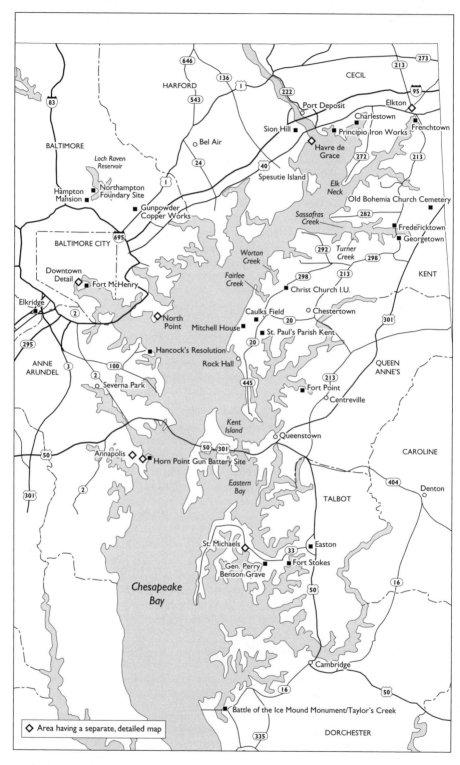

Maryland Eastern Shore and Head of the Chesapeake

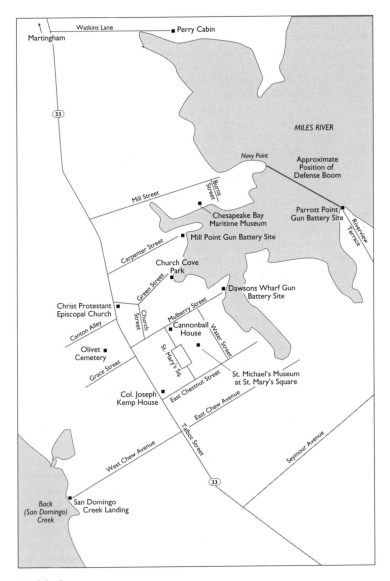

St. Michaels

getting within a few yards of a small battery [Parrott Point] *before those who were stationed in it discovered them, when they opened a fire from a nine pounder charged with round shot & langrage, and supposed that considerable execution was done. There being but 14 or 15 men in the fort, and the enemy all around it, they spiked their cannon and retreated. Two small batteries placed in the town* [Mill Point and Dawsons Wharf], *with a few 6's in them, then opened their fire upon the barges, and in a few minutes compelled them to retreat with considerable precipitation, and they were seen about day-light towing a barge after them. It is not known what damage was done to the enemy, but it is supposed considerable fr. the great hurry with which they left the shore.*

A British account of the engagement was reported by Lt. James Polkingthorne to Capt. Henry Baker on August 10, 1813: *I proceeded with the division of Boats ... up the St. Michael's [Miles] river. We advanced along Shore close to the Town of St. Michaels, and were discovered by the Enemies Patrol who fired on us, a few minutes after a Battery [Parrott Point] mounting Six Twelve and Six pounders gave us a round of Grape and Cannister, when we immediately landed I got possession of the Battery and drove the Enemy into the Town after Spiking the guns; Splitting the Carriages and destroying the Ammunition and Stores, I reembarked with the loss of only two wounded; by this time the Enemy had collected in considerable numbers, and commenced firing from two field pieces [Mill Point and Dawsons Wharf] in the Town. The destruction of the Battery being complete, and not a Vessel to be seen, I deemed the object of the enterprise fulfilled, and returned on board with the Boats.*

Three gun batteries and supposedly a floating boom across the harbor defended St. Michaels. An earthwork was constructed at the entrance to the harbor at Parrott Point, and traveling cannons were hastily established at Dawsons Wharf and Mill Point within the harbor. Both the Americans and the British claim to have spiked the cannons at Parrott Point. It appears one cannon was spiked by the militia before fleeing, and the British spiked the remaining three after taking the gun battery. The cannons at Dawsons Wharf and Mill Point drove the British back to their boats. H.M. sloop *Conflict,* positioned out of reach of the American guns, then cannonaded the town.

A second engagement took place at St. Michaels on August 26, 1813, when a British force of approximately 2,100 men landed at Wades Point, about 6 miles from town. One detachment of about 300 troops headed south to attack a militia camp near Harris Creek, while the main body, consisting of about 1,800 men, headed east toward St. Michaels. At a narrows bounded by Porter Creek on the north and Broad Creek on the south, about 1.5 miles west of St. Michaels, the British met an American force of 500 men supported by cavalry and artillery. After a few shots were fired, the British withdrew. The detached British force near Harris Creek captured 14 militiamen who had fled to their homes. They were paroled the next day.

An American account of the second engagement was reported by Gen. Perry Benson and published in the Easton *Star* on August 29, 1813: *about day-light the enemy was discovered by our videts stationed at Col. [Hugh] Auld's point [Wades Point], to be landing from upwards of 60 barges—They immediately moved in column about two miles toward our camp at this place [St. Michaels]. They then posted a picquet of men in advance, within four miles of us—They had two field pieces, and a number of rockets on the road, in rear of the picquet. At the same time we discovered three schooners and a brig beating up the river, crowded with troops, evidently with all intentions of cutting off our retreat, and destroying this place, should we march down to attack them ... A flag from one of the schooners landed and informed several persons on the water, that the British troops would land in a few hours, and if they would remain in their houses, their property should not be injured. The vessels, after grounding several times, came to anchor. After this, [Rear] Admiral [George] Cockburn, at the head of 300 men, marched below in search of a militia company stationed there; the greater part of whom made their retreat across Harris's creek ... Fourteen were afterwards taken at their own houses. They burnt two small vessels, and plundered the inhabitants of clothing, &c. to a large amount. From information received that morning from five seamen who deserted after landing, their force on shore was 300 under [Colonel] Sir [Thomas] Sidney Beckwith. At six, P.M. they re-embarked, taking with them the 14 prisoners, whom they released the next day on parole.*

St. Michaels is known as "the town that fooled the British" because of a legend. It is said that during the first engagement Americans hung lanterns from the tops of buildings and trees and on mastheads of vessels in the harbor to induce the British to fire over the town. However, the cannonade that followed the attack actually took place in early morning light. The British would have been able to at least faintly see the town, even with the overcast conditions that morning. Furthermore, in the official report by Gen. Perry Benson, he wrote that several homes (such as the Cannonball House discussed below) were hit, suggesting the British were not fooled. In fact, the Americans were taken totally by surprise and had no time to hang lanterns. This story of the lanterns did not surface until many years after the war.

The **CANNONBALL HOUSE,** located at 200 Mulberry Street, near southeast corner of St. Mary's Square, was built circa 1805 by shipwright William Merchant. It was struck on August 10, 1813, by a cannonball during the British cannonade. A cannonball reportedly penetrated the roof of this house, then rolled across the attic and down the staircase, frightening Mrs. Merchant, who was carrying her infant daughter downstairs at the time. The Cannonball House is privately owned and not open to the public.

> ### The Battles of St. Michaels
>
> Gen. Perry Benson commanded the American forces that repulsed the British in the first and second attacks on St. Michaels. The first engagement is often referred to as the "Battle of St. Michaels," although only a few score Americans took part in it. The second action, which involved hundreds of men on each side, is little known and has no common name.

CHESAPEAKE BAY MARITIME MUSEUM. Location: Navy Point at end of Mill and Cherry streets. **Parking:** free for museum visitors. **Hours:** 10 a.m. to 5 p.m. spring and fall; 10 a.m. to 6 p.m. summer; and 10 a.m. to 4 p.m. winter. **Fees:** $13 adults, $10 seniors, $6 children aged 6 to 17, and children under 6 free. **Facilities:** exhibits, visitor information at entrance kiosk, museum store, restrooms on grounds. **Contacts:** 410-745-2916; www.cbmm.org. **Comment:** this museum is worth a visit and plan at least two hours or more.

The **CHESAPEAKE BAY MARITIME MUSEUM** includes a small exhibit on the War of 1812. Among the exhibits is an engraving showing the privateer *Rossie,* commanded by Com. Joshua Barney, taking the British mail packet *Princess Amelia* in 1812. The museum and the Inn at Perry Cabin, located north of the museum on the waterfront, were once part of the Perry Cabin Farm, owned by Samuel Hambleton, U.S. Navy purser during the War of 1812. Hambleton named the point where the museum is now located Navy Point.

CHRIST PROTESTANT EPISCOPAL CHURCH, at the intersection of Talbot and Green streets, was founded in 1672, although the present structure, the third at this location, dates from 1878. American troops reportedly occupied an earlier frame structure that served as the church during the first engagement of St. Michaels. During a reconstruction of the church in 1814, muskets left behind during or shortly after the attack were said to be discovered under the floorboards.

The **COL. JOSEPH KEMP HOUSE,** located at 412 Talbot Street, was built between 1805 and 1807. Kemp commanded the Saint Michaels Patriotic Blues of the 26th Regiment, Maryland militia. During the first engagement of St. Michaels, he led a cavalry patrol along San

Domingo Creek (now Back Creek). Kemp is buried at St. Luke's Methodist Cemetery. The Kemp House is privately owned and not open to the public.

The site of the **PARROTT POINT GUN BATTERY** is located on the south side of the harbor entrance, at the northwest end of Riverview Terrace, off Seymour Avenue. A defensive boom was supposedly erected across the harbor mouth from Parrott Point to Cedar Point. A four-gun battery erected at Parrott Point fired two shots before being captured by British troops who landed before sunrise in eleven barges. Although the British were driven away by the Mill Point and Dawson Wharf gun batteries, they spiked the cannons at Parrott Point before leaving. The shoreline of this residential area has been severely altered by erosion and erosion-control measures. No vestige of the battery is extant. Please respect private property and do not disturb owners.

Parrott Point Commander

Capt. William Dodson commanded the Parrott Point gun battery. He later commanded one of the Chesapeake Flotilla barges and participated in the Battle of Bladensburg. Dodson is buried at St. Luke's Methodist Church Cemetery, St. Michaels. In May 1813, the ladies of St. Michaels presented to Captain Dodson a flag embroidered with the names of the officers of the Talbot County militia.

The site of the **DAWSONS WHARF GUN BATTERY** is located at the foot of Mulberry Street at the Town Dock Restaurant. Here Lt. John Graham commanded a two-gun battery positioned on shipwright "Impy" Dawson's wharf. The site of the **MILL POINT GUN BATTERY** is located at the foot of Carpenter Street at the Two Swan Inn. Here Capt. Clement Vickers commanded a two gun-battery.

PERRY CABIN, also Perry's Cabin, now called Inn at Perry Cabin, is located at the east end of Perry Cabin Drive. Samuel Hambleton (1777–1851), born in Talbot County, served as a U.S. Navy purser and aide-de-camp to Capt. Oliver Hazard Perry during the September 10, 1813, Battle of Lake Erie. He was wounded in this battle. Some sources credit him with suggesting the slogan "Don't Give Up the Ship" on Perry's flag, which was made by seven women in Erie, Pennsylvania. The flag is now in the U.S. Naval Academy Museum (*see* Annapolis Tour *in part 2*). Hambleton retired in 1816 to Perry Cabin, an estate named after his former commander. The original north wing of the Inn at Perry Cabin is said to resemble Perry's cabin on his flagship, the U.S. brig *Niagara*. This original structure, now part of a restaurant/hotel complex, is but a small hidden part of a greatly expanded structure.

ST. MARY'S SQUARE, located between Mulberry and East Chestnut streets, is where a public market house was built in 1805, and, reportedly, cannons used in the defense of St. Michaels were stored there. During the early morning of August 10, 1813, the houses and churches that bordered the square were

The Other Perry

Oliver Perry's brother, Com. Matthew Calbraith Perry, is best remembered as commander of the East Asia Squadron expedition to Japan and negotiator of the Treaty of Kanagawa in 1854. But he was also aboard the U.S. frigate *President* when it engaged H.M. sloop-of-war *Little Belt* on May 18, 1811, and served under Com. John Rodgers during the War of 1812. Later, Matthew Perry supervised the construction of the Navy's first steam frigate, U.S.S. *Fulton* II, launched in 1837.

billeting militia. Of the two cannon mounted on the square, one is said to be a Revolutionary War cannon. The smaller 6 pounder cannon is said to have been used in the defense of St. Michaels during the War of 1812. This cannon was dedicated in 1913 by the Centennial Commission on the 100th anniversary of the battle.

ST. MICHAELS MUSEUM AT ST. MARY'S SQUARE. Location: St. Mary's Square, between Mulberry and East Chestnut streets. **Parking:** street parking. **Hours:** open May to October; Friday and Sunday, 1 to 4 p.m.; Saturday, 10 a.m. to 4 p.m.; and Monday 10 a.m. to 1 p.m.; or by appointment. **Fees:** $3 adults, $1 children 6-17. **Facilities:** exhibits, small gift shop, restrooms. **Contacts:** 410-745-9561; stmichaelsmuseum.com. **Comment:** self-guided and guided walking tours of the historic town are available at the museum.

In the **ST. MICHAELS MUSEUM AT ST. MARY'S SQUARE** there is a model depicting the town during the war that shows the location of Parrott Point gun battery and the floating boom across the harbor mouth. There are also mementoes of the St. Michaels 100th Anniversary Committee commemoration of the Battle of St. Michaels. Among the exhibits are three "Flash Backs" that appeared in the comic section of the Sunday *Washington Post* featuring St. Michaels in the War of 1812; "The Two-Shot Battle" (which refers to the claim that only two shots were fired from Parrott Point gun battery before it was abandoned by the militia), "The Town That Fooled the British," and "The Cannonball House."

In **CHURCH COVE PARK,** located at the foot of Green Street, are two replica War of 1812 6 pounder cannons, mounted in the park in 1975. The original cannons were donated to the town in 1813 by Jacob Gibson as a peace offering after a mischievous prank. On April 17, 1813, he had disguised his boat to look like a British naval vessel when he tied a red bandana to its masthead and approached St. Michaels via San Domingo Creek (now Back Creek). His prank so frightened the town's inhabitants that women and children were sent to the country and the militia assembled. At the beginning of the American Civil War, federal troops from the arsenal at Easton confiscated the cannons. Views of **SAN DOMINGO CREEK,** can be found at the west end of West Chew Avenue.

These replica guns serve as a reminder of a prank that took place in St. Michaels in 1813. (Ralph Eshelman 2005 photograph)

CAULKS FIELD BATTLEFIELD MONUMENT. Location: north side of Caulks Field Road, 0.3 mile northwest of its intersection with Tolchester Beach Road (Route 21), Kent County. **Parking:** shoulder parking. **Hours:** daylight hours. **Facilities:** none. **Comment:** the Caulks house and surrounding farm fields are private property. Please respect private property and do not trespass.

CAULKS FIELD BATTLEFIELD, also called Battle of Moorefield, is the site of a battle between Maryland militia and British forces. On the night of August 30, 1814, the British landed approximately 260 troops near Fairlee Creek off Chesapeake Bay, about 5 miles northwest of Caulks Field. Capt. Peter Parker, commander of the British forces, called the maneuver a "frolic with the Yankees." The British advanced on an American encampment of approximately 200 militiamen under the command of Lt. Col. Philip Reed. Under a moonlit night, the British attacked the Americans at Caulks Field. Captain Parker was mortally wounded early on the morning of August 31. Parker had previously conducted a diversion up Chesapeake Bay to make the Americans think the British were advancing on Baltimore and not Washington. The British, unaware that the Americans were nearly out of ammunition, withdrew. British casualties were 15 soldiers killed and another 27 wounded. American casualties were 3 wounded. The Americans viewed the engagement as a victory and

Sketch of the Battle of Caulks Field as drawn by Lt. Henry Crease within thirty-six hours of the action. Key: A. American militia camp is near where the Caulk House (not shown) still stands. B. Defile through which the British passed to reach the battlefield. A detachment of American troops fired on the British from the trees on right and withdrew to the American line. C. Position of the American line and artillery. (Courtesy National Archives United Kingdom, London)

news of Parker's death may have helped buoy American morale during the Battle for Baltimore, less than two weeks later. The 1743 Caulk House, which overlooks the battlefield, belonged to Isaac Caulk, who earlier had been a captain in the 21st Regiment under Lieutenant Colonel Reed. It contains mementoes of the battle, including a copy of a portrait of Capt. Peter Parker.

A British account of the battle by Lt. Henry Crease to Vice Adm. Alexander F. I. Cochrane on September 1, 1814: *An intelligent black man gave us information of two hundred Militia being encamped behind a Wood distant half a mile from the beach . . . On arriving at the Ground we discovered the Enemy had shifted his Position . . . of a mile farther . . . after a march of between four and five miles . . . we found the Enemy posted on a Plain, surrounded by Woods, with the camp in their Rear; they were drawn up in a line and perfectly ready to receive us; a single moment was not to be lost, by a smart fire and instant charge we commenced the attack, forced them . . . in full retreat, to the rear of their Artillery where they again made a stand, shewing a disposition to out flank us on the right; a movement was instantly made by Lieut. [Robert] Pearce's Division to force them from that Quarter, and it was at this time while animating his Men in the most heroic manner that Sir Peter Parker received his mortal wound which obliged him to quit the field and he expired in a few minutes. Lieut. Pearce with his Division soon routed the Enemy, while that under my Command gained and passed the Camp; one of the Field pieces was momentarily in our possession, but obliged to quit it from superior numbers; The Marines . . . formed our Centre and never was bravery more conspicuous. Finding it impossible to close on the Enemy from the rapidity of their Retreat, having pursued them upwards of a Mile I deemed it prudent to retire toward*

Mitchell House Myth

Local tradition holds that Capt. Peter Parker was taken to the Mitchell House located at 8796 Maryland Parkway, off Tolchester Beach Road, after he was mortally wounded. A report after the incident claimed that "On their retreat they called at a house some distance from the field of battle and got a blanket and sheet, it is supposed to wrap Sir Peter in" (Baltimore *Federal Gazette,* September 7, 1814). It had been assumed by many that the house was the Mitchell House, but that house is not located along the known British route. In fact, Parker's body was taken directly to the British boats and never to any house.

Mitchell House, however, is the site of an early morning British raid on September 3, 1814, during which Maj. Joseph Mitchell and his wife were roused from their bed and Mitchell's horses shot. Major Mitchell was taken prisoner as he was believed to be a commissary general for Maryland but was actually a militia contractor for Kent County. Mrs. Mitchell was permitted to visit her husband later that same day and the following day, bringing him fruit, butter, and cider. Some accounts claim Major Mitchell was sent as a prisoner of war to England and did not return until 1817.

British Soldier Burials Disputed

Local tradition asserts that the nearby St. Paul's Parish Kent, located at 7579 Sandy Bottom Road, Sandy Bottom, west of Chestertown, served as a barracks during the war and that wounded soldiers from the battle at nearby Caulks Field were treated here. Local lore also suggests that British soldiers were buried at St. Paul's. A survey of the grounds conducted by the University of Delaware's Center for Archaeological Research in 1992 failed to find any supporting physical evidence.

Reed and Parker Burials

Lt. Col. Philip Reed is buried at nearby Christ Episcopal Church, located at 25328 Lambs Meadows Road, near the intersection of Route 298 and Smithville Road, at Worton. Capt. Peter Parker's body was shipped back to London via Bermuda in a coffin filled with whiskey and buried at St. Margaret's Church next to Westminster Abbey, London.

A monument erected to Peter Parker at Westminster Abbey claims he "defeated an enemy, supported by cavalry & artillery, three times the number of his own force." The Americans were not directly supported by cavalry, the British slightly outnumbered the Americans, and the battle was at best a draw for the British, not a victory.

the Beach, which was effected in the best possible Order, taking with us from the field twenty five of our wounded, the whole we could find, the Enemy not even attempting to regain the ground they had lost.

An American account of the battle by Lt. Col. Philip Reed to Brig. Gen. Benjamin Chambers on September 3, 1814: *Orders were immediately given to . . . form on the rising ground about three hundred paces in the rear—the right towards Caulk's house, and the left retiring on the road, the artillery in the centre, supported by the infantry on the right and left . . . The head of the enemy's column soon presented itself and received the fire of our advance party, at seventy paces distance, and, being pressed by numbers vastly superior, I repaired to my post on the line; having ordered the riflemen to return and form on the right of the line. The fire now became general along the whole line, and was sustained by our troops with the most determined valor. The enemy pressed our front; foiled in this he threw himself upon our left flank . . . Here, too, his efforts were unavailing. His fire had nearly ceased, when I was informed that in some parts of our line cartridges were entirely expended, nor did any of the boxes contain more than a few rounds, although each man brought about twenty into the field.—The artillery cartridges were entirely expended. Under these circumstances I ordered the line to fall back to a convenient spot where a part of the line was fortified, when the few remaining cartridges were distributed amongst a part of the line, which was again brought into the field, where it remained for a considerable time, the night preventing pursuit. The artillery and infantry for whom there were no cartridges were ordered to this place (Belle Air, [now Fairlee]). The enemy having made every effort in his power, although apprized of our having fallen back, manifested no disposition to follow us up, but retreated about the time our ammunition was exhausted.*

Later that morning, Parker's bloody right shoe was found with his name written in it. British Midshipman Frederick Chamier's remembrances of the affair were published in 1850: "It was the height of madness to advance into the interior of a country we knew nothing about, led by a black man [guide], whose sincerity in our cause was very questionable." Parker's cousin, Lord Byron, wrote a poetic eulogy to his memory in 1815.

On October 18, 1902, the Tolchester Steamboat Company steamer *Kitty Knight* arrived from Baltimore carrying eighteen guests who were taken by carriage to the battlefield for the dedication of a monument. A lunch, consisting of ham, oysters, bread, and coffee, was served at the Caulk House. The monument was dedicated to the "victor and vanquished." It was restored by a local farmer, Charmayne Dieker, and the Colonel Reed Chapter of the 4-H Club in 1967 on the 153rd anniversary of the battle.

GEORGETOWN and FREDERICKTOWN. Location: Fredericktown occupies the north side of the Sassafras River in Cecil County, and Georgetown occupies the south side in Kent County. **Parking:** street parking. **Facilities:** *see* Kitty Knight House *below.*

Rear Adm. George Cockburn burned **FREDERICKTOWN** and **GEORGETOWN** on May 6, 1813, after the militia dared to offer resistance. The Americans had built fortifications at Pearce Point, on the Kent County side of the Sassafras River, and Fort Duffy, on the Cecil County side of the river.

An American account of the engagement was published in the Baltimore *American & Commercial Daily Advertiser* on May 14, 1813: *The enemy still approaching gave three cheers, which was returned by the militia, and directly after, a volley from their small arms. The fire was immediately returned by the enemy, by a general discharge of grape, cannister, slugs, rockets, and musketry, which made such a terrible noise that one-half of the men shamefully ran, and could not be rallied again, whether it was from their political aversion to the present war, their dislike of shedding blood, or actually through fear, I cannot determine; but so it was that not more one half of the original number remained, to contend against the whole force of the enemy. This gallant little band resisted for near half an hour, in spite of the incessant fire of the enemy, until they were in danger of being surrounded, when they retreated in safety with the loss of but one man wounded. The enemy threw several rockets in the town (or rather village) and reduced the whole place to ashes, except two or three houses, saved by the entreaties of the women. Not satisfied with this destruction, they extended their ravage to the neighboring farm-houses, several of which were burned quite down.*

A British account was reported by Rear Adm. George Cockburn to Adm. John Borlase Warren on May 6, 1813: *having intercepted a small Boat with two of the Inhabitants . . . I sent forward the two Americans in their Boat to warn their Countrymen against acting in the same rash manner the People of Havre-de-Grace had done* [who opened fire upon the British], *assuring them if they did that their Towns would inevitably meet with a similar Fate* [burning], *but on the contrary, if they did not attempt Resistance no Injury should be done to them or their Towns, that Vessels and Public Property only, would be seized, that the strictest Discipline would be maintained, and that whatever Provisions or other Property of Individuals I might require for the use of the Squadron should be instantly paid for in the fullest Value . . . I soon found the more unwise alternative was adopted, for on our reaching within about a mile of the Town between two projected elevated Points of the River, a most heavy Fire of Musquetry was opened on us . . . the hot Fire we were under this Morning cost us five Men wounded one only however severely.*

An American eyewitness account of the burning was published in the Washington *Daily National Intelligencer* on May 14, 1813: *Yesterday morning I witnessed a scene that surpasses all description. It was the little villages of George and Frederick towns, nearly all in flames. It would have excited sympathy in any human heart, except a savage, or still more ferocious Englishmen; and they you know are so much inured to villainy and destruction, that there is no mercy in their composition. It was* [Rear] *admiral* [George] *Cockburn*

Fort Duffy

An earthwork built to defend the towns, Fort Duffy was destroyed circa 1985 during improvements at Skipjack Marina. A plaque dedicated to the thirty-six men who defended the fort is located at the intersection of Duffy Creek Lane and Sassafras Street.

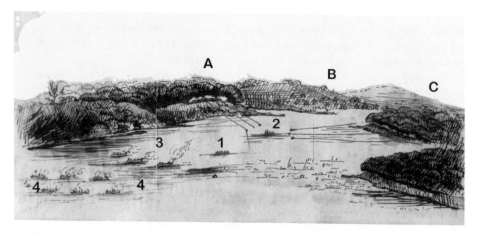

This 1813 British sketch depicts the attack on Fredericktown and Georgetown. Key: 1. Rear Adm. George Cockburn's boat. 2. Capt. Henry D. Byng's boat with 1st Lt. Frederick Robertson. 3. Launches with Congreve rockets. 4. Boats with Royal Marines. A. Fort Duffy. B. Georgetown. C. Fredericktown. Note that B and C are reversed; Fredericktown is actually on the north side (left) and Georgetown on the south side (right). The American battery on the left side of the sketch is Fort Duffy and the battery on right side is Pearce Point Fort. (*Attack upon George & Frederick's towns by a detachment of boats from the R[ight] Honorable Sir. J. B. Warren's Squadron under Rear Admiral Cockburn in April 1813, Hon. Capt. Byng, Commanding;* Library of Congress)

himself, who led on the morn that tiger banditti, who committed the devastation. In the afternoon I repaired to the smoking, burning ruins, and found only a few houses standing, that had been spared at the entreaties of the women and aged; and these few, with one or two exceptions, nearly plundered of their all. Desks, bureaus, clocks, looking glasses, and such things as could not be carried off, were broken to pieces, and even beds cut open, the ticking taken off, and the feathers scattered to the winds. Even negroes cabins were reduced to ashes, or plundered of their scanty pittance of furniture and meat.

KITTY KNIGHT HOUSE. Address: 14028 Augustine Herman Highway (Route 213). **Parking:** free. **Hours:** Sunday through Thursday, 11 a.m. to 10 p.m.; Friday through Saturday, 11 a.m. to 12 p.m. **Facilities:** meals and lodging. **Contacts:** 410-648-5200; www.kittyknight.com. **Comment:** The Kitty Knight House Inn has gone through several changes in ownership with periods of closing between owners. It is best to call to make sure the establishment is open.

The Archibald Wright House, better known as the **KITTY KNIGHT HOUSE**, is one of ten or eleven houses that survived the British sacking of Georgetown. Kitty Knight is credited with saving this house by pleading with the British that an elderly lady occupied it. Miss Knight was renting the house at the time so she also had a personal interest in saving the structure that she ultimately bought in 1836. She lived there until her death in 1855. The William Henry House was later joined to the Archibald Wright House in what is now known as the Kitty Knight House Inn. Letters and writing samples from Kitty Knight, many written during the war, were at one time displayed in the house. Their whereabouts today is unknown. In the sitting area is a twentieth-century mural depicting the attack of Georgetown and Fredericktown as well as a painting of Miss Kitty as a ghost at the door. A rocking chair now in the hall is said to have belonged to her. The original front door of the Henry House reportedly once showed damage from a British boarding ax.

On **TAYLORS ISLAND**, there is a monument dedicated to the Battle of the Ice Mound that took place on February 7, 1815, the last engagement of the war in Maryland.

Goodnight, Miss Kitty

Kitty Knight's grave is located approximately 8 miles northeast of Georgetown at the historic Old Bohemia Church near Warwick. Her tombstone reads as per her wishes "Miss Catherine Knight." Despite her reputed beauty, she remained unmarried throughout her life.

BATTLE OF THE ICE MOUND MONUMENT. Location: north side of Taylors Island Road, Route 16, west side of Slaughter Creek Bridge on Taylors Island. **Parking:** parking lot. **Facilities:** interpretation, tourism brochures.

The monument consists of the "Becky Phipps" carronade captured from a British tender to H.M. sloop *Dauntless* after it became stuck in ice at nearby James Island. The 12 pounder carronade was mounted here about 1950 and was refurbished in 1999. It was fired to celebrate political elections until it exploded during President Woodrow Wilson's inauguration in 1913. The DAR marker here has several mistakes. The carronade was captured in 1815, not 1814. Pvt. Joseph Fookes Stewart is referred to as a captain. While he may have been a captain of a nonmilitary vessel, there is no documentation that he held that rank in the militia. The carronade was nicknamed "Becky Phipps" for the tender's captured black cook Becky and the commander, Lt. Matthew Phipps. The cook's name was actually "Becca" and the commander's name was "Phibbs." "Becca Phibbs" was corrupted to "Becky Phipps."

This ends the Maryland Eastern Shore Tour.

Head of the Chesapeake Tour

Particulars Havre de Grace is a good place to seek lodging and food, although Elkton is another possibility. Excellent views of the water and bicycling options can be found at Havre de Grace and Charlestown. Both also have paddling opportunities and Havre de Grace has boat excursions (*see* appendixes C *and* D).

Historical Background The British blockaded the Chesapeake in February of 1813 and, in the spring of that year, sent naval ships to the head of Chesapeake Bay. Frenchtown, Elk Landing (present-day Elkton), Havre de Grace, and Principio Iron Works were attacked and all suffered damage (with the exception of Elkton, which repulsed the British). Charlestown capitulated to the enemy, the only jurisdiction in Maryland to do so. It was only the second instance in the Chesapeake—the other being Alexandria, Virginia. Some Annapolis authorities considered surrendering, but the measure failed to gain enough votes to pass. Elkton is one of only two jurisdictions in Maryland that twice succeeded in repulsing British attacks—the other was St. Michaels on Maryland's Eastern Shore.

HAVRE DE GRACE VISITOR CENTER. Address: 450 Pennington Avenue. **Parking:** free. **Hours:** generally 9 a.m. to 5 p.m. on weekdays and 11 a.m. to 4 p.m. on weekends. **Facilities:** maps, brochures, restrooms. **Contacts:** 1-800-851-7756; www.hdgtourism.com. **Comment:** Havre de Grace is a National Historic District. Boat excursions are available (*see* appendix D). Small craft such as kayaks may be used to explore the area, but there is a wide fetch here so be cautious if winds should pick up (*see* appendix C).

HAVRE DE GRACE is the site of a savage British attack after a brief exchange of fire with the local militia at dawn on May 3, 1813. A force of four hundred British troops in nineteen barges, supported by a rocket-vessel, cannonaded, landed at, and burned most of Havre de Grace.

British Rear Adm. George Cockburn reported the attack to Adm. John Borlase Warren on May 3, 1813: *I observed Guns fired and American Colours hoisted at a Battery lately erected at Havre-de-Grace . . . a warm fire was opened on the Place at Daylight from our Launches and Rocket Boat, which was smartly returned from the Battery for a short time, but . . . Captain [John] Lawrence . . . judiciously directed the landing of the Marines on the Left . . . Lieut. G[eorge] . A. Westphal . . . in the Rocket Boat close to the Battery . . . pulled directly up under the work and landing with his Boat's Crew got immediate possession of it, turned their own Guns on them, and thereby soon obliged them to retreat with their whole Force to the furthest Extremity of the Town, . . . they were closely pursued and no longer feeling themselves equal to the manly and open Resistance, they commenced a teasing and irritating fire from behind their Houses, Walls, Trees &c . . . soon succeeded in dislodging the whole of the Enemy from their lurking Places . . . setting Fire to some of the Houses to cause the Proprietors (who had deserted them and formed Part of the Militia who had fled to the Woods) to understand and feel what they were liable to bring upon themselves by building Batteries and acting towards us with so much useless Rancor, I embarked in the Boats the Guns from the Battery, and having also taken and destroyed about 130 Stand of small arms.*

John O'Neill of Havre de Grace published his account of the attack in the Baltimore *Niles' Weekly Register* on May 15, 1813: *we were attacked by fifteen English barges at break*

Detail of a 1799 map of the Upper Chesapeake Bay showing Havre de Grace region. Key: 1. Havre de Grace. 2. Principio Iron Works. 3. Charlestown. 4. Concord Point. 5. Sion Hill. ("A Map of the Head of Chesapeake Bay and Susquehanna River" by C. P. Hauducoeur 1799; courtesy of Enoch Pratt Free Library, Central Library / State Library Resource Center, Baltimore, Maryland)

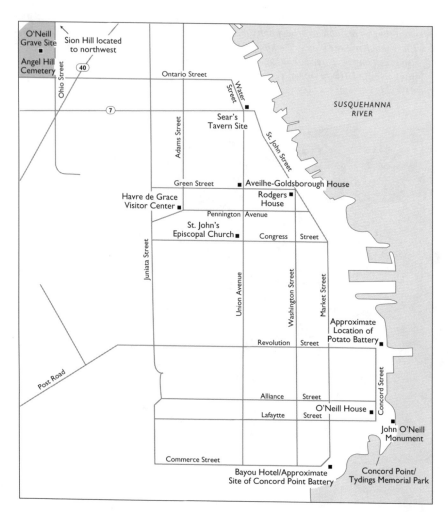

O'Neill
Grave Site

Sion Hill located
to northwest

Angel Hill
Cemetery

Ohio Street

40

Ontario Street

Water Street

7

Adams Street

Sear's
Tavern Site

St. John Street

SUSQUEHANNA
RIVER

Green Street

Aveilhe-Goldsborough House

Havre de Grace
Visitor Center

Rodgers
House

Pennington Avenue

St. John's
Episcopal Church

Congress   Street

Juniata Street

Union Avenue

Washington Street

Market Street

Approximate
Location of
Potato Battery

Revolution   Street

Post Road

Concord Street

Alliance   Street

Lafaytte   Street

O'Neill House

John O'Neill
Monument

Commerce Street

Bayou Hotel/Approximate
Site of Concord Point Battery

Concord Point/
Tydings Memorial Park

Havre de Grace

of day. We had a small breastwork erected, with two six and one nine-pounder in it, and I was stationed at one of the guns. When the alarm was given I ran to the battery and found but one man there, and two or three came afterwards. After firing a few shots they retreated, and left me alone in the battery. The grape-shot flew very thick about me. I loaded the gun myself, without any one to serve the vent, which you know is very dangerous, and fired her, when she recoiled and ran over my thigh. I retreated down to town, and joined Mr. Barnes, of the nail manufactory, with a musket, and fired on the barges while we had ammunition, and then retreated to the common, where I kept waving my hat to the militia who had run away, to come to our assistance, but they proved cowardly and would not come back. At the same time an English officer on horseback, followed by the marines, rode up and took me with two muskets in my hand. I was carried on Board the Maidstone frigate, where I remained until released, three days since.

The Baltimore *Niles' Weekly Register* published an eyewitness account of the attack on May 22, 1813: *On the report of guns we immediately jumped out of our beds; and from the top of the house could plainly see the [cannon] balls [probably Congreve rockets] and hear the cries of the inhabitants. We ran down the road, and soon began to meet the distressed people, women and children half naked; children enquiring for their parents, parents for their children, and wives for their husbands. It appeared to us as if the whole town was on fire. I think this act, committed without any previous warning, has degraded the British flag.*

The enemy robbed every house of everything valuable that could be carried away, leaving not a change of raiment to one of ten persons; and what they could not take conveniently they destroyed by cutting in pieces or breaking to atoms . . . An officer put his sword through a large elegant looking glass, attacked the windows, and cut out several sashes. They cut hogs through the back, and some partly through, and then left them to run. Such wanton barbarity among civilized people, I have never heard of.

During the attack, one British naval officer was wounded, while one American militiaman, a Mr. Webster, was killed by a Congreve rocket. Of the town's sixty-two private homes, approximately forty were burned. The Maryland government provided $1,000 for the needy after the conflagration.

1814 etching depicting the British raid on Havre de Grace. Rear Adm. George Cockburn is shown with his sword tip resting on the ground. Soldiers are pilfering private articles, shooting a hog, and burning private buildings. To the right a British officer is endeavoring to ride over two citizens. On the river is a barge loaded with a coach taken by Cockburn as a gift for his wife. A rocket-vessel is also depicted. ([William Charles] *Admiral Cockburn Burning & Plundering Havre de Grace on the 1st of June 1813. Done from a Sketch Taken on the Spot at the Time;* courtesy of The Maryland Historical Society)

Shortly after the raid, American satirist James Kirke Paulding (best known for his tongue-twister "Peter Piper picked a peck of pickled peppers") anonymously wrote a lengthy poem about the devastation of Havre de Grace called *The Lay of Scottish Fiddle: A Tale of Havre de Grace.* In it he wrote: "Childe Cockburn carried in his hand / A rocket and a burning brand, / And waving o'er his august head / The red-cross standard proudly spread, / Whence hung by silver tonsil fair / A bloody scalp of human hair."

A good place to begin your tour is at **CONCORD POINT.**

CONCORD POINT. Location: Millard E. Tydings Memorial Park, east end of Lafayette Street. **Parking:** free. **Hours:** daylight hours. **Facilities:** waterside promenade, picnic facilities. **Comment:** there is good interpretation about the lighthouse keeper's house where War of 1812 hero John O'Neill later lived. Tours of the lighthouse and keeper's house can be arranged by calling 410-939-3213.

A gun battery was erected at Concord Point probably upon the elevation behind this point where the former Bayou Hotel, now private apartments at the south end of Market Street, stands. Erosion of the bluff may have destroyed part or all of the original battery site. Concord Point was one of at least two earthworks built to defend Havre de Grace.

The second battery, named the Potato Gun Battery because of its shape, was located further to the north between the east ends of Bourbon and Fountain streets near the intersection with Market Street where Tidewater Marina is now located. Rather than at Concord Point, as most accounts claim, this second battery site is where John O'Neill heroically fought. The monument and cannon erected in 1914 at Concord Point to commemorate John O'Neill should actually be located further north at the Potato Gun Battery Site. For his bravery, O'Neill received a sword from the City of Philadelphia that can be seen at the Maryland Historical Society (*see* Baltimore Tour *in part 2*). During the war, O'Neill apparently lived in a house on Washington Street between Fountain and Bourbon streets. The respect for this man can be gleaned from the tax roll of 1814 when O'Neill's entry was recorded by the assessor as "List of property owned by the brave John O'Neal." This is the only known case in which the county assessor used this language.

One account claims that John O'Neill's fifteen-year-old daughter Matilda successfully pleaded with Rear Adm. George Cockburn for the release of her father after he was captured during the attack. For her bravery, Cockburn supposedly gave her a gold-mounted tortoise shell snuff box, which can be seen at the Maryland Historical Society. Although the story is widely reported, actual documents indicate O'Neill was released on parole upon application of the magistrates of Havre de Grace. One contemporary report indicated a "Miss O'Neill" among the town's committee members who visited the admiral under a flag of truce. She may very well have pleaded for her father's release and received the snuff box, but if so she was far from alone.

The Maryland Historical Roadside Marker here claims there were "two small batteries on Concord Point." Only one gun battery was located at Concord Point; the other was the Potato Gun Battery located a few blocks farther to the north. A plaque on a cannon at Concord Point states that O'Neill served at the Concord Point Battery, but he was actually at the Potato Battery. Finally, the plaque claims that O'Neill served the guns of the battery "until disabled and captured." O'Neill was not captured at the gun battery but later in town, where he unsuccessfully attempted to rally the militia.

The **O'NEILL HOUSE,** more appropriately called the lighthouse keepers house, is just across the street west of the lighthouse at Concord Point. For his heroism in the unsuccessful defense of Havre de Grace, John O'Neill was appointed as the first keeper of the newly built Concord Point Lighthouse by President John Quincy Adams in 1827. O'Neill retained this position and lived in the keeper's house until his death in 1838.

Other places worth visiting include the **RODGERS HOUSE,** also called the Ferry House and Elizabeth Rodgers House.

RODGERS HOUSE. Address: 226 North Washington Street. **Parking:** street parking. **Hours:** daylight hours. **Facilities:** none. **Comment:** private, exterior views only; please respect private property.

Built in 1788, Rodgers House is the oldest documented structure in Havre de Grace. It was set on fire by the British three times yet survived.

The Rev. James Jones Wilmer wrote in 1813: *The enemy, however, set fire three times to Mrs. Rogers' house . . . but it fortunately each time was extinguished, though they defaced and mutilated much valuable furniture, broke the windows and doors and stole valuable clothing belonging to the ladies.*

The 1801 stuccoed brick **AVEILHE-GOLDSBOROUGH HOUSE,** located at 300 North Union Avenue, is another one of the few homes that survived the burning of the town. Mary Goldsborough, sister of Com. John Rodgers (*see* Sion Hill *below*), lived here after 1816.

ST. JOHN'S EPISCOPAL CHURCH, located at the northwest corner of Union and Congress avenues, dates from circa 1805, but the present structure, built in 1809, is among the oldest surviving in the city. The interior, however, was gutted by fire in 1832. The British agreed to spare the church but destroyed the pews, pulpit, and windows. John O'Neill served as a vestryman here. He is buried at Angel Hill Cemetery on the northwest side of town.

The Rev. James Jones Wilmer wrote in 1813: *They burst the doors, broke the window and sash, entered and beat the drum. One would* [have] *suppose . . . they would have shown some respect to this building, as it was called after their own name generally, "The English Church" . . . But it seems all sense of shame was lost, and every spark of grace was removed.*

Benjamin Latrobe wrote to Robert Fulton on May 4, 1813: *Not a house or shed is left standing, except an old church.*

The Rodgers House, shown here as it appeared in the 1850s, was set on fire three times during the British attack. (Lossing, *Pictorial Field-Book of the War of 1812*)

The interior of St. John's Episcopal Church was damaged during the raid. This depiction illustrates the church as it appeared in the 1850s, before the belfry was added circa 1884. (Lossing, *Pictorial Field-Book of the War of 1812*)

The Baltimore *Niles' Weekly Register* reported on May 8, 1813: *The church at Havre de Grace . . . was not fired; but to shew their respect for "religion," [the enemy] assailed the house [of religion], and finding nothing to steal "magnanimously" attacked the window with brick-bats and stones, and demolished them.*

Though on private land and not open to the public, **SION HILL** (NHL) can be glimpsed among a clump of mature trees on the south side as one ascends the hill overlooking the Chesapeake on Level Road (please respect private property and do disturb the occupants). This three-part brick house, begun in 1787 by the Rev. John Ireland, became the home of Com. John Rodgers (1772–1838), naval hero in War of 1812, when he married Minerva Denison, daughter of the second owner of Sion Hill, on October 21, 1806. They were married in the north parlor.

Rodgers is credited with personally firing the first shot of the War of 1812 on June 23, 1812. He lit a fuse of one of his guns aboard the U.S. frigate *President* as he fired on the H.M frigate *Belvidera*. A popular bar-ballad saluted him: "And Rodgers with his gallant crew,/O'er the wide ocean ride,/To prove their loyal spirits true,/And crush old Albion's pride."

Benjamin Latrobe wrote to Robert Fulton on May 4, 1813: *[the British] set fire to everything, threw over the stages into the river, killed the horses in the stables, and then methodically burnt every house and shed in the village . . . The women and children fled to the woods . . . It is supposed that the circumstance of Commodore [John] Rodgers, being a native of Havre de Grace, this unmanly warfare is to be attributed.*

Actually the British attacked Havre de Grace because one of the gun batteries fired a shot of defiance at them when they initially passed by.

From Havre de Grace, follow Pulaski Highway (U.S. Route 40) east across the Susque-hanna River toll bridge. (Another option is travel on I-95. Both routes have a toll charge.)

From the Cecil County line at Perryville continue approximately 1.4 miles to Mill Creek Road on right (south), follow it 0.5 mile to Principio Furnace Road (Route 7) and turn left (east). Follow Principio Furnace Road 1.3 miles to **PRINCIPIO IRON WORKS.**

PRINCIPIO IRON WORKS. NRHP. Location: south side of Principio Furnace Road just west of Principio Creek. **Parking:** free. **Hours:** daylight hours. **Fees:** none. **Facilities:** none. **Contacts:** 410-642-2358. **Comment:** ruins of the iron works can be seen from the parking lot. Access to the ruins is permissible by tour only, which must be arranged in advance. The ruins visible from the parking area are all believed to date from after 1814. For a history of this site see www.cchistory.org/Principio.htm.

Principio Iron Works, also called Principio Furnace and Cecil Furnace, began operation in 1725. By 1727, the Iron Works operated the first blast furnace and refinery forge in Maryland. Since at least 1796, Principio Iron Works produced cannon used by Maryland privateers and the U.S. Navy. In 1807 the furnace supplied 24 pounder long guns for the U.S. frigate *Constitution*. In 1813, the complex consisted of a blast furnace, two air furnaces, a boring mill capable of boring five cannon at one time, a stamping mill, a stone grist mill, managers and workmen's houses, coal house, stables, and a blacksmith shop.

The Baltimore *Patriot* reported on April 22, 1813: *We* [defenders of Frenchtown and Elk Landing] *yesterday got 7000 weight of cannon balls from Cecil Furnace, to be returned if not used.*

Sion Hill was spared burning by the pleading of prominent women in the village. (E.H. Pickering 1936 photograph; HABS, Library of Congress)

On May 3, 1813, the British destroyed a gun battery consisting of five 24 pounder cannons erected to protect the iron works, twenty-eight 32 pounder cannon ready to be shipped, and eight other cannons and four carronades of different caliber. The British effectively destroyed the foundry and cannon boring machinery and burned the mills, coal houses, and the bridge across Principio Creek. The total loss to the owner was around $20,000. Rear Admiral Cockburn is reputed to have said the Americans knew better how to make guns than to use them.

Rear Adm. George Cockburn reported to Adm. John Borlase Warren on May 3, 1813: *the Cecil or Principio Foundery . . . was one of the most valuable Works of the Kind in America, the Destruction of it therefore at this moment will I trust prove of much national Importance* [to the British war effort].

Col. Samuel Hughes, owner of the works, rebuilt the complex the same year and on December 16, 1813, received a contract for forty 24 pounder cannons. But Hughes never recovered from his debts and was forced to sell his business.

The Baltimore *Federal Gazette* reported on July 15, 1814: *cannon for the United States frigate* Guerriere, *are casting at Cecil Furnace, about 6 miles from the Susquehannah. It is not improbable that this Furnace is the object of the enemy's approach to that neighourhood.*

Continue east on Principio Furnace Road back to Pulaski Highway and turn right (southeast) on Old Philadelphia Road (Route 7) into **CHARLESTOWN** via Baltimore Street (Route 267).

Charlestown is a small village with many historic homes (NHD), ideal to explore by walking or bicycling. (*See* appendix C *for information on boat launching.*) Charlestown capitulated to the British on May 6, 1813, to prevent destruction of the town.

Rear Adm. George Cockburn reported to Adm. John B. Warren on May 6, 1813: *I also had a Deputation from Charleston in the North East River, to assure me that that Place is considered by them as at your Mercy, and that neither Guns nor Militia Men shall be suffered there.*

At the end of Conestoga Street, near the intersection with Water Street, a gun battery was established, but it was never used in defense of the town. Suffering from neglect, it was washed down by heavy rains. There are excellent views of North East River here at the stone wharf. From Charleston return to Pulaski Highway and travel east to **ELKTON.**

ELKTON VISITOR CENTER. Address: 101 East Main Street. **Parking:** street parking. **Hours:** vary, call ahead. **Fees:** none. **Facilities:** brochures, maps. **Contact:** 410-398-5076. **Comment:** this visitor center is operated by the Elkton Alliance and has irregular hours. The **CECIL COUNTY TOURISM OFFICE** is located at Perryville Outlets, exit 93 off I-95. **Hours:** Monday through Friday, 10 a.m. to 5 p.m., Saturday, 10 a.m. to 4 p.m., and Sunday, 11 a.m. to 2:30 p.m. **Parking:** free. **Facilities:** brochures, maps. **Contacts:** 1-800-232-4595; www.ccgov.org/tourism.

Elkton, also called Head of Elk and Elk Landing, was threatened by the British in the spring of 1813.

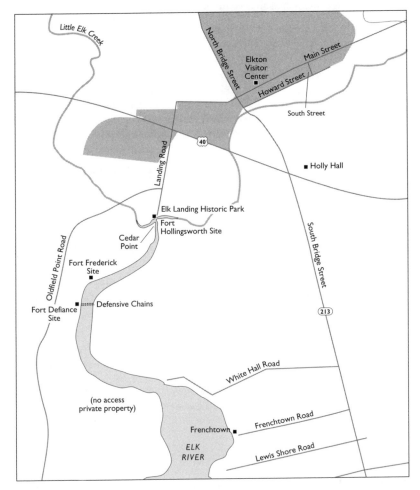

Elkton

The Baltimore *Patriot* reported on April 22, 1813: *a meeting of the people of the town and county was called, when not less than 200 convened at the court-house, and in a few minutes $1,000 was raised; a committee of three appointed; and on Saturday the ground laid out for three breast-works* [Forts Hollingsworth, Defiance, and Frederick].

Brig. Maj. James Sewall reported to Maj. Gen. Samuel Smith on May 7, 1813: *We have two forts* [Defiance and Frederick] *(tho small) and a chain across the river as an obstruction. An attack is more seriously apprehended by land and in this way we are as well prepared as the short term & the few troops I have heretofore permit.*

On April 29, 1813, the American militia at Fort Defiance repulsed a British force of approximately 150 marines in at least ten barges, saving Elkton and thirty bay craft from almost certain destruction.

The Alexandria *Gazette* published an account of the skirmish on August 18, 1813: *the enemy made an attack . . . with 10 or 12 barges. From the extreme darkness of the night they succeeded in getting within a few yards of a small battery* [down river at Frenchtown] *before those who were stationed in it discovered them, when they opened a fire from a nine pounder charged with round shot & langrage, and supposed that considerable execution was done. There being but 14 or 15 men in the fort, and the enemy all around it, they spiked their cannon and retreated. Two small batteries* [Forts Frederick and Defiance] *placed in the town, with a few 6's in them, then opened their fire upon the barges, and in a few minutes compelled them to retreat with considerable precipitation, and they were seen about day-light towing a barge after them. It is not known what damage was done to the enemy, but it is supposed considerable fr. the great hurry with which they left the shore.*

The following year, on July 12, 1814, British barges attempted a surprise attack on Elkton but were again beaten off by an eleven-gun battery.

Brig. Gen. Thomas Marsh Forman wrote to his wife, Martha Ogle Forman, on July 12, 1814: *Five barges were discovered on the river and about one o'clock they opened upon our view from behind a point, and point blank shot, say ½ a mile. We gave them in all eleven guns, so well directed, that they hastily put about and retreated down the river having fired but three at us, which did us no injury.*

With more attacks likely, a contingent of 250 men from the Delaware Flotilla was sent with two cannon to reinforce the Elkton defenses. Elkton was considered a possible landing place for a British attack on Philadelphia; thus Delaware and Pennsylvania militia established a camp here.

Rear Adm. George Cockburn reported to Vice Adm. Alexander Cochrane on July 17, 1814: *If Philadelphia is supposed to be an Object of greater Importance than the Places I have just mention'd* [Baltimore, Washington, and Annapolis], *I should deem the landing at Elkton the most advisable Mode of approaching it, as the intended Point of Attack would thereby be masked til the Army would be actually landed and on its March on the Road from Elton to Wilmington . . . this Movement need not prevent such Ships . . . from proceeding up the Delaware.*

Elkton and St. Michaels (*see* Maryland Eastern Shore Tour *in part 2*) are the only places in the Chesapeake region known to have twice successfully repulsed British attacks.

FORT DEFIANCE and **FORT FREDERICK** were earthworks located on the Elk River. Fort Frederick, located about 300 yards above Fort Defiance, was fitted with a double chain across the 60-foot-wide river channel. The chains rested on the river bottom to allow passage of vessels but were raised by a windlass from within the fort to impede enemy vessels from moving up the river toward Elkton. Fort Defiance was the first fortification on the river below Fort Frederick. On April 29, 1813, Fort Defiance fired several shots at approaching British barges, forcing them to withdraw. Both earthwork sites are on private property and not accessible to the public.

The Baltimore *Patriot* published on April 22, 1813: [Forts Defiance and Frederick] *when finished, will mount seven cannon, one of them, a long 12 pounder, and its situation commands Frenchtown and Elkton. The channel can be swept the whole distance; it is 30 feet higher than the water, and the channel not 60 feet wide. An old vessel and a chain will be put across it.*

The **FORT HOLLINGSWORTH** site can be visited at **ELK LANDING HISTORIC PARK.**

ELK LANDING HISTORIC PARK. Location: south end of Landing Lane off Pulaski Highway (U.S. Route 40). **Parking:** free. **Hours:** daylight hours. **Fees:** none. **Facilities:** historic house open by appointment. **Contact:** 410-620-6400. **Comment:** if the gate is locked, park and walk in. Please respect this historical property. The Fort Hollingsworth site is located near the stone house (NRHP) ruins by the river. Look for the interpretive sign.

Fort Hollingsworth, under the command of Capt. Henry Bennett, served as the upper defensive earthwork on Elk River at Elk Landing. On April 29, 1813, Fort Hollingsworth fended off a British landing party that had marched overland to Cedar Point, opposite the fort. At the same time, Fort Defiance repulsed a British barge probing up the Elk River.

When news of the Treaty of Ghent reached Elkton in February 1815, the citizens gathered at Fort Hollingsworth to celebrate. A frozen "clod" (a lump or chunk of earth or clay) was placed in one gun. When fired, it exploded, seriously injuring Capt. Ezekiel Forman Chambers.

HOLLY HALL (NRHP), home of Brig. Maj. James Sewall, commander of the Second Battalion at Fort Defiance, is located at Cecil Center, 259 South Bridge Street (Route 213) near the entrance to Big Elk Mall. The house is not open to the public and only exterior views are possible.

Optional Side Trip **HAGLEY MUSEUM.** From Big Elk Mall it is about 23 miles northeast to the Hagley Museum, near Wilmington, Delaware, the site of the Du Pont Gunpowder Plant.

HAGLEY MUSEUM. NHD. Address: 298 Buck Road East, off New Bridge Road (Route 141), northwest of Wilmington, Delaware. **Parking:** free. **Hours:** open seven days a week; tours 9:30 a.m. to 4:30 p.m.; Winter hours, January 4 through March 12, one tour at 1:30 p.m. weekdays and open 9:30 a.m. to 4:30 p.m. on weekends. **Fees:** $11 adults, $9 students and seniors, $4 children 6 to 14, children under 6 free. **Facilities:** museum, historic houses, gunpowder yard, live demonstrations, museum store, restrooms, restaurant, picnic facilities. **Contacts:** 302-638-2400; www.hagley.lib.de.us. **Comment:** allow at least two hours or more if you plan to visit the museum, historic houses, and gunpowder yard.

Hagley Museum occupies and interprets the Du Pont Gunpowder Company, founded in 1801 on the Brandywine River by Éleuthère Irénée du Pont de Nemours (1771–1834). He is better known as Irénée du Pont, or E. I. du Pont, a French-born American chemist and industrialist who worked at a French gunpowder mill near Paris and emigrated to the United States in 1799. The E. I. du Pont de Nemours and Company produced its first gunpowder in 1804 and by 1811 was the largest producer in the United States. In 1813, the U.S. government requisitioned 500,000 pounds of powder from the firm. To fill this order, du Pont purchased the adjacent Hagley Estate downriver.

Fort McHenry purchased gunpowder from du Pont during the War of 1812. So, too, probably, did Fort Severn, Fort Norfolk, and other Chesapeake Bay–area military installations. Organ Cave, Virginia (now West Virginia; *see optional side trip under* Central Virginia Tour *in part 2*), produced saltpetre, a necessary ingredient for the making of gunpowder. Some of the Organ Cave saltpetre is believed to have been processed into gunpowder by du Pont. E.I. du Pont is buried in the family cemetery near the du Pont family home at Eleutherian Mills, part of the museum park complex.

The Brandywine powder mills offered a prime target for the British during the war.

British Vice Adm. Alexander Cochrane wrote to Rear Adm. George Cockburn on July 1, 1814: *I am uninformed of the plans of Government but . . . Suppose that they must be pointed against Philadelphia, Baltimore & Washington, if to the first the landing should be made at or near New Castle & Chester upon the Delaware or at the head of Elk* [Elkton, Maryland] *; at Brandywine the principal Mills for* [gun] *Powder & Flour are Situated which may be destroyed in passing.*

William Frazer of Rich Neck Farm, Talbot County, Maryland, wrote to his son William C. Frazer, Lancaster, Pennsylvania, on September 1, 1814: *with the Expectation that the British will come up this* [Chesapeake] *Bay as they are now reinforced to the amount of 2500 and in all probability will go against Baltimore and then proceed on to Wilmington & Brandywine to destroy the public Property & Powder Mills if so there will come a part of them up this* [Delaware] *Bay to meet the others and there let them Embark onboard the Fleet.*

During the War of 1812, E.I. du Pont and his older brother Victor both served as officers in the South Brandywine Rangers. Extraordinary measures were taken to protect the Brandywine mills from a British attack.

Victor du Pont wrote on August 19, 1814: *All those men who did belong last year to the volunteer Corps of the Brandywine Rangers are hereby informed that the Captain is authorised by order of* [Brig.] *General* [Joseph] *Bloomfield to reorganize the Company under the immediate orders of the President of the United States—for the purpose of protecting the works on the Brandywine. They will be exempt from militia service and are not to be sent out further than the vicinity of Wilmington.*

An inventory for June 30, 1814, lists over $52,000 worth of "Powder, in magazine or with agents" and puts the total worth of the mill at $351,704.11.

Several structures from the War of 1812–era can be seen, including a restored mill (number 3 distinguished by the double abutments on the land side), a glazing mill, a graining mill, and the walls of the packing mill. Although the external appearance of these restored buildings is the same or similar to what it was in 1812, the mill was transformed from a stamping mill into a rolling mill in the 1820s, and the glazing and graining equipment is of a later era. The ruins of a magazine from 1813 are located at the sharp turn in the road between the Composition House and the Steam Engine House. The original Eleutherian Mills, farther upstream, produced gunpowder that was used during the War of 1812. The saltpetre works and the first magazine were also located here. A model in the museum shows the site as it would have appeared in 1806. The du Pont office during the war was a three-story "lean-to" attached to the south side of the house. It was removed when du Pont's son built the current office near the house.

This ends the Head of the Chesapeake Tour.

Frederick Tour

Historical Background Frederick, located 44 miles northwest of Washington, D.C., was considered safe from attack when the British occupied that city. Hence, federal government funds and some archives were temporarily stored there. Commandant of the U.S. Marine Corps Lt. Col. Franklin Wharton and his paymaster took refuge in Frederick as did the Secretary of Treasury George Campbell and Secretary of War John Armstrong.

After the Battle of Bladensburg, an unnamed man, who served as a British guide from Benedict to Upper Marlboro, went to Frederick and mixed with the soldiers, making inquiries about numbers and locations of troops. These were normal questions an American citizen might ask, but, when he was recognized by one of the American officers who knew he had been with the British Army, he was arrested as a spy. What became of him afterwards is unknown. Another six British subjects of suspicious character were also held in custody.

The day after news reached Frederick of the American defeat at the Battle of Bladensburg, Capt. John Brengle raised a company of about fifty men during a four-hour march through Frederick. Brengle's Company later served in the defense of Baltimore at Hampstead Hill. Many of these veterans are buried in Mount Olivet Cemetery in Frederick. Begin your tour at the **FREDERICK VISITOR CENTER.**

FREDERICK VISITOR CENTER. Address: 19 East Church Street. **Parking:** limited metered street parking, garages recommended. **Hours:** 9 a.m. to 5 p.m. daily. **Fees:** none. **Facilities:** maps, brochures, restrooms. **Contacts:** 1-800-999-3613; www.fredericktourism.org. **Comment:** Frederick has a pleasant downtown district filled with historic buildings, shops, museums, and restaurants. The historic area, which encompasses most of the downtown, is designated a National Historic District. The Hessian Barracks are 0.5 mile south and the Francis Scott Key Monument an additional 0.2 mile south of the barracks. Walking and biking are recommended.

One hundred and seven British prisoners were held in the county jail and American troops were housed in the **HESSIAN BARRACKS.**

HESSIAN BARRACKS. NRHP. Address: 101 Clark Place off South Market Street, on grounds of Maryland School for the Deaf. **Parking:** free. **Hours:** exterior viewing daylight hours; interior tours by appointment, call 301-360-1455. **Fees:** none. **Facilities:** none. **Comment:** this property is a school for the deaf, drive cautiously.

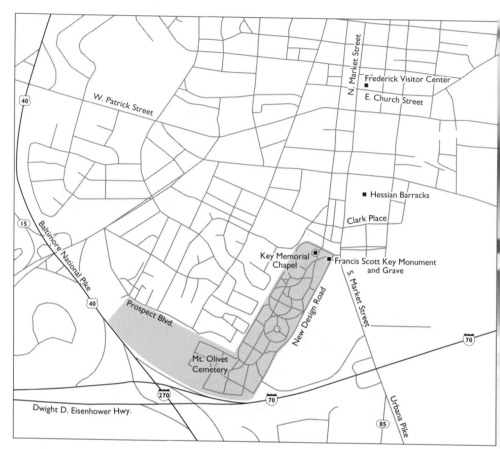

Frederick

The stone Hessian Barracks, also called the Frederick Barracks, were built between 1777 and 1778. Some British prisoners from the Battle of Bladensburg may have been held here. **THE FRANCIS SCOTT KEY MONUMENT** and grave are located at Mount Olivet Cemetery.

FRANCIS SCOTT KEY MONUMENT. Address: 515 South Market Street. **Parking:** free. **Hours:** daylight hours. **Facilities:** none. **Contacts:** 1-888-662-1164; www.mountolivetcemeteryinc.com. **Comment:** monument and grave are located just inside the main entrance of Mount Olivet Cemetery.

Francis Scott Key and his wife and son, who had been buried twice before, were re-interred on October 1, 1866, in the family lot here with a simple gravestone. Key and his wife were moved to a crypt under the Key monument in 1898. The monument, a gift of the Ladies

Monument Association of Frederick, was designed by Alexander Doyle of New York City and executed by Pompeo Coppini, an emigrant from Italy. School children across the county contributed toward the cost of the monument. The central figure is a woman representing Columbia, the goddess of patriotism. She holds a staff in her right hand on which hangs the Fort McHenry garrison flag. On her left side is a teenage boy with his hand resting upon a sword, representing war. On her right is a young boy representing song or music, holding a lyre in his left hand and grasping the folds of the flag with his right hand. Beneath a bronze plaque is the seal of the State of Maryland. At the rear of the monument, near the base, is another bronze plaque bearing the words of the national anthem. On June 7, 1987, the Key Monument was restored and rededicated.

On the grounds of the cemetery, just behind the monument, is the Key Memorial Chapel, constructed in 1911 (open by appointment only). It contains the contents of the time capsule, removed from the base of the Key Monument in 1998, including Key's bible, as well as memorabilia from the monument centennial dedication. The American flag flies continuously over the Francis Scott Key Monument.

While visiting this cemetery it is worth exploring and looking for the graves of veterans from the Revolutionary War, War of 1812, and the Civil War. There are approximately 43 Revolutionary War soldiers and patriots graves here, 83 War of 1812 graves, and over 440 Civil War graves including both Union and Confederate soldiers. (*See* Ralph E. Eshelman, Scott S. Sheads, and Donald R. Hickey, *The War of 1812 in the Chesapeake: A Reference Guide to Historic Sites in Maryland, Virginia, and the District of Columbia* [2009] for a list of the War of 1812 veterans buried here.)

This ends the Frederick Tour and the Maryland Tour.

VIRGINIA

Alexandria Tour

Particulars Alexandria is best known for it colonial architecture and is reported to have more surviving original eighteenth-century structures than Colonial Williamsburg. It is therefore no surprise that the downtown historic portion of the city is designated a National Historic District. Alexandria has a wide selection of hotels, motels, and restaurants to meet most budgets and tastes. The waterfront is a popular area with good walking paths and scenic views of the Potomac River. Boat excursions are also available (*see* appendix D). Visitors may plan their tour to suit their own interests and time constraints.

Historical Background British naval forces occupied Alexandria from August 28 through September 3, 1814, after the city capitulated to a British naval squadron. Commanded by Capt. James Alexander Gordon, the squadron consisted of the 36-gun H.M. frigate *Euryalus,* the 38-gun H.M. frigate *Sea Horse,* the 18-gun H.M. rocket-vessel *Erebus,* the 8-gun H.M. bomb-vessel *Aetna,* the 8-gun H.M. bomb-vessel *Devastation,* the 8-gun H.M. bomb-vessel *Meteor,* and the 2-gun H.M. schooner/dispatch ship *Anna Maria.*

The American State Papers in 1832 published a letter issued by the Alexandria Committee of Vigilance in 1814, despairing its situation and fearing the city would be burned, recommended to the Alexandria Council Committee: "That, in case the British vessels should pass the fort [Washington], or their forces approach the town by land, and there should be *no sufficient force* on our part, to oppose them, with any reasonable prospect of success, they should appoint a committee to carry a flag to the officer commanding the enemy's force, about to attack the town, and to procure the best terms for the safety of persons, houses, and property, in their power."

When the British squadron threatened the city, Thomas Herbert, President of Alexandria Common Council, ordered the following declaration:

Reprinted in Baltimore *Niles' Weekly Register* on September 10, 1814: *The forts erected for the defence of the district having been blown up by our men* [U.S. regular troops], *and abandoned without resistance, and the town of Alexandria having been left without troops or any means of defence against the hostile force now within sight, the Common Council of Alexandria have with reluctance been compelled, from a regard to the safety of the inhabitants, to authorize an arrangement with the enemy, by which it has been stipulated that, during their continuance before the town, they shall not be molested. No superior power having, in this emergency, appeared to defend or direct, the Common Council has considered itself authorized, from extreme necessity, to make the above stipulation; they, consider it binding on themselves and on the nation, require a faithful observance of it from all the inhabitants of the town.*

Prior to the British occupation of Alexandria, six hundred small arms were destroyed and two cannon, the only artillery in the city, were removed to prevent their capture. The Americans also burned the Long Bridge joining Washington with the Virginia shore and scuttled twenty-one vessels in the port. In order to keep their city from being plundered or possibly burned, members of the Alexandria Council Committee reluctantly accepted Captain Gordon's terms of capitulation.

JOHNNY BULL and the ALEXANDRIANS.

"Johnny Bull and the Alexandrians" is a cartoon satirizing the capitulation of Alexandria. The Bull demands all the flour and tobacco except Porter and Perry (beer and a pear cordial), a punning reference to the otherwise victorious American naval officers who ironically were unsuccessful in opposing the British during their withdrawal down the Potomac River. Johnny Bull holds the "Terms of Capitulation." Local residents plead on their knees for mercy on the grounds that they were always friendly to the British, even trading with them when it was outlawed by the embargo. (1814 etching by William Charles; Library of Congress)

In exchange for the acceptance of these terms, the British agreed not to invade private dwellings or to molest the citizens of Alexandria. The British carried away three ships, four brigs, ten schooners, and three sloops as prizes. They burned one sunken ship which they could not raise. They also captured a gunboat from the Washington Navy Yard, mounting a long 18 pounder cannon and a 32 pounder carronade that had been sent to Alexandria for safekeeping. The British confiscated about 16,000 barrels of flour, about 1,000 hogsheads of tobacco, 150 bales of cotton, as well as wine, sugar, and other articles, all amounting to upwards of $5,000 in value.

Alexandria Mayor Charles Simms wrote to his wife, Nancy Simms, on September 3, 1814: *It is impossible that men could behave better than the Brittish behaved while the town was in their power, not a single inhabitant was insulted or injured by them in their person or houses.*

However, many Virginians and non-Virginians were outraged by the capitulation of Alexandria to the British.

The Richmond *Enquirer* reported on August 31, 1814: *In what terms can we express our indignation against the conduct of the citizens of Alexandria? Thanks be to the Almighty God:*

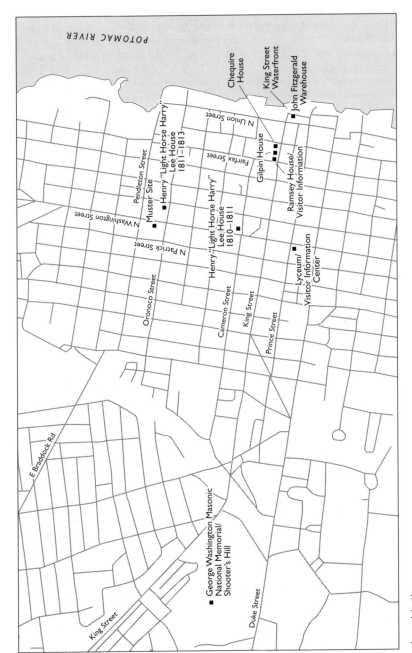

POTOMAC RIVER

Chequire
House

King Street
Waterfront

John Fitzgerald
Warehouse

N Union Street

Henry "Light Horse Harry"
Lee House
1811–1813

Fairfax Street

Gilpin House

Pendleton Street

Ramsey House/
Visitor Information

Muster Site

N Washington Street

N Patrick Street

Henry "Light Horse Harry"
Lee House
1810–1811

Lyceum/
Visitor Information
Center

Oronoco Street

Cameron Street

King Street

Prince Street

E Braddock Rd

George Washington Masonic
National Memorial/
Shooter's Hill

Duke Street

King Street

Alexandria City

that this degraded town no longer forms a part of the state of Virginia [this portion of Virginia had been deeded as part of the Nation's Capitol and later returned to Virginia].

The Washington *Daily National Intelligencer* reported on September 1, 1814: *The degrading terms dictated by the Commander of the British squadron below Alexandria, to the civil authority of that town, connected with the offer of the townsmen,* before *the squadron had even reached the fort* [Washington], *to surrender without resistance, and their singular submission to* [Rear] *Admiral* [George] *Cockburn whilst he was in this city, have everywhere excited* astonishment and indignation.

Even after the British had retired 20 miles down the Potomac River, Alexandria officials did not raise the American flag until U.S. Navy Capt. John Rodgers threatened to fire on the town if they did not consent to his hoisting of the American colors. Dolley Madison told friends that the Alexandrians should have let their town burn rather than accept such humiliating terms. Charlestown (*see* Head of the Chesapeake Tour *in part 2*), Maryland, is the only other town in the Chesapeake region known to have capitulated to the British. The chairman of the Annapolis Committee of Safety recommended that the Maryland capital city surrender if threatened by attack, but his resolution did not pass, and Annapolis was never attacked.

If you are driving to Alexandria, begin your tour at the **LYCEUM,** where you will find visitor information as well as exhibits about the historic city.

LYCEUM. NRHP. Address: 201 South Washington Street. **Parking:** free. **Hours:** Monday through Saturday, 10 a.m. to 5 p.m.; Sunday, 1 p.m. to 5 p.m. **Fees:** free for visitor information; $2 for museum. **Facilities:** maps, brochures, exhibits, restrooms. **Contacts:** 703-838-4994; http://oha.alexandriava.gov/lyceum. There is also a visitor center at the 1724 Ramsay House, located at 221 King Street (open 9 a.m. to 5 p.m. daily; 1-800-388-9119). Street parking in the city is at a premium so parking garages are advised.

A small exhibit on the War of 1812, including a carronade recovered from the shoreline of the Potomac River near its confluence with Hunting Creek, is in the 1839 Creek Revival Lyceum. It is possible this gun was scuttled prior to the British occupation of Alexandria to keep it out of British hands.

At the east end of **KING STREET** at Union Street (then the original waterfront), the British loaded the prize goods taken from Alexandria. John Fitzgerald's warehouse, on the southeast corner of King and Union streets, as well as three warehouses on the north side of the 100 block of King Street, all date from before the war and are little altered. The Chequire House, built 1797 and located at 202 King Street, and Gilpin House, built 1798 and located at 208 King Street, are typical merchants' houses of the time, consisting of shops on the ground floor and living quarters above. In 1812, Francis Peyton exhibited wax figures, including those of George Washington and Stephen Decatur, at his house located at the intersection of King and Patrick streets.

Other places worth visiting include the 1796 **HENRY LEE HOUSE,** better known as the Boyhood Home of Robert E. Lee.

David Porter Incident

U.S. Navy Capt. David Porter, Jr. (1780–1843) reconnoitered the British occupied town of Alexandria. At a warehouse near the intersection of Princess and Union streets, Captain Porter spotted a young British lieutenant, John West Fraser, and a squad of men rolling out barrels of flour. Porter grabbed Fraser by his neck scarf and would have abducted him had not the scarf given away.

British Capt. Charles Napier wrote of the incident: *An enterprising* [American] *midshipman* [actually captain] *thought it would be fine fun to carry off an officer; and . . . dashed into the town on horseback . . . came boldly down to the boats, and seized a midshipman* [lieutenant] *by the collar. The fellow was strong, and attempted to get him on his horse. The youngster, quite astonished, kicked and squalled most lustily; and after being dragged a hundred yards, the American was obliged to drop his brother officer. This operation . . . created a considerable alarm; the men retreated to the boats, and prepared their carronades, and were with difficulty prevented from firing. This occurrence soon found its way to the mayor, who came off in great alarm for the town. Captain* [James Alexander] *Gordon, with great good humour, admitted his apology, and treated it . . . as a midshipman's spree; but recommended that proper precautions should be taken as a repetition . . . might lead to the destruction of the town.*

Mayor Charles Simms wrote to his wife, Nancy Simms, on September 3, 1814: *Capt.* [David] *Porter, Lieutenant* [Master Commandant John O.] *Creighton and Lieutenant* [Midshipman Charles T.] *Platt naval officers rode into Town like Saracens and seized on a poor unarmed Midshipman* [John Fraser] *a mere strapling, and would have carried him off or killd him had not his neck handkerchief broke. This rash act excited the greatest alarm among the Inhabitants of the Town, Women and children runing and screaming through the Streets and hundreds of them layed out that night without Shelter. I immediately prepared a message to Commodore* [Captain James Alexander Gordon] *explaining the manner and circumstances of this insult and sent it on board . . . while I was preparing the message One of the Captains* [probably Captain Charles Napier] *rushed into the parlour with the strongest expressions of rage in his countenance bringing with him the midshipman who had been so valiantly assaulted by those Gallant Naval Officers, I explained to him by whom the outrage was committed, that the Town had no control over them; and ought not be held responsible for their conduct, and I was at that time preparing a message of explanation to the Commodore he said it was necessary that it should be explained, after which his fury seemd to abate and he went off, before Mr. Swann* [attorney] *and Mr. Lee* [former member of the Alexandria Common Council] *got on Board the Signal of Battle was hoisted and all the Vessels were prepared for action when Mr. Swan and Mr. Lee made their explanation & the Commodore said he was satisfied and ordered the signal of Battle to be annulld thus the Town was providentially preserved from destruction, by the accidental circumstance of the midshipmans neck handkerchief giving way for had he been killd or carried off, I do not believe the Town could have been saved from destruction.*

HENRY LEE HOUSE. NRHP. Address: 607 Oronoco Street. **Comment:** private residence; please respect privacy. Views of exterior of house from public street only; no access. Go to http://leeboyhoodhome.com for a virtual tour.

Henry "Light Horse Harry" Lee, his wife, and their five children, including Robert E. Lee of Civil War fame, lived here from 1811 to at least 1813. They had lived the previous year at 611 Cameron Street. Henry Lee, a Federalist, defended the printing office of the antiwar Baltimore *Federal Republican* newspaper during the Baltimore Riots of 1812. Lee sustained serious injuries from the enraged and drunken mob and remained an invalid until his death.

The area north of Oronoco and North Washington streets was then the edge of the city and consisted of fields that served as a muster site for troop training during the French and Indian War, the Revolutionary War, and the War of 1812. In 1755, at age twenty-three, George Washington met here with British Gen. Edward Braddock during the French and Indian War.

The **GEORGE WASHINGTON MASONIC NATIONAL MEMORIAL** on Shooter's Hill is worth a visit for the view alone.

GEORGE WASHINGTON MASONIC NATIONAL MEMORIAL. Address: 101 Callahan Drive. **Parking:** free. **Hours:** April through September, 9 a.m. to 4 p.m.; October through March, 10 a.m. to 4 p.m.; tours: 10, 11:30, 1:30, and 3 daily. **Fees:** none. **Facilities:** exhibits, restrooms. **Contacts:** 703-682-2007; www.gwmemorial.org. **Comment:** the view of Alexandria from Shooter's Hill is best in the late afternoon or early evening, with the sun behind you.

It was on Schooter's Hill that Brig. Gen. John Pratt Hungerford, commander of the Northern Neck of Virginia militia, was ordered to encamp by the War Department. When the British withdrew from Alexandria, President James Madison, Secretary of Navy William Jones, Brig. Gen. John Hungerford, and Capt. David Porter, Jr., met at Shooter's Hill to plan countermeasures for attacking the British as they descended the Potomac River. Here the plans to erect batteries at White House on the Virginia shore and Indian Head on the Maryland shore were made.

A War of 1812 banner, carried by the Alexandria Independent Blues, is exhibited inside the George Washington Museum of the George Washington Masonic National Memorial, built on what was then called Shuter's or Shooter's Hill.

Optional Side Trip **MOUNT VERNON.** About 9 miles south of Alexandria is the former home of George Washington, the first president of the United States. At 5 p.m. on August 26, 1814, British warships ascended the Potomac River to Alexandria, passing Mount Vernon, then owned by Bushrod Washington, his nephew.

MOUNT VERNON. NHL. Address: 3200 Mount Vernon Memorial Highway. **Parking:** free.
Hours: April through August, 8 a.m. to 5 p.m.; March, September, October, 9 a.m. to 5 p.m.;
November through February 9 a.m. to 4 p.m. **Fees:** $15 adults, $14 seniors, $7 children
6 to 11, children under 6 free. **Facilities:** historic house, outbuildings, visitor center,
museum, museum shop, food court, restaurant, restrooms. **Contacts:** 703-780-2000; www.
mountvernon.org.

George Washington first suggested fortifications be built at Fort Washington (*see* Southern Maryland Tour *in part 2*). The fort, named for Washington, was blown up by the Americans when threatened by a British naval squadron in 1814.

British Capt. Charles Napier wrote on August 26, 1814: *Mount Vernon,—the retreat of the
illustrious* [George] *Washington,—opened to our view, and showed us, for the first time since
we entered the Potomac, a gentleman's residence.*

The British squadron assembled near here in preparation for descending the Potomac
and passing the White House and Indian Head gun batteries, located on the Virginia and
Maryland shores respectively.

The Boston *Weekly Messenger,* published on September 16, 1814: *The British squadron (assembled at Mr. Marshall's Point* [Maryland side] *and a little below Mount Vernon) began to
move downwards about two o'clock on Monday at the pitch of high tide and a most favorable
fresh wind at N.E. The preceding ship was the Commodore* [Capt. Charles Gordon] *in the Sea
Horse frigate of 38 guns with the first division of the prize craft.*

Optional Side Trip **NATIONAL MUSEUM OF THE MARINE CORPS.** If you are particularly interested in the U.S. Marines you may want to take the optional side trip to the National
Museum of the Marine Corps, roughly 23 miles south of Mount Vernon. Part of the Marine
Corps Heritage Center, it offers exhibits that deal with the War of 1812; for example, an
1810 shako (tar bucket type hat) with a plate marked "MARINES" is on display.

NATIONAL MUSEUM OF THE MARINE CORPS. Address: 18900 Jefferson Davis Highway,
Triangle, Prince William County. **Parking:** free. **Hours:** 9 a.m. to 5 p.m. daily. **Fees:**
none. **Facilities:** exhibits, museum store, restrooms. **Contacts:** 1-877-635-1775; www.
usmcmuseum.org.

This ends the Alexandria Tour.

Greater Norfolk Tour

Particulars This tour includes sites in Norfolk, Hampton, Portsmouth, and Newport News, all located in an area known to mariners as Hampton Roads, near the mouth of Chesapeake Bay. Nearby Lynnhaven Roads, sometimes referred to as Lynnhaven Bay by the British, is located just east of Norfolk and west of Cape Henry. It served as an important anchorage for the Royal Navy throughout the war. It was from here that the British fleet conducted its blockade at the mouth of the Chesapeake. The region is a popular tourist destination with lodging options ranging from waterfront hotels to lower-priced motels. Eating options range from expensive fresh seafood restaurants to fast food. The tour starts in Norfolk, but you can start at any of the tidewater cities and plan your tour to suit your own interests and time.

Historical Background Craney Island served as the first line of defense for Norfolk and Portsmouth as well as for the Gosport Navy Yard and the U.S. frigate *Constellation* that was blockaded here (*see below*). Despite its importance, Craney Island was defended by only

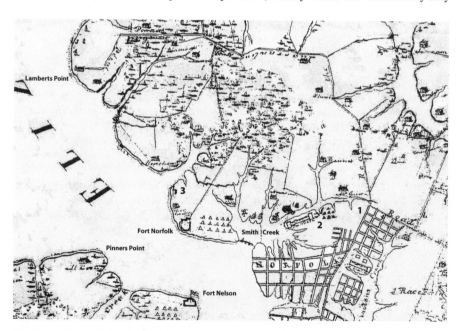

Sketch map circa 1813 showing the location of Forts Nelson and Norfolk and adjacent encampments (designated by tents) on Elizabeth River. Key: 1. Fort Barbour. 2. Earthwork and encampment near Fort Tar. 3. Earthwork near Fort Norfolk. Some labeling added for clarity. (Detail of "Map of the Country contiguous to Norfolk Taken by actual Survey under the direction of Brigadier Gen'l Robt. B. Taylor"; National Archives and Records Administration)

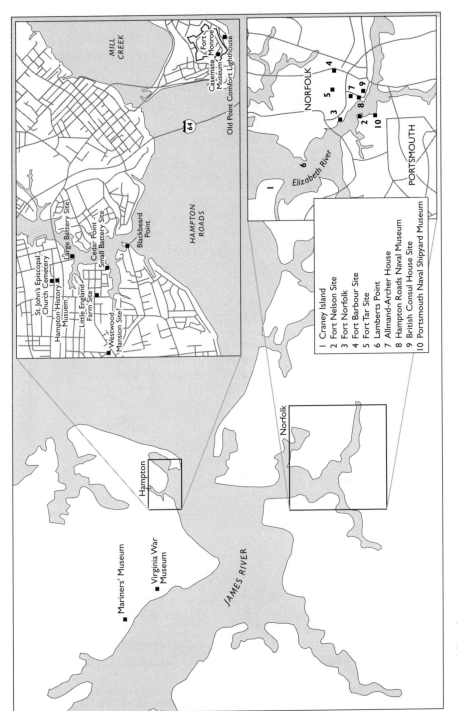

Greater Norfolk Region

MILL CREEK

Fort Monroe
Casemate Monroe Museum
Old Point Comfort Lighthouse

64

HAMPTON ROADS

St. John's Episcopal Church Cemetery
Large Battery Site
Cedar Point
Small Battery Site
Blackbeard Point
Hampton History Museum
Little England Farm Site
Westwood Mansion Site

NORFOLK
4
7
9
5
3
8
2
10
6
Elizabeth River
1
PORTSMOUTH

1 Craney Island
2 Fort Nelson Site
3 Fort Norfolk
4 Fort Barbour Site
5 Fort Tar Site
6 Lamberts Point
7 Allmand-Archer House
8 Hampton Roads Naval Museum
9 British Consul House Site
10 Portsmouth Naval Shipyard Museum

Hampton

Norfolk

JAMES RIVER

Mariners' Museum

Virginia War Museum

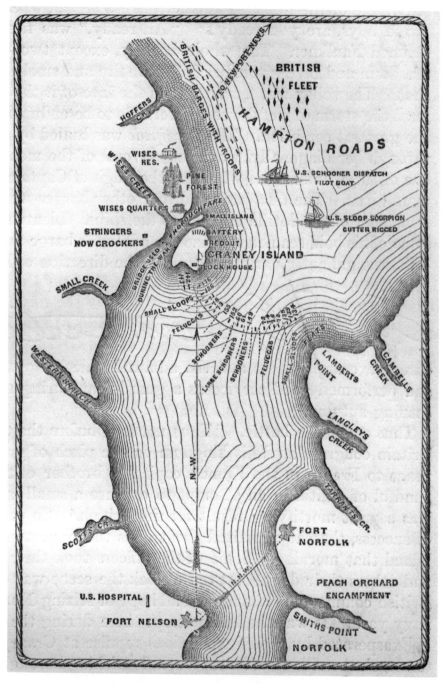

Sketch of Battle of Craney Island showing location of forts and batteries and position of American and British vessels. (Lossing, *Pictorial Field-Book of the War of 1812;* based on map now in Library of Congress by James Travis, a soldier in the U.S. Army at Norfolk during the war)

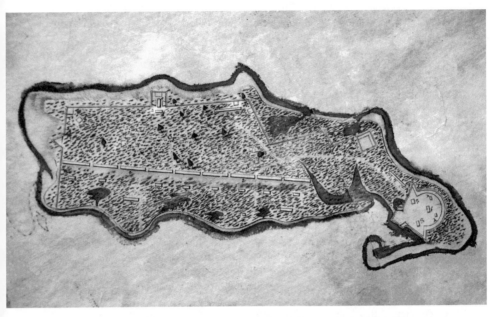

The defenses of Craney Island as surveyed in 1819. (National Archives and Records Administration, Cartographic Section)

800 men and its fortifications were incomplete when the British launched a two-pronged attack on June 22, 1813. One British force of 2,400 men landed on the mainland, 2.5 miles to the west, but, because of a high tide, the troops could not ford a channel to get to Craney Island. A second British force of 1,500 men approached the island in approximately 50 barges. While American artillery rained down on them, the British boats ran into thick mud, making an amphibious landing nearly impossible. The British troops withdrew. Thus ended the only attempt in the war to take the navy yard, the U.S. frigate *Constellation*, and Norfolk.

Three days later, the British took out their revenge on Hampton, sweeping aside the defending militia and occupying the city. The occupation force included the Independent Companies of Foreigners, some of whom went on a rampage of murder, rape, robbery, and arson. These acts were long remembered in the United States. Hampton became a byword among Americans for enemy atrocities during this war.

Norfolk

Norfolk is located on the east side of the confluence of the Elizabeth and James rivers.

NORFOLK VISITOR INFORMATION CENTER. Address: 9401 4th View Street; exit 273 off I-64 West. **Parking:** free. **Hours:** 9 a.m. to 5 p.m. daily. **Fees:** none. **Facilities:** brochures, maps, restrooms. **Contacts:** 1-800-368-3097; www.norfolkcvb.com.

The famous *Chesapeake–Leopard* affair occurred off the nearby Virginia capes on June 22, 1807. H.M. frigate *Leopard* hailed U.S. frigate *Chesapeake* and insisted that it muster its crew. Com. James Barron, commander of the *Chesapeake,* refused, whereupon the British opened fire, killing three Americans and wounding eighteen others, including Commodore Barron. After firing only one shot *Chesapeake* struck its colors. Four crewmen from the *Chesapeake* were accused of being British deserters and taken prisoner. The *Chesapeake* sailed back to Norfolk with its mortified officers and crew. A public meeting was held in Norfolk and it was resolved that no intercourse of any kind was to be had with the British squadron then in the area. No pilots or water were to be provided and no supplies were to be sold to any British ships.

Citizens donated to a fund for the families of the men who had been killed. Robert Mac-Donald, one of the wounded sailors, died on June 27, 1807, bringing the death toll to four. In Norfolk harbor, American vessels displayed their colors at half mast, while artillery fired salutes from the shore. An estimated four thousand citizens gathered on Market Square. They formed a long procession that marched to the beat of muffled drums to Christ Church (probably St. Paul's Episcopal Church).

As news of the *Chesapeake–Leopard* affair spread, Americans everywhere became outraged. A mob destroyed British naval property in Norfolk. Governor William H. Cabell ordered detachments of militia to the Hampton Roads area to prepare for a possible British attack. Although the British formally apologized for the incident in 1811, emotions ran high, fueling the war movement.

On February 3, 1813, upon approaching the mouth of Chesapeake Bay, U.S. frigate *Constellation,* under command of Capt. Charles Stewart, sighted a British squadron. Captain Stewart wisely sought the protection of Forts Norfolk and Nelson, which defended Norfolk, Portsmouth, and the Gosport Navy Yard. Although now blockaded in the river for the duration of the war, the *Constellation* was an added enticement for the British to attack Norfolk, but *Constellation* also provided additional men and cannon for protection of the cities.

Capt. George de la Roche wrote on February 3, 1813: *Stood out to Sea, but when off Cape Henry were chased back by four British frigates. Ran up and moored the frigate* [Constellation] *between forts Norfolk & Nelson in Elizabeth River for the defences of Norfolk, being blockaded by the British Squadron.*

To protect Norfolk, Portsmouth, Gosport Navy Yard, and the U.S. frigate *Constellation,* Forts Barbour, Nelson, Norfolk, and Tar were placed on alert and blockships (hulks) were sunk in the Elizabeth River channel off Lamberts Point.

An anonymous letter about the blockade, written on March 18, 1813, was reprinted in the Baltimore *Patriot* on March 22, 1813: *Our port is so completely blockaded, that nothing can go in or out. Three ships of the line and two frigates are in Hampton Roads and their boats are constantly in motion. The Constellation and the gunboats are now between our forts. Our channel has been obstructed by sinking three vessels; two more will be sunk, and then no vessel can pass drawing more than 16 feet.—We feel no apprehension of an attack on our harbor by ships. The enemy might attempt to and in the night and assail our forts; which is the only possible way of annoying us at present—and it would not find expedient at least until the talked of brigade of marines arrive from England.*

Sites worth visiting include the **ALLMAND-ARCHER HOUSE,** reported to be the oldest standing house in Norfolk.

ALLMAND-ARCHER HOUSE. NRHP. Address: 327 Duke Street. **Parking:** limited street parking. **Comment:** only the exterior of this private house can be seen. Please respect the privacy of the owners.

The Allmand-Archer House was built in the 1790s by Matthew Heary, who sold it in 1802 to Harrison Allmand, a Norfolk merchant known as "Old Gold Dust" because of his great wealth. The Allmand-Archer House served as a headquarters for the American forces in Norfolk during the War of 1812.

The site of the **BRITISH CONSUL HOUSE**, where Col. John Hamilton resided, is located at 118 Main Street. The house was saved from destruction by an angry mob after the *Chesapeake–Leopard* affair only because of Colonel Hamilton's popularity. The structure was demolished during city development in the twentieth century and is now occupied by Town Point Garage.

Nothing remains of **FORT BARBOUR**, which was located east of Church Street and south of Princess Anne Road, and **FORT TAR**, which was located at Fort Tar Lane, northwest off Saint Pauls Boulevard, north of the intersection with Virginia Beach Boulevard. **FORT NORFOLK**, however, is one of the best-preserved examples in the United States of pre-1812 fortifications. It has survived largely unchanged.

FORT NORFOLK. NRHP. Address: 803 Front Street. **Parking:** free. **Hours:** 8 a.m. to 6 p.m. daily. **Fees:** none. **Facilities:** none. **Contacts:** 757-640-1720; www.norfolkhistorical.org/fort. **Comment:** photo ID is required to gain access to the grounds of the fort. A brochure is available from the guard at the gate. None of the buildings in the fort is open to the public except via a tour that may be arranged through the Norfolk Historical Society. **Contacts:** 757-640-1720; www.norfolkhistorical.org.

This important War of 1812–era fort, located at "The Narrows" on the Elizabeth River, served as the second line of defense, backing up Craney Island at the mouth of the river. Like Fort Nelson on the opposite (west) side of the river (*see* Portsmouth *below*), Fort Norfolk was originally constructed during the Revolutionary War. The present asymmetrical and oddly shaped Fort Norfolk, with two bastions, was begun as part of a national defense effort in 1794. The *Chesapeake–Leopard* affair caused the military to upgrade the fort and by July 1808 it was reported to be "in excellent order" and mounted nine 18

British Consul House in Norfolk as it appeared in 1865. (Lossing, *Pictorial Field-Book of the War of 1812*)

Fort Norfolk as it appeared in 1853. (Lossing, *Pictorial Field-Book of the War of 1812*)

pounder cannon. The main gate, with attached brig (jail), carpenter's shop and storeroom, barracks, and officers' quarters, date from 1810. In March of 1813, the fort mounted twenty-seven 24 pounder and two 9 pounder cannons. The fort is within U.S. Army Corps of Engineers property.

HAMPTON ROADS NAVAL MUSEUM. Address: Nauticus, One Waterside Drive. **Parking:** parking garage suggested. **Hours:** Generally 10 a.m. to 5 p.m., see Web page for details. **Fees:** none. **Facilities:** exhibits, restrooms. **Contacts:** 757-322-2987; www.hrnm.navy .mil/ **Comment:** this excellent museum is almost hidden within the Nauticus complex; ask at the information desk for directions (it is located on the second floor). You do not need to pay the Nauticus entrance fee if you visit only the museum. Allow at least an hour if you also plan to visit the U.S. battleship *Wisconsin*.

The **HAMPTON ROADS NAVAL MUSEUM** has a small War of 1812 exhibit that includes a model of U.S. gunboat *No. 135*, employed in the Elizabeth River during the Battle of Craney Island. On June 22, 1813, the American's successfully repulsed a British attack on Norfolk and Portsmouth. A second gunboat model, *No. 2*, was designed by Com. James Barron. Also on display is a piece of wood from the U.S. frigate *Chesapeake*, captured by H.M. frigate *Shannon* after mortally wounded Capt. James Lawrence supposedly uttered the words, "Don't give up the Ship." Taken to England as a prize, *Chesapeake* was broken up in 1820 and its timbers were used to build a mill, which still stands in Wickham. This *Chesapeake* wood fragment was obtained from that mill.

Portsmouth

PORTSMOUTH NAVAL SHIPYARD MUSEUM. Address: 2 High Street. **Parking:** street parking. **Hours:** Wednesday through Saturday, 10 a.m. to 5 p.m.; Sunday, 1 to 5 p.m. **Fees:** $3 adults, military discount, $1 children 2 to 17. **Facilities:** exhibits, gift shop, restrooms. **Contacts:** 757-393-8591; www.portsnavalmuseums.com. **Comment:** tour of lightship included in fee.

The **PORTSMOUTH NAVAL SHIPYARD MUSEUM** focuses on the history of America's oldest shipyard. It features a few War of 1812 artifacts, including a smooth bore .69 caliber muzzle-loading flintlock musket made at the Virginia Manufactory of Arms in Richmond (*see* Richmond and Petersburg Tour *below*) based on U.S. models 1812 and 1816. Although made after the war, it illustrates the common-issue musket used by the Virginia militia during the war.

Cape Henry

CAPE HENRY. Location: within Fort Story military installation, north off Shore Drive (U.S. Route 60), Virginia Beach. **Parking:** free. **Hours:** dusk to dawn. **Fees:** none. **Facilities:** restrooms and picnic facilities. **Comment:** have photo ID ready and be prepared for vehicle search. During periods of high security alert the base might be restricted to public access. The first Cape Henry Lighthouse (NRHP) can also be visited but there is a fee. **Contacts:** 757-898-2410; www.nps.gov/came.

1798 plan for Fort Nelson, now the grounds of the Portsmouth Naval Hospital. In concert with Fort Norfolk on the opposite side of the Elizabeth River, these forts protected Norfolk, Portsmouth, and the navy shipyard. (National Archives and Records Administration, Cartographic Section)

Bird's-eye view of Portsmouth Naval Hospital and Elizabeth River. Key. 1. Fort Norfolk. 2. Fort Nelson site. (Photographer and date unknown; HABS, Library of Congress)

Cape Henry, located at the confluence of Chesapeake Bay and Atlantic Ocean, was an important landmark distinguished by the Cape Henry Lighthouse, completed in 1792. The British conducted a raid on the lighthouse on February 14, 1813, taking meat from the keeper's smokehouse. The raid was described in the following humorous account:

published by the Wilmington *American Watchman & Delaware Republican* on February 24, 1813: *British valor and discipline. A band of veterans from Admiral* [John Borlase] *Warren's squadron landed at the lighthouse on Cape Henry and with the most undaunted heroism attacked the pantry and smoke house of the keeper, captured his hams, mince pies and sausages, leaving not a link behind!—after when they effected their retreat in the greatest good order and regularity to their ships, with flying colors, without the loss of a ham! So much for British heroism and discipline—*HUZZA! *"England expects every man to do his duty!" This gallant and brilliant smokehouse exploit was achieved on the 14th inst.*

The Americans extinguished the light at Cape Henry to make British navigation more difficult.

British Capt. James Scott remembered the lighthouse in 1843: *The enemy, contrary to his own interest, (a rare occurrence with citizens of the United States,) had extinguished the light on Cape Henry: this gratuitous act saved us the trouble of "dowsing the glim."*

Cape Henry served as the southern end of the blockade at the mouth of Chesapeake Bay. (*see* New Point Comfort *under* Other Tidewater Virginia Sites *below for a discussion of how Baltimore clippers attempted to run the British blockade at the mouth of the Bay.*) Cape Henry served as a watering area for the British blockading fleet.

The Baltimore *Patriot* described the British watering details at Cape Henry on July 19, 1813: *The* [H.M. ship-of-the-line] Plantagenet, *74* [guns], *has for some days past been lying off Cape Henry Light-House, near enough in shore to protect the landing of her men, who were sent on shore to procure water.—The enemy had sunk wells for this purpose on the Cape Point, where there is excellent water, and every day visited them in their barges, supplying themselves with water and plundering the inhabitants.*

A description of fifty local militiamen who positioned themselves among the sand dunes to ambush a watering party in the early morning of July 14, 1813, was published in the Baltimore *Patriot* on July 19, 1813: *At half past 5 this morning, a barge, full of men from the ship* [H.M. Ship-of-the-Line *Plantagenet*], *was seen rowing towards the shore. They landed about 6 o'clock, and all hands proceeded to the wells, where they received a full fire from the militia, who, until that moment were concealed from their view by the sand-hills. The enemy were panic struck. They threw down their arms, and ran in confusion to their boat. Some were cut off in their running, and those who reached the boat immediately laid themselves down in her, and durst not shew their heads . . . and were all taken prisoners. The enemy's force consisted of 3 lieutenants 16 seamen, and 9 marines; and they had three marines killed, and 1 lieut. 2 seamen, and 2 marines wounded. We had not a man injured. As the barge could not be moved without exposure to the guns of the 74, a piece of cannon which was in her bow, and whatever else that could be detached from her, were taken out and she was scuttled.*

The prisoners were taken to Hampton. On June 15, 1813, a second British landing took place at Ragged Island Lake Plantation near Cape Henry, destroying a corn mill after the owner refused to provide sheep and oxen. When a small contingent of militia arrived, the British cannonaded the plantation, destroying a second mill.

The Norfolk *Public Ledger* published an account of the landing on July 19, 1813: *Captain* [Frederick] *Hickey, commanding the British ship* [sloop], *Atalante, sent a boat on shore a few miles to south-*

Torpedo Makes Big Splash

In 1805, a commission recommended that the U.S. Navy support Robert Fulton's new invention, the "torpedo" (water mine). In the summer of 1813, Secretary of Navy William Jones gave encouragement to Elijah Mix, who worked with Capt. Charles Stewart of the U.S. frigate *Constellation,* to use a mine to blow up H.M. ship-of-the-line *Plantagenet* off the Chesapeake capes. Mix rowed near *Plantagenet* in an open boat named *Chesapeake's Revenge* and dropped a torpedo into the water hoping it would drift into the vessel and explode. Despite several attempts, Mix was never successful, although on July 24 a torpedo exploded so near *Plantagenet* that it caused a cascade of water to fall on its deck. The British referred to these mines as "Powder Machines."

The Washington *Daily National Intelligencer* published an account of the incident on August 2, 1813: *It was like the concussion of an earthquake attended with a sound louder and more terrific than the heaviest peal of thunder. A pyramid of water 50 feet in circumference was thrown up to the height of 30 or 40 feet . . . on ascending to its greatest height, it burst at the top with a tremendous explosion and fell in torrents on the deck of the ship which rolled into the yawning chasm below.*

ward of Cape Henry, and made a demand of some fresh provision, accompanying the demand with a threat, that if it was not complied with, he would burn a wind-mill, belonging to the citizen at whose house the boat landed—the demand was not complied with, and . . . destroyed the wind-mill.

Hampton

Little England Farm, then on the outskirts of Hampton, was home to the Barron family, members of whom served in the navy during the Revolutionary War, the War of 1812, and the Civil War. James Barron (1789–1851) commanded the U.S. frigate *Chesapeake* during the infamous encounter with H.M. frigate *Leopard* on June 22, 1807. Barron was court-martialed and sentenced to five years' suspension without pay for neglecting, with the probability of an engagement, to clear his ship for action. An exchange of correspondence between Barron and Com. Stephen Decatur, who served on the court martial board, resulted in Barron killing Decatur in a duel. The impressment of American sailors—typically from merchant vessels rather than a warship as in the incident above—was one of the leading causes of the War of 1812.

Soon after their abortive attempt to take Craney Island on June 22, 1813, the British attacked Hampton (on June 25). While the British fleet cannonaded an American camp defended by two batteries on the Little England Farm southeast of Hampton, some 2,000 British troops landed just before daylight 2 miles west of Hampton on the James River near Newport News. They then marched along Celey's Road to attack Hampton from the rear. At the same time, British barges approached from the waterside at Blackbeard Point. Maj. Stapleton Crutchfield, in command of the 450 American forces, believing that the waterborne attack was only a feint, fired upon the barges from his four-gun battery, but he moved the bulk of his forces north to defend against the British land attack. Near the head of the west branch of Hampton Creek, where Celey's Road joins Yorktown Road, the Americans held back the British advance about three-quarters of an hour before their lines gave way and the militia fled into the thick woods. Artillerymen, protecting a bridge, spiked their cannon and fled. During the confusion, British troops landed from barges at Hampton. Outflanked and outnumbered, the American forces escaped to the north. The British occupied Hampton for ten days, destroying all ordnance and commandeering supplies for their ships. British casualties were 5 killed, 33 wounded, and 10 missing. Among the killed was Lt. Col. Richard Williams. American casualties were 7 killed, 12 wounded, 11 missing, and one taken prisoner. Several of the missing had apparently fled to their homes.

An American account of the action was provided by Capt. John Cassin in his report to the Secretary of Navy William Jones on June 26, 1813: *I am sorry to inform you the Enemy succeeded in Hampton yesterday morning, after a very obstinate resistance, and no doubt great loss on both sides; the Enemy landed several hundred Troops near Newportnews at 4 A.M. marched round, commencing the Action with their Rockets, while the barges forty in number entered the Creek, so few troops tho I believe brave as Ceazer [Caesar] did not exceed five hundred, were overpower'd by numbers, and the Rockets thrown in such way as to confuse them; from the best information we can receive the Inhabitants had flown and little or nothing left in town but the shells of houses.*

A British account of the action was provided by Col. Thomas Sidney Beckwith in his report to Adm. John Borlase Warren on June 28, 1813: *landed half an hour before day light . . . about two miles to the westward of the town . . . With a view to turn the enemy's position our march was directed towards the great road leading from the country into the rear of the*

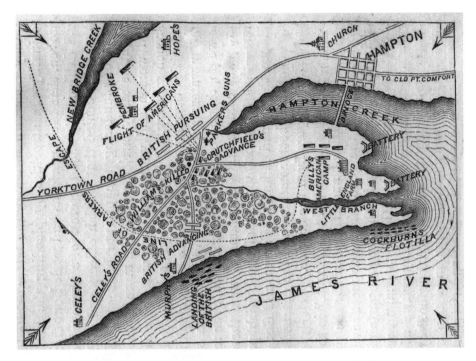

Sketch of the Battle of Hampton showing the locations of Celey's Road; site of death of Lt. Col. Richard Williams; Pembrooke or Westwood Mansion, where Williams was buried; Little England Farm; and the large (upper) battery and the small (lower) battery. Blackbeard Point is not identified but is the lowermost point at the entrance to Hampton Creek where Rear Admiral Cockburn's Flotilla is located. (Lossing, *Pictorial Field-Book of the War of 1812*)

Town . . . to engage the enemy's attention . . . armed launches and rocket boats to commence a fire upon their batteries this succeeded so completely that the head of our advance guard, had cleared a wood and were already on the enemy's flank before our approach was perceived. They then moved from their camp to their position in the rear of the town and here they were vigorously attacked . . . a detachment . . . push'd thro' the town and forced their way across a bridge of planks into the enemy's Encampment, of which, and the batteries, immediate possession was gained—In the mean time some Artillery men stormed and took the enemy's remaining field force . . . Lieut. Colonel [Richard] William will have the honor of delivering to you a stand of colours of the 68th Regt. James City Light Infantry, and one of the 1st Battn. 85th Regt.

The Washington *Daily National Intelligencer* published the news of the attack on June 29, 1813: *HAMPTON TAKEN . . . About 5 o'clock the British made an attack by land and water upon Hampton. One party landed about 5 miles above that place, while another proceeded directly by water . . . the firing was kept up for 1 hour and 45 minutes when it ceased . . . the barges rowed into the creek and land at Hampton. The firing from the fort ceased with that of the musketry. We cannot state what became of the troop stationed there, but is to be hoped they have escaped. The force was as we understand, between 6 and 800. Two houses were set on fire by the rockets.*

Hampton Battlefield Sites

Unfortunately, most of the Hampton battlefield sites are inaccessible to the public. The Americans first detected British barges approaching Hampton from Blackbeard Point, located on the west side of the mouth of Hampton Creek at the east end of Ivy Home Road. This commercial site is privately owned and posted with "no trespassing" signs.

The American encampment and two gun batteries were located on the James Barron family Little England Farm, a five-hundred-acre estate located a short distance southwest of the 1813 town limits. A historic marker about Little England Farm is located at 4400 Victoria Boulevard. Two gun batteries protected the water approach to Hampton. The Large Battery Site, consisting of four guns, was located on the north mouth of Salters Creek, approximately at the south end of King Street. The Small Battery Site, consisting of three guns, was located at Cedar Point, the north mouth of Sunset Creek at the south end of Cedar Point Drive and south off Bridge Street. Cedar Point Drive is a private road. Glimpses of the battery site can be seen from the end of Victoria Boulevard, at the Hampton Yacht Club, but the waterfront area here is off-limits to the general public.

A British land force of two thousand troops approached from the north and was met by an American force of about four hundred men at the junction of Celey's and Yorktown roads. Unfortunately these sites do not retain any historic integrity nor do they have any interpretation.

1852 view of Hampton Creek from Hampton looking south toward Little England Farm, the home of Com. James Barron. Key: 1. Large battery. 2. Small battery. 3. Blackbeard Point. (Lossing, *Pictorial Field-Book of the War of 1812*)

The British victory at Hampton was tainted by the pillaging, murder, and rape committed by members of two companies of Independent Foreigners who participated in the attack. These companies consisted of French deserters and prisoners from the Peninsular War. The British claim these men were spoiling for revenge after the loss of thirty Independent Foreigners during the Battle of Craney Island.

An American account of the plundering was published in the Baltimore *Patriot* on July 23, 1813: *That the town and country adjacent, was given up to the indiscriminate plunder of a licentious soldiery . . . In many houses not even a knife, a fork or a plate was left . . . The church was pillaged and the plate belonging to it was taken away . . . The wind-mills in the neighborhood were stript of their sails. The closets, private drawers and trunks of the inhabitants were broken open, and scarcely any thing semed to be too trifling an object to excite the cupidity of those robbers.*

Margaret Ann Bonyer wrote of the atrocities to her sister Sally Wyatt Bibb in a letter dated June 30, 1813: *The enemy took possession of Hampton . . . During their stay, their conduct exhibited deeds of infamy and barbarity which none but British savages could have been so callous and lost to the tender feelings of human nature. They pillaged the place of every article they could convey . . . they murdered the sick and dying and committed the most hard and cruel insults to the defenseless young ladies. From such nefarious enemies good Lord deliver us, is the prayer of your affectionate sister.*

British Col. Thomas Sidney Beckwith acknowledged the unacceptable behavior of these troops to Adm. John Borlase Warren in his report of July 5, 1813: *It is with great Regret I am obliged to entreat your Attention to the Situation & Conduct of the Two Independent Companies of Foreigners embarked on this Service . . . Their Behavior on the recent Landing at Hampton . . . dispersing to plunder in every direction; their brutal Treatment of several Peaceable Inhabitants, whose Age or Infirmities rendered them unable to get out of their Way . . . and whose Lives they threatened . . . I take the Liberty of submitting to You, the necessity of their being sent away as soon as possible.*

Reports of Hampton Man's Death Biased

Biased American newspaper accounts spread many stories of the atrocities committed during the British occupation of Hampton, but one story of the deliberate killing of a very sick and aged man named Kirby is not credible.

The Washington *Daily National Intelligencer* reported the account on July 2, 1813: *A Mr. Kilby, near Hampton was dying in his house in the arms of his wife, when the British troops approached, and one of them cooly pulled out his pistol, shot poor Kilby and the ball lodged in the hip of the wife. "Expect no quarter," said an officer to his friend here.*

The Baltimore *Patriot* reported the incident on July 23, 1813: *Kirby, who for seven weeks or more had been confined to his bed, and whose death the savages only a little hastened, was shot in the arms of his wife . . . go to his wounded wife and hear her heart-rendering tale.*

Benson J. Lossing visited this widow in 1853 and wrote the following: *her version of the story was that, with vengeful feelings, the soldiers chased an ugly dog into the house, which ran under Mr. Kirby's chair, in which he was sitting, and, in their eagerness to shoot the dog, shot the aged invalid, the bullet grazing the hip of Mrs. Kirby. Mrs. Kirby always considered the shooting of her husband an accident.*

Hampton was heavily damaged during the American Civil War, yet some interesting structures from the War of 1812 survive. Begin you tour at the **HAMPTON HISTORY MUSEUM.**

HAMPTON HISTORY MUSEUM. Address: 120 Old Hampton Lane. **Parking:** free. **Hours:** Monday through Saturday, 10 a.m. to 5 p.m.; Sunday, 1 to 5 p.m.; **Fees:** $5 adults, $4 seniors, military, children 4 to 12, children under 4 free. **Facilities:** exhibits, tourist information; restrooms. **Contacts:** 757-727-1610; www.hampton.gov/history_museum.

This museum provides a good overall history of Hampton including a small exhibit about life during the War of 1812. Artifacts include a musket made by Archibald Rutherford in 1810, one of seventy-five delivered to the Hampton Volunteer Rifle Company. This one was taken as a war trophy to England after the British attack on Hampton. "115 REGT VA MA ELIZABETH CITY" is stamped on the musket barrel.

Immediately north of the museum is **ST. JOHN'S EPISCOPAL CHURCH.**

ST. JOHN'S EPISCOPAL CHURCH. NRHP. Address: 100 West Queens Way. **Parking:** free street parking and free parking garage. **Hours:** daylight hours; church and parish museum, 9 a.m. to 3 p.m. weekdays, and 9 a.m. to noon Saturdays. **Fees:** none. **Contacts:** tours can be arranged by calling 757-722-2567; www.stjohnshampton.org. **Comment:** the communion silver service was made in London in 1618.

St. John's Episcopal Church, founded in 1610, is the oldest Anglican Parish in America. The present structure, the fourth, was completed in 1728 and the belfry was added in 1762. The British are said to have sacked the church and used the cemetery grounds as a slaughterhouse for the butchering of cattle taken from the inhabitants of Hampton. A historic marker on the grounds of the church proclaims that the walls that surround the church "have suffered during the Revolutionary War, the War of 1812 and the War Between the States." Parts of the circa 1759 wall can be seen at the southwest corner of the graveyard (left of main entrance as one faces the church). Interpretive markers describe the wall.

From the Hampton History Museum and St. John's Episcopal Church, it is approximately 3 miles to **FORT MONROE,** located on the north side of the confluence of James River and Chesapeake Bay.

FORT MONROE. NRHP. Location: south end of NcNair Drive (U.S. Route 258). **Parking:** free. **Hours:** daylight hours. **Fees:** none. **Facilities:** historic fort, views of Chesapeake Bay, waterside walk. **Contact:** www.fmfada.com/community/facilities.php. **Comment:** photo ID required for entrance. The fort is a good place to walk and bicycle.

Fort Monroe was begun in 1819 to beef up American coastal defenses, which had been far from adequate during the War of 1812. Completed in 1834, the fort is named for James

Monroe, who served as secretary of state and secretary of war during the War of 1812 and later became the fifth president of the United States (1817–25). Several officers who served at Fort Monroe took part in the War of 1812. Among them are John Walbach, Abraham Eustis, Charles Gratiot, and Walker K. Armistead. René DeRussy, one of the engineers who designed the fort, and John E. Wool, commander of the fort, fought at the Battle of Plattsburgh (September 11, 1814).

CASEMATE MUSEUM. Location: northwest interior casement of fort. **Parking:** free. **Hours:** 10:30 a.m. to 4:30 p.m. daily except Christmas, New Year's and Thanksgiving days. **Fees:** none. **Facilities:** exhibits, restrooms, gift shop; handicap accessible. **Contacts:** 757-788-3391 or 3935. **Comment:** the museum is located inside the fort, which is accessible by foot, bicycle, or by vehicle. Obey traffic singles and be prepared for narrow gate entrances.

In the **CASEMATE MUSEUM,** artifacts related to the War of 1812 include the flag of the 3rd Regiment, U.S. Artillery with campaign ribbons for the unit's participation at the Battle of Chippawa (July 5, 1814), Battle of Lundy's Lane (July 25, 1814), and the Battle of Fort Erie (August 15, 1814), all in Upper Canada. An 8-inch siege mortar, made at the Woolwich Arsenal in England, was captured by the Americans at Fort George, Canada, in May 1813. It was used in the defense of Plattsburgh, New York, on September 11, 1814. This mortar was kept as a trophy and is believed to be among the original armaments of the fort.

OLD POINT COMFORT LIGHTHOUSE. NRHP. Location: north side of Fenwick Road. **Parking:** street parking. **Hours:** daylight hours. **Fees:** none. **Facilities:** restrooms at Casemate Museum. **Comment:** the interior of the lighthouse is not accessible; exterior views only. For further history on this lighthouse *see* www.nps.gov/history/maritime/light/oldpt.htm.

The British used the **OLD POINT COMFORT LIGHTHOUSE** tower as an observation station in 1813. The Virginia Historical Roadside Marker, located on Fenwick Road near the lighthouse, claims that the tower was used as a lookout by the British during their attack on Washington. This text is misleading as the lighthouse was not specifically used during the 1814 attack on Washington but during the attack on Hampton in 1813.

On March 8, 1813, a schooner off Old Point Comfort was attacked and taken by a British naval force.

The Baltimore *Niles' Weekly Register* reported the incident on March 13, 1813: *A small black schooner with one gun, supposed from Baltimore, was attacked on Monday morning off Old Point Comfort by 13 boats, after fighting them for some time was overpowered and carried* [taken].

Newport News

MARINERS' MUSEUM. Address: 100 Museum Drive, south off J. Clyde Morris Blvd. (Avenue of the Arts), south off Warwick Boulevard (Route 312). **Parking:** free. **Hours:** Monday through Saturday, 10 a.m. to 5 p.m.; Sunday, noon to 5 p.m. **Fees:** $14 adults, $13 AAA, military, students, $12 seniors, $8 children 6 to 12, children under 6 free. **Facilities:** exhibits, restrooms, café, gift shop. **Contacts:** 1-800-581-7245; www.mariner.org. **Comment:** plan to stay at least two hours for a complete tour of the museum.

Among the exhibits at the **MARINERS' MUSEUM** is an anchor from H.M. troop-ship *Dictator* recovered from the Patuxent River, Maryland, in the 1950s. *Dictator* was one of the transport ships that took part in the British invasion of Maryland in August 1814. The anchor is in the Chesapeake Bay Gallery.

VIRGINIA WAR MUSEUM. Address: 9285 Warwick Boulevard. **Parking:** free. **Hours:** Monday through Saturday, 9 a.m. to 5 p.m.; Sunday, 1 to 5 p.m. **Fees:** $6 adults, $5 seniors, military, AAA, $4 children 7 to 18, children under 7 free. **Facilities:** exhibits, restrooms, picnic tables. **Contacts:** 757-247-8523; www.warmuseum.org.

Among the War of 1812 artifacts on exhibit at the **VIRGINIA WAR MUSEUM** are: the uniform of Greenleaf Dearborn, an officer during the war; a circa 1878 oil painting depicting the Battle of Lake Erie; a circa 1812 guard officer's coatee (military coat with short tail) worn by Moses Myers (1752–1835), active in the Norfolk Junior Volunteers; circa 1812 knee breeches and trousers worn by members of the Myers family; and a wooden canteen used during the war by George Schrader of Norfolk.

This ends the Greater Norfolk Tour.

Richmond and Petersburg Tour

Particulars The Richmond-Petersburg area offers a full range of lodging and dining options—from expensive to inexpensive—owing to the many tourists who visit Civil War–related sites. Visitors may plan their tour to suit their own interests and time constraints.

Historical Background Neither Richmond nor Petersburg was ever attacked during the War of 1812, although Richmond, an important center for arms manufactory at the head of navigation on the James River, felt threatened. By the fall of 1814, seven camps were established around the city and Fort Powhatan defended the river. The Petersburg U.S. Volunteers distinguished themselves at the siege of Fort Meigs in May and June 1813, on the Maumee River, northwestern Ohio, and later became famous for their leather cockade hats.

Richmond

RICHMOND VISITOR CENTERS. Addresses: Downtown: 405 North 3rd Street; and Bass Pro Shops: 11550 Lakeridge Parkway, Ashland (off I-95). **Parking:** downtown: free 20-minute street parking on block; Bass Pro Shops: free. **Hours:** downtown: Friday through Sunday, 9 a.m. to 5 p.m.; Bass Pro Shops: Friday through Saturday, 9 a.m. to 7 p.m.; Sunday, 9 a.m. to 6 p.m. **Fees:** none. **Facilities:** brochures, maps, reservations, restrooms. **Contacts:** Downtown: 804-783-7450; Bass Pros Shops: 804-496-4700; www.VisitRichmondVA.com.

In late June 1814, British ships ran up the James River raiding plantations but primarily seeking to replenish their fresh water supplies. Nevertheless, exaggerated reports caused citizens of Richmond to fear that an attack was imminent. Before calm could be restored, plans were underway to remove the women and children, public records, and bank specie from the Virginia capital.

By mid October 1814, nearly 11,000 troops were present defending Richmond in a number of camps including Camp Malvern Hill, Camp Holly Springs, Camp Carter, Camp Mims, Camp Fairfield, Camp Mitchell's Springs, and Camp Bottoms Bridge. Although the exact location of most of these camps in unclear, Camp Malvern Hill was located 12 miles southeast of Richmond on heights near the James River, and Camp Holly Springs was 10 miles east of Richmond. Camp Bottoms Bridge was just east of the Henrico–Charles City line on the old Richmond-Williamsburg road. Camp Carter was 2 miles west. Fort Powhatan, on the James River, also defended Richmond.

The Virginia legislature authorized the construction of an armory in 1797 to manufacture weapons for the state. Built in 1801, the **VIRGINIA MANUFACTORY OF ARMS** began production the next year. Virginia was the only state after the Revolutionary War to arm its own forces with locally made weapons. Other states depended upon federal armories at Harpers Ferry, Virginia (now West Virginia), or Springfield, Massachusetts, or on private contractors like one at Edinburg, Virginia. The Virginia armory closed in 1821. The manufactory consisted of a boring mill and a two-and-a-half story U-shaped structure where the manufacture of arms took place. This complex later became the Richmond Manufactory.

VIRGINIA MANUFACTORY OF ARMS Site, Richmond Civil War Visitor Center. **Address:** 470 Tredegar Street, foot of 5th Street. **Parking:** charge for parking at center; free parking nearby. **Hours:** 9 a.m. to 5 p.m. daily. **Fees:** none. **Facilities:** visitor information, exhibits, gift shop, restrooms. **Contacts:** 804-771-2145; www.nps.gov/rich/planyourvisit/visitorcenters. htm. **Comment:** the stone foundations near the intersection of 5th and Tredegar streets are believed to represent the remains of the Virginia Manufactory.

In the Richmond National Battlefield Civil War Visitor Center (second floor), there are three models of the Tredegar area. The early industries model shows the location of the Virginia Manufactory of Arms in relation to the Tredegar Iron Works established in 1836. A model 1817 muzzle-loading flintlock musket made here is exhibited at the Portsmouth Naval Shipyard Museum.

Model of Virginia Manufactory of Arms. (Richmond National Battlefield Civil War Visitor Center; Ralph Eshelman 2006 photograph)

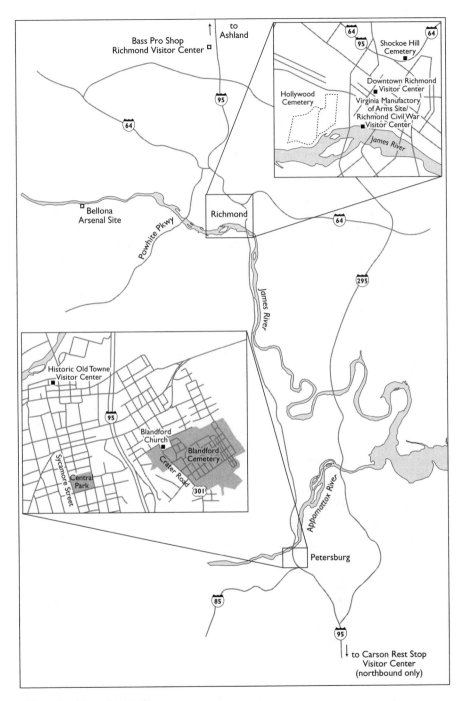

Richmond and Petersburg Region

Petersburg

On September 1, 1812, the War Department asked Virginia to provide fifteen hundred armed militiamen for the North Western Army in Ohio. This request grew out of the surrender of Detroit to the British on August 16. The control of Lake Erie and the Michigan Territory was at stake. Governor James Barbour put out a call for volunteers from the various militia units of the state. One of the first units to respond was the Petersburg Volunteers. A public meeting was held at the courthouse on September 8, 1812, and a committee of eleven was appointed to raise funds by public subscription to finance the creation of the unit.

A resolution was adopted and published in the Richmond *Virginia Argus* on September 17, 1812: *That the town of Petersburg will ever hold in high remembrance those Noble & Patriotic young men, who, unmindful of every other consideration, save love of country, have volunteered their services to retrieve the reputation of the republic, so shamefully, ignominiously and disgracefully sullied by the imbecile (if not treacherous) conduct of General* [William] *Hull* [referring to Brigadier General Hull, commander of the "North Western Army" who was bluffed into surrendering Detroit, August 16, 1812].

Cockade City

Petersburg is reputed to have been named "The Cockade City of the Union" by President James Madison when the Petersburg Volunteers visited Washington during their return from Fort Meigs, where they had distinguished themselves in 1813. Their leather cockade hats supposedly prompted President Madison to make the statement. In reality the Petersburg Volunteers returned in several groups taking many different routes to Petersburg, although some soldiers may have stopped in Washington. The sobriquet may have been conferred when Capt. Richard McRae, the unit's commander, visited Washington in July of 1814. However, the appellation "The Cockade of the Union," seems to have first appeared in a toast on July 4, 1838, and then showed up several times in the press between 1843 and 1848. The term "The Cockade City" does not appear until after 1850. The Cockade Monument, also known as the Petersburg Volunteers Monument, is inscribed "Cockade City of the Union," but it was not erected until 1857. Thus it is unclear who coined the phrase or when it was first used.

CENTRAL PARK. Location: northeast corner of Sycamore and Filmore streets. **Parking:** street parking. **Hours:** daylight hours. **Fees:** none. **Facilities:** none. **Comment:** A granite monument commemorating this site as a muster and drill grounds is located near the northwest corner of the park.

CENTRAL PARK, then known as Poplar Lawn, was the muster and drill grounds used by the Petersburg Volunteers at the beginning of the War of 1812. On October 21,

1812, the Volunteers assembled at Centre Hill (NRHP), the old historic section of Petersburg on the hill above the Appomattox River near Courthouse Avenue and Adams Street. En route to Canada via Richmond, they were followed by carriages filled with ladies. The Volunteers marched down Sycamore Street and across the Pocahontas Bridge over the Appomattox River, where a small cannon saluted them from a schooner. These volunteers were present at the siege of Fort Meigs in May and June 1813 and remained in service until October 1813.

When the Petersburg Volunteers returned to Petersburg after defending Fort Meigs, festivities honoring the company were held January 8, 1814. Guns were fired at Centre Hill, and after appropriate salutes, the company proceeded to Poplar Lawn. A band played and patriotic songs were sung. A dinner and a ball followed. Poplar Lawn was decorated with flags including a war-worn banner from Fort Meigs.

OLD BLANDFORD CHURCH AND CEMETERY. NRHP. Address: 319 South Crater Road (U.S. Route 301) and Rochelle Lane. **Parking:** free. **Hours:** 10 a.m. to 5 p.m. daily; **Tours:** 10 a.m. to 4 p.m. **Fees:** grounds free; tours $5 adults, $4 military, seniors, and children 7 to 12, children under 7 free. **Facilities:** exhibits, gift shop, restrooms. **Contacts:** 804-733-2396; www.craterroad.com/oldblandfordchurch.html.

The Capt. Richard McRae obelisk is surrounded by a cast iron fence incorporating into its design an eagle with spread wings, the U.S. shield, cockade hats, muskets, swords, powder horns, belts, a bullet pouch, a drum, and cannonballs. Each corner post is in the form of a battle axe. (Ralph Eshelman 2007 photograph)

The **OLD BLANDFORD CHURCH** was erected in 1735, abandoned, and then restored in 1882. In 1901 it became a memorial chapel to Confederate veterans. Within the 189 acre cemetery dating from 1702 are buried Revolutionary War, War of 1812, and Civil War veterans. A replica of the Petersburg Volunteers War of 1812 uniform, including the famous leather cockade hat, is on display in the church reception center. A monument was erected over the grave of Capt. Richard McRae in 1856 to honor him and the Petersburg Volunteers. The 10-foot obelisk monument features an American shield surmounted by an American eagle gilded with 23 karat gold and surrounded by an ornate cast iron fence topped by seventeen stars representing the states of the Union at the time of the war. Since Louisianan joined the Union on April 30, 1812, there should be eighteen stars. The monument was damaged during the Federal cannonading of Petersburg during the Civil War, but it was later restored by the Cockade City Garden Club. The gilded eagle was stolen several years ago and later found in a pawn shop in Richmond. A replica now surmounts the obelisk, while the original is on display in the reception center at Blandford Church.

This ends the Richmond and Petersburg Tour.

Tappahannock Tour

Particulars Tappahannock has motels, bed and breakfast establishments, and several dining options. It is a good place to wander by foot or bicycle, but I advise you to stay off congested U.S. Route 17 and Route 360. For a map of the town and walking tour of historic structures see www.essex-virginia.org/ta_walk.htm. Boat excursions are also available (*see* appendix D). Visitors may plan their tour to suit their own interests and time constraints.

Historical Background Located on the Rappahannock River, Tappahannock retains many structures dating from before the War of 1812; including the custom house (1720), the old debtors' prison (1769), the old clerk's office (1808), and the Meriwether Ritchie House (1706). The historic downtown including the St. Margaret's School grounds are designated a National Historic District. The latter two structures are located on the corner of Prince and Cross streets. The Rappahannock River, where the British loaded tobacco and flour during their raid here on December 2–3, 1814, can be viewed from the end of Prince Street.

In late November of 1814, British Capt. Robert Barrie received information that the Virginia militia regiments, lately stationed on the banks of the Rappahannock, had disbanded for the winter. Most of the troops had returned to their homes. Taking advantage of this intelligence, Captain Barrie planned an attack on Tappahannock to "annoy the Enemy by obliging him to reassemble his Militia, and by landing in different parts of the River, keep his Troops constantly on the alert, which in this Country at this advanced season of the year is most harassing Service." The attack of approximately 500 troops, including some 150 Colonial Marines made up of former slaves, began on December 2, 1814, and ended the next day. The outnumbered local militia withdrew to the nearby hills when the British landed. Congreve rockets forced the militia to retreat farther. The British burned the custom house, a jail, and a large granary. The following day, the county courthouse and a second jail were also torched.

Lt. Col. Archibald Ritchie wrote his account of the raid to Governor James Barbour, published in the Richmond *Enquirer* on December 6, 1814: *all the houses had been pillaged of everything; except some fine pieces of furniture. Some furniture they carried off, other of the most valuable broken to pieces, all the beds, their furniture, etc. which were left, taken off, except in one house, where the beds were ripped open, the feathers left on the floor, but the ticking carried off, the glass in the windows of many houses entirely broken.*

Brig. Gen. John Hartwell Cocke wrote another account of the raid to Governor James Barbour on December 4, 1814: *landed here . . . were three companies, of about 50 each, of negroes* [Colonial Marines] *in uniform and apparently well trained, commanded by white officers.—They were said to be Virginia & Maryland negroes, trained at Tangier Islands—. . . The plundering of the Enemy has been confined* [to the] *bay Shores of inconsiderable amount, & on a few plantations . . . There has been much wanton destruction of private property here* [Tappahannock] *—in breaking windows & furniture—and one deed of damnation has been performed which out does all their former atrocities—The family Vault of the Ritchies was broken open and the Coffins searched—I have seen the shocking spectacle.*

Capt. Robert Barrie wrote his account of the raid to Rear Adm. George Cockburn on

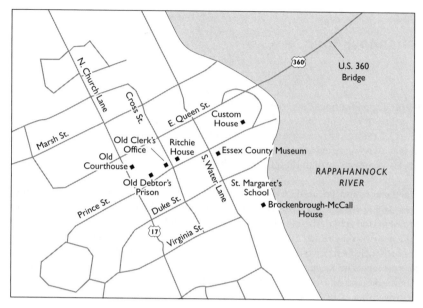

Tappahannock

December 7, 1814: *we* [British] *observed a considerable body of Troops drawn out with their Field Pieces . . . proceeded with the Boats abreast of the Town* [Tappahannock], *and when within Grape Shot commenced our Fire, which the Enemy did not return and observing them abandoning the Town . . . the Inhabitants with the exception of two had entirely deserted the Town, and removed all their effects except about forty hogsheads of Tobacco and some Flour. The Enemy in his haste to abandon the Town left behind him a Stand of Colours, several Musquets, Bayonets, and a quantity of Ammunition and Camp Equipage . . . the Enemy, being in sight drawn up on a Hill, about a Mile and a half above the Town . . . Rockets . . . fell among the Enemy who soon retreated into the Wood behind the Hill, wishing to entice him to attack us in the Town, I caused to be set on fire the Custom House and a Jail, but as he envinced no disposition to quit his fastness, I embarked the Troops at Sunset, and at daylight on the 3rd. I again landed and completed Shipping the Flour and Tobacco; in the course of the day, a second Jail and the Court House was consumed without molestation from the Enemy though he frequently shewed himself with increased Force.*

Vice Adm. William Stanhope Lovell remembered the raid in 1879: *We first took the town of Rappahannock* [Tappahannock], *driving the enemy out of it, who ran away so fast that they dropped their colours, which we took. On one side of them, under the American eagle, was this motto, "Death or victory"; on the other, "Down with the tyrants." However, they were "scared" from death and ran away from victory.*

Capt. Frederick Chamier wrote down his memories of the plundering in 1850: *We were particularly desired not to land; but seeing boots and shoes walking into a captain's gig,—half a butcher's shop in another, the cockswain of a third with two geese dangling to his hands—we became hungry from fancy, and impatient under our restrictions; and therefore edged near the beach, and landed in the vicinity of a large house which belonged to one Doctor Bolingbroke* [Austin Brockenbrough?]. *In about five minutes the house was turned out of the windows, and every man carried off some of the property. A large staircase clock was clapped upon a few geese at the bottom of the boat to keep them quiet; then came a bundle of books and some cabbages, a feather-bed, and a small cask of peach brandy. The boat was soon deeply laden, and we all re-embarked, like good boys.*

A Virginia Historical Highway Marker on Richmond Road (Route 360), entitled "Historic Tappahannock," states "The British Admiral Cockburn shelled the town, December 1, 1814." While cannon may have been fired on the town on December 1, the raid took place on December 2 and 3.

Begin your tour at the **ESSEX COUNTY MUSEUM.** Among the exhibits is a cavalryman's saber dating from the War of 1812.

ESSEX COUNTY MUSEUM. Address: 218 Water Lane. **Parking:** street parking. **Hours:** Monday, Tuesday, and Thursday through Saturday, 10 a.m. to 3 p.m. **Fees:** none. **Facilities:** exhibits, restrooms, and visitor information. **Contacts:** 804-443-4690; www.essexmuseum.org.

It is only a short walk to **BROCKENBROUGH-MCCALL HOUSE.**

BROCKENBROUGH-MCCALL HOUSE. Location: South Water Lane near intersection with Virginia Street. **Parking:** street parking. **Comment:** this house is now the admissions office of St. Margaret's School. Exterior views of house only. Please respect private property.

The Brockenbrough-McCall House was built in 1763 and owned by the Brockenbrough family during the War of 1812. A black marble fireplace mantel in the east parlor (drawing room) was reportedly damaged when it was hit by cannon fire during the British attack. The fireplace hearth in the east parlor is made from what appears to be a broken slab of fossiliferous black marble, possibly originally from the mantle. The cannonball that is said to have caused the damage has been kept next to the fireplace as a remembrance of the event. The approximately 4.5-inch diameter of the cannonball suggests it was fired from a 12 pound cannon. The white marble fireplace mantle, in the ground floor south bedroom, provides a clue as to what the original black marble mantle may have looked like before the cannonball damage. The other five fireplace mantles in the house, including the present mantle in the east parlor, are all wood.

Col. Archibald Ritchie wrote to the Governor of Virginia on December 1, 1814: *The Enemy fired many cannon, one of which struck the easternmost part of Dr. Brockenbrough's large House; some struck in the Lots, and some passed over.*

One account mentions the plundering of the Bolingbroke House. It is probable that this was the Brockenbrough house, the name having been corrupted. Dr. Austin Brockenbrough, who served in the 6th Virginia Regiment and occupied the house during the War of 1812, is buried at the Blake-Brockenbrough Cemetery, located on Water Street near the museum.

The **CUSTOM HOUSE,** located at 109 Prince Street, sits on the bank of the Rappahannock River where the British landed. Reports state that the British burned the custom house, so either the damage was slight or the structure was rebuilt.

The Brockenbrough-McCall House. Upper left: white marble fireplace mantle from lower floor south bedroom. Lower left: cannonball on lower floor east parlor hearth. Right: east parlor fireplace mantel with presumed broken black marble fireplace mantel re-utilized as hearth. (Ralph Eshelman 2009 photographs)

There were as many as four jails. Two of them were reportedly burned by the British. The exact location of the jails that were burned is unclear. The Treasurer's Office now occupies a building then referred to as the "debtors' jail." It is located on the north side of Prince Street, just west of the intersection with Church Lane.

The **OLD COURTHOUSE,** later the Beale Memorial Baptist Church, is located at 202 Church Lane. Dating from 1729, this structure served as a courthouse until 1848, when the court moved to its present location on Prince Street. The old courthouse was burned by the British. Some accounts claim that the walls of that old structure were reused in the rebuilding of the courthouse on that site, while others claim the original building was a total loss. A church tower was added to the structure when it served as the Beale Memorial Baptist Church. The historic property is now again owned by Essex County.

This ends the Tappahannock Tour.

Central Virginia Tour

The Piedmont of Central Virginia produced a number of politically important men who had significant roles either leading up to or during the War of 1812—arguably more than any other region of the Chesapeake. Among them were three presidents (Thomas Jefferson, James Madison, and then–Secretary of State [and later President] James Monroe) and a governor (James Barbour). Their homes (with the exception of Barbour's, which is in ruins) are open to the public. An interesting, but distant, side trip, is to eastern West Virginia (what was then Virginia) to visit Organ Cave where saltpetre was produced to make gunpowder during the war.

James Monroe, who served as secretary of state and secretary of war during the War of 1812, lived at **ASH LAWN–HIGHLAND** for twenty-four years. Monroe was compelled to sell the property for financial reasons and moved to Oak Hill.

ASH LAWN–HIGHLAND. NRHP. Address: 1000 James Monroe Parkway (Route 795), southwest off Thomas Jefferson Parkway (Route 53), south of Charlottesville, Albemarle County. **Parking:** free. **Hours:** April through October, 9 a.m. to 6 p.m.; November through March, 11 a.m. to 5 p.m. **Fees:** $10 adults, $9 seniors, $5 children 6 to 11 and local residents, children under 6 free. **Facilities:** historic house, gift shop. **Contacts:** 434-293-8000; www.ashlawnhighland.org. **Comment:** Ash Lawn–Highland is operated by the College of William and Mary, Monroe's alma mater.

The Petersburg U.S. Volunteers stopped at **MONTICELLO**, Thomas Jefferson's home, in the fall of 1812 on their way to Fort Meigs, Ohio. Jefferson was the third president of the United States from 1801 to 1809. During his presidency, he orchestrated economic embargos with countries who interfered with American commerce and reduced construction of large naval vessels in favor of less expensive gunboats.

MONTICELLO. NHL. Address: 931 Thomas Jefferson Parkway, Charlottesville, Albemarle County. **Parking:** free. **Hours:** November through February, 9 a.m. to 4:30 p.m.; March through October, 8 a.m. to 5 p.m. **Fees:** $15 adults November through February, $20 March through October, $8 children 6 to 11 throughout year, children under 6 free. **Facilities:** historic house, grounds, exhibits, museum shop, café, restrooms. **Contacts:** 434-984-9822; www.monticello.org.

The Richmond *Enquirer* on November 20, 1812, and the *Niles' Weekly Register* on November 28, 1812, claimed that the Petersburg Volunteers were entertained by Thomas Jefferson. However, other accounts, such as the Federalist newspaper Richmond *Virginia Patriot*, differ.

On December 8, 1812, the newspaper published the following account: *As a singular instance of the small reliance that can be put . . . on newspaper paragraphs I here subscribe an extract from my son's letter, who joined the Petersburg Volunteers . . . we . . . went three miles out of our way to gratify Mr. Jefferson's curiosity; and our expectations were highly raised, for we all expected to see and partake of every thing the house could afford, as having met the most bountiful treatment elsewhere; but we were all disappointed and horrified; though hungry, thirsty and tired, we got neither meat nor drink; not even water. We had a distance view of Mr. Jefferson and house.*

Alfred M. Lorrain published his remembrance of the event in 1862: *We drew up, in military array, at the base of the hill on which the great house* [Monticello] *was erected. About half way down the hill stood a very homely old man, dressed in plain Virginia cloth, his head uncovered, and his venerable locks flowing in the wind . . . But how we were astonished when he advanced to our officers and introduced himself as Thomas Jefferson! The officers were invited in to a collation, while we were marched off to the town, where more abundant provisions had been made.*

The ruins of Governor James Barbour's house and the Barbour family cemetery, where he is buried, are on the grounds of the **BARBOURSVILLE** Vineyards.

What Levy Left

Uriah Phillips Levy (1792–1862) owned Monticello from 1834 until his death. Although court-martialed six times and dismissed from the U.S. Navy three times, he became the navy's first Jewish captain and later its first Jewish commodore. During the War of 1812, Levy served as a supernumerary sailing master on the 18-gun U.S. brig *Argus.* The *Argus* captured or destroyed at least fifteen British ships. Levy was placed in command of the prize merchant-ship *Betsey,* but this vessel was captured by H.M. sloop-of-war *Pelican* the next day. Levy spent the next sixteen months in Dartmoor Prison. He abolished flogging in the U.S. Navy, leading to the approval of a congressional anti-flogging bill in 1850. An admirer of Thomas Jefferson, Levy purchased Monticello eight years after Jefferson's death, refurbished it, and even increased its acreage. Years before Mount Vernon was restored, Levy can be credited with saving Monticello. Marc Leepson wrote in his 2001 book, *Saving Monticello: The Levy Family's Epic Quest to Rescue the House That Jefferson Built,* that Levy was possibly "the first American to act upon the idea of preserving a historic dwelling." A bronze statue of Thomas Jefferson, located in the rotunda of the U.S. Capitol, was donated by Uriah Levy. This is the only privately funded statue in the Capitol. The Jewish Chapel at the U.S. Naval Academy, opened in 2005, is named for Uriah Levy.

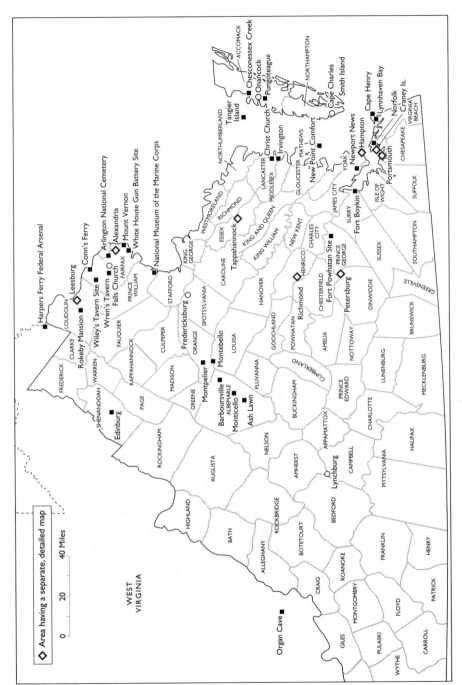

Miscellaneous Virginia Sites

BARBOURSVILLE. NRHP. Address: 17655 Winery Road, 0.2 mile west off Route 777, 0.2 mile south off Route 678, 0.6 mile east off Route 20, Barboursville, Orange County. **Parking:** free. **Hours:** grounds: daylight hours; winery visitor center: Monday through Saturday, 10 a.m. to 5 p.m., and Sunday, 11 a.m. to 5 p.m. **Fees:** none. **Contacts:** 540-832-3824; http://barboursvillewine.net/winery/estate-and-history/the-barbour-era. **Comment:** the vineyards are also worth a visit. Historic photographs of Barboursville and free wine tasting available at the visitor center.

Governor Barbour viewed the war as the only means by which to end British threats to American sovereignty. He therefore sought to prepare Virginia for war. Barbour's father had trained the Orange County militia, and his son was well aware of the inadequacies of Virginia's militia. Thus, on January 27, 1812, the governor addressed the General Assembly and sought appropriations for training and arming a stronger militia. Barbour toured the tidewater region from April 21 to May 10, 1812, to form a plan for the defense of Virginia against the British.

James Madison served as the fourth president of the United States and chief executive throughout the War of 1812. Dolley Payne Madison, his wife, is credited with saving important state papers and the portrait of George Washington from certain destruction by the British. James and Dorothea (Dolley) Madison lived at **MONTPELIER** and are buried there.

Ruins of the Governor James Barbour house; known as "the war governor" for his energetic service during the War of 1812. (Ralph Eshelman 2006 photograph)

MONTPELIER. NHL. Address: 11395 Constitution Highway (Route 20), Montpelier Station, Orange County. **Parking:** free. **Hours:** November through March, 9 a.m. to 4 p.m.; April through October, 9 a.m. to 5 p.m. **Fees:** $16 adults, $8 children 6 to 14, children under 6 free; discount for National Trust members. **Facilities:** visitor center, house, grounds, museum shop, restrooms. **Contacts:** 540-672-2728 X 140; www.montpelier.org.

The gravestone for President Madison was erected in 1856 and one for Dolley about 1858. The boyhood home of Governor James Barbour, known as Bloomingdale (*see also* Barboursville *above*), was on the grounds of Montpelier.

Optional Side Trip **ORGAN CAVE.** For those with time to explore (about a three-hour drive one way), I recommend a trip to Organ Cave, which preserves an impressive thirty-seven saltpetre leaching hoppers, including fragments of at least three that date from the War of 1812. The remaining hoppers are from the Civil War period. Saltpetre (potassium nitrate) was used in making gunpowder and may have been mined here as early as the American Revolution. The date 1704 is inscribed on the wall in a saltpetre-producing area of the cave.

ORGAN CAVE. NRHP. Address: 417 Masters Road (Route 63), south of Roncevorte, Greenbrier County, West Virginia (formerly Virginia). **Parking:** free. **Hours:** Monday through Saturday, 10 a.m. to 5 p.m.; closed Sunday. **Fees:** $14 adults, $7 children 6 to 12, children under 6 free. **Facilities:** restrooms, picnic facilities, souvenir store. **Contacts:** 304-645-7600; www.organcave.com. **Comment:** Organ Cave is open for public tours, but the "1812 Room" can only be visited by making a strenuous guided "wild cave" tour, which involves much crawling. Only fragments of the original 1812 saltpetre hoppers survive. However, Civil War–era hoppers, in excellent condition and on display on the public tour, give an idea of what the 1812 hoppers might have looked like.

The name Henry Cadiz is inscribed on the walls of Organ Cave about 0.5 mile beyond the "1812 Room." Cadiz is believed to have contracted with E.I. du Pont to supply saltpetre for making gunpowder. Tradition holds that the saltpetre was dragged by sled to the entrance of the cave and then shipped to nearby Union. From there it was probably transported to E.I. du Pont's Gunpowder Company (*see under* Head of the Chesapeake Tour *in part 2*) near Wilmington, Delaware, where gunpowder was made and then shipped to military installations like Fort McHenry.

During the War of 1812, the market price for saltpetre was between 75 cents and $1.00 per pound, making good nitre caves extremely valuable. An estimated 250 caves in the United States were mined during the Revolution, the War of 1812, and the Civil War. During the War of 1812, saltpetre was mined from caves in Indiana, Kentucky, Tennessee, and Virginia (including present-day West Virginia). Mammoth Cave, Kentucky, is perhaps the best known. It is unclear how many Maryland and Virginia caves were mined for saltpetre, although Thomas Jefferson mentions that there were several caves in Virginia with saltpetre potential. The following Virginia caves, in addition to Organ Cave, are believed to have been mined during the War of 1812: Haynes Cave, Monroe County; Trout Cave and/

or New Trout Cave, Pendleton County (both now in West Virginia); Madison Cave, Augusta County; and an unnamed cave near Natural Bridge, Rockbridge County. Grand Caverns, Augusta County, has been open to the public sporadically since 1806. Legend holds that it was mined during the War of 1812, but no documentary evidence supporting this claim has been found.

This ends the Central Virginia Tour.

Other Tidewater Virginia Sites

Although all the sites in this section are in Tidewater Virginia, they require some driving time in between. Plan accordingly *(see the map on page 213 for relative distances between sites)*. All are worth visiting, however.

Irvington

IRVINGTON (NHD), Lancaster County, is located off the Rappahannock River and bounded by Carter Creek on the west and Eastern Branch on the east. It was attacked three times by the British. The 92nd Virginia Regiment, under Lt. Col. John Chewning, Jr., repulsed the first British landing at Chewning Point on April 4, 1813.

The Alexandria *Gazette* reported on April 12, 1813: *The British landed at capt.* [Lt. Col. John] *Chowning's* [Chewning, Jr.], *robbed his plantation, took work oxen from the ploughs, pillaged the house, and broke open Mr. C's desk.*

On April 18 and April 22, 1814, the British again raided Carter Creek, causing heavy damage to private property including Corotoman.

The Baltimore *Patriot* reported on May 4, 1814: *On the 18th instant four British barges passed up the river to Carter's Creek, where they captured two schooners, one the "Felicity," belonging to that Creek and the other the "Antilope," Hughes, of Baltimore with 250 barrels of flour on board. They also took some sheep. It was Election and court day, of which they were supposed to be apprized, and they met no opposition.—On the 22d, . . . the same number of barges passed up to Carter's Creek, and took some negroes. They were fired at by five or six militia.*

For more information about the attack at Corotoman, visit the **CHRIST CHURCH** museum that includes information, artifacts, and a drawing of how the plantation might have appeared.

CHRIST CHURCH. NRHP. Address: southwest intersection of Christ Church (Route 646) and Gaskins roads, north of Irvington, Lancaster County. **Parking:** free. **Hours:** grounds: daylight hours; church and Carter Reception Center: April through November, Monday through Saturday, 10 a.m. to 4 p.m.; Sunday, 2 to 5 p.m. **Fees:** $5 per person suggested donation. **Facilities:** exhibits, 1812 war veteran graves, restrooms. **Contacts:** 804-438-6855; www.christchurch1735.org. **Comment:** excellent interpretation of Corotoman Plantation.

Corotoman Plantation (NRHP) was located at Orchard Point at the west entrance to Carter Creek. Only the foundation of the plantation house remains today, and the property is privately owned. The first Corotoman Plantation house, owned by Robert "King" Carter,

The Spinsters (Spinning) House at the Corotoman Plantation stood until the 1970s. It had been plundered by the British on April 4, 1814. (Photographer and date unknown; HABS, Library of Congress)

was completed in 1725 and burned in 1729. On April 22, 1814, the British landed and removed sixty-nine slaves from the adjoining plantations of Joseph C. Cabell and Charles Carter.

Fort Boykin

FORT BOYKIN, also called Fort at Rock Wharf, is located on the James River. As a consequence of the *Chesapeake–Leopard* affair in 1807, which heightened potential hostilities between England and America, the fort was strengthened into a five-pointed, star-shaped (local legion claims a seven-pointed star) earthwork with log palisade.

FORT BOYKIN HISTORIC PARK. NRHP. Address: 7410 Fort Boykin Trail (Route 705), Mogarts Beach, Smithfield, Isle of Wight County. **Parking:** free. **Hours:** 8 a.m. to dusk daily. **Fees:** none. **Facilities:** picnic. **Contacts:** 1-800-365-9339; www.virginia.org/site/description .asp?attrid=14449.

In 1623, this site was chosen by the early Jamestown colonists to be a point of defense. It was known as the Castle or Fort Warraskoyack, and was strategically located on a forty-five-foot height bounded on the north side by a deep natural ravine, on the south and west side by gentle slopes, and on the east by a steep bank of the James River where the channel runs close to the shore along a bend in the river. This strategic location made enemy ships vulnerable to the fort's cannon. It was refortified during the Revolution and renamed for Maj. Francis Boykin of the Continental Army. Francis Marshall Boykin II (1806–63), son of Lt. Col. Francis Marshall Boykin, a War of 1812 veteran and grandson of Maj. Francis Boykin, owned the property after the War of 1812. The land on which the fort is located was never public property until the site was donated to Virginia in the late 1970s.

This strategic spot was fortified yet again during the American Civil War by the Confederates. The 1812 fort included barracks, a powder magazine, a well, and six gun positions. The present configuration of the fort dates from the Civil War era, although the south exterior wall and possibly one gun emplacement wall may in part date from the War of 1812. Erosion along the river bank has destroyed some of the War of 1812–era earthworks. The fort is operated by the Isle of Wight Public Recreation Facilities Authority. A small interpretive shelter is located at the entrance to the fort.

The British ascended the James River in July 1813, raiding and plundering along the way. Just to the west of the fort at Rocks Plantation, also known as Edward Bennett's Plantation, on Burwell Bay, the British attempted a landing on July 2, 1813, but were driven off by militia under the command of Capt. David Dick and Capt. Charles Wrenn of the 29th Regiment. Rocks Landing development now occupies the Rocks Wharf area.

The Washington *Daily National Intelligencer* published on July 9, 1813: *3 barges from the frigate then laying off the mouth of Pagan Creek, full of men, went up the creek* [James River?] *as far as the rocks* [Fort Boykin], *(about three miles below Smithfield) they were fired upon by a small detachment of militia, (from 12 to 15) and after returning their fire for about ten minutes, decamped. None of our men were injured, though the balls flew around them like hail. An attack on Smithfield was hourly expected; they have, however, respectable force at that place. But even if they should succeed in getting possession of it, they will find nothing but bare walls, as every article of value is removed, and all the inhabitants, except those under arms, have left the town.*

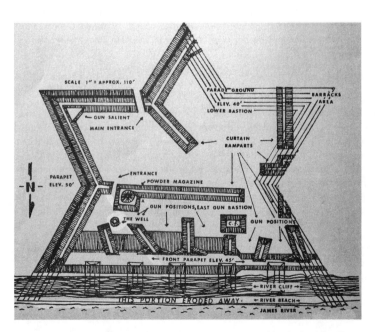

This sketch of Fort Boykin, based on conjecture, was prepared by the late Floyd Painter. (Courtesy of the artist)

New Point Comfort

NEW POINT COMFORT, located at the north confluence of Mobjack Bay with Chesapeake Bay, is the site of New Point Comfort Lighthouse, completed in 1804 and apparently used by the British as a lookout station during the war.

NEW POINT COMFORT NATURAL PRESERVE AREA. NRHP. **Location:** end of Lighthouse Road (Route 600), south off New Comfort Highway (Route 14), Matthews County. **Parking:** free. **Hours:** dusk to dawn daily. **Fees:** none. **Facilities:** boardwalk and interpretation panels, some of which deal with the War of 1812. **Contacts:** 434-295-6106; www.nature.org/wherewework/northamerica/states/virginia/preserves/art1237.html. **Comment:** boardwalk provides excellent water views of the area.

American privateers stood near New Point Comfort, waiting for severe weather to allow them to escape the British blockade at the mouth of Chesapeake Bay. The point also served as one of many watering places used by the British.

British Rear Adm. George Cockburn reported to Vice Adm. Alexander F. I. Cochrane on April 2, 1814: *I am in great Hope that we shall find enough* [water on islands in the Middle Chesapeake] *by digging a number of Wells, and if they should at any time fail us unexpectedly, our Watering place at New Point Comfort is so near as to make this a matter of less moment.*

British Capt. James Scott wrote of his memories of the area during the war published in 1834: *Wells were sunk near the light-house, and a plentiful supply obtained; we were only reminded of the enemy's presence by an occasional shot from his field-pieces, whenever he fancied a boat within reach of them.*

On March 17, 1814, a skirmish between about fifty British troops and Virginia militia took place near here.

The Richmond *Virginia Patriot* published an account of the incident on March 30, 1814: *near New Point Comfort . . . had the pleasure of seeing one of the handsomest skirmishes I ever witnessed . . . The fire commenced equally severe on both sides for about fifteen minutes, when the enemy was compelled to take shelter under the cover of some sand hills. At this moment a barge came to their assistance and commenced a fire from a 12 pound cannon, which was returned from a concealed six; which was continued with great warmth for a few minutes, when she had to make the best of her way to the beach, being in a sinking condition, having several shot through her . . . although . . . his* [Capt. Frederick Weedon] *horse shot down . . . we lost not a man.*

The British burned the lighthouse keeper's dwelling and oil vault, shattered the lantern glass, and removed the window frames and door from the tower.

This ends the tour of Other Tidewater Virginia Sites and the Virginia Tour.

Washington, D.C., Tour

Particulars Washington, D.C., is a major tourist destination with a full complement of restaurants and overnight accommodations. Roads are congested, street parking is difficult, and garages are an expensive alternative, so private vehicles are not the best option. Fortunately, Washington is easy to get around either by walking, biking, or using taxis or public transportation (both bus and metro [subway]). Guided War of 1812 tours by foot and vehicle are available by noted historian Tony Pitch (301-294-9514; info@dcsightseeing.com). Visitors may plan their tour to suit their own interests and time constraints, although both Capitol Hill and the White House/Lafayette Park are good starting points. (*See* appendix A *for approximate distances between sites.*)

Historical Background The 100-square-mile District of Columbia boasted 15,500 people in 1810, only 0.2 percent of the nation's total population. The City of Washington accounted for a little over half the district's total population. With only 8,200 people, it was still the fourteenth largest city in the nation. This small southern city was the center of federal activity during the war. Here the president recommended war preparations and war strategy, and here Congress adopted a war program and then passed the war bill. For the next thirty-two months, the president and his cabinet devised strategy and managed the war effort from Washington, while Congress met periodically to raise men and money and adopt other war-related legislation. The war began when the president signed the war bill into law in the White House on June 18, 1812. It officially ended when he ratified the Treaty of Ghent in the Octagon House (*see separate listing below*) on February 16, 1815.

Also located in the federal district were the Washington Navy Yard and the Greenleaf Point Federal Arsenal, where arms and ammunition were stored. There were several war industries in Washington as well, most notably the Columbian Foundry (then called Foxall's Foundry), which made shot and cannon, and three rope walks, which made rope for the standing and running rigging of the U.S. warships as well as for other war-related purposes.

The nation's capital suffered a terrible blow when the British occupied it in August 1814. The British burned most of the public buildings and destroyed the federal arsenal. American officials torched the Navy Yard and two warships under construction there and destroyed most of the bridges across the Potomac and Anacostia rivers. The British for unknown reasons missed the U.S. Marine barracks. It survived the occupation intact.

Begin your visit at the **WASHINGTON D.C. VISITOR INFORMATION CENTER.**

WASHINGTON D.C. VISITOR INFORMATION CENTER. Address: Ronald Reagan Building, 1300 Pennsylvania Avenue, N.W. **Parking:** garage parking, public transportation recommended. **Hours:** March 15 through Labor Day, Monday through Friday, 8:30 a.m. to 5:30 p.m., Saturday, 9 a.m. to 4 p.m.; day after Labor Day through March 14, Monday through Friday, 9 a.m. to 4:30 p.m., closed weekends. **Fees:** none. **Facilities:** brochures, maps, restrooms, food court.

View of Pennsylvania Avenue from the west terrace of the Capitol. The poplar trees that line the avenue were planted at the suggestion of Thomas Jefferson in 1803. Some sources claim this view dates from circa 1800, 1810, or 1813, but the image was actually executed circa 1828. (John Rubens Smith, "Washington Looking up Pennsylvania Avenue from the Terrace of the Capitol," in *A System of Universal Geography*. vol. 2, 1834)

West elevation of the U.S. Capitol as it appeared between 1811 and 1814. (Glenn Brown, *History of the United States Capitol,* vol. 1, *The Old Capitol—1792–1850,* 1900)

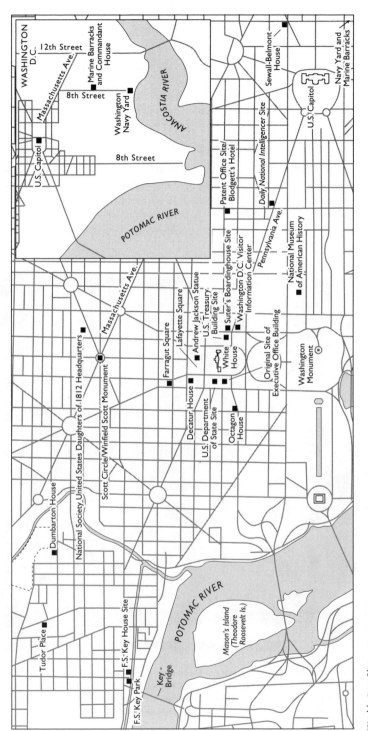

Washington City

Capitol Hill Area

The **U.S. CAPITOL** (NHD) was not complete in 1814. There was no central core with a dome, only a north wing containing the Senate chamber, the Supreme Court chamber, and various other offices, and the south wing containing the larger House chamber and accompanying offices. The wings were connected by a wooden causeway about a hundred yards long.

U.S. CAPITOL VISITOR CENTER. Location: intersection between Maryland and Pennsylvania avenues and Constitution and Independence avenues. **Parking:** parking garages, public transportation recommended. **Hours:** Monday through Saturday, 8:30 a.m. to 4:30 p.m. **Fees:** none. **Facilities:** exhibits, tours, restrooms, coat room, gift shop. **Contacts:** 202-226-8000; www.visitthecapitol.gov. **Comment:** tours fill quickly so I recommend that you arrive early.

On the ceiling of the ground floor east corridor of the House wing is a 1974 fresco by Allyn Cox entitled *British Burn the Capitol 1814*. On the left of the painting, Major General Ross confers with Rear Admiral Cockburn as British troops march by with the Capitol ablaze in the background. On the right, British soldiers tear off shutters from the Sewall-Belmont House to be used as fuel to set it ablaze. (Ralph Eshelman 2001 photograph)

Dr. William Thornton, an aide to Gen. George Washington, was the first architect of the Capitol. Thornton also designed Tudor Place and Octagon House (*see separate listings below*). The Capitol housed the three thousand-volume Library of Congress and the Supreme Court library. The Capitol building was burned by the British around 9 p.m., August 24, 1814. Separate fires were started in the House of Representatives Chamber, now known as Statuary Hall, South Wing, and the Old Senate Chamber or North Wing.

British Lt. George Robert Gleig published his remembrance in 1821: *Like other infant towns, it* [Washington] *is but little ornamented with fine buildings; for, except the Senate house* [U.S. Capitol], *I really know of none worthy to be noticed. This, however, is, or rather was, an edifice of great beauty. It stood, where its ruins now stand, upon a mound called the Capitol hill . . . from which circumstances, these modern republicans are led to flatter themselves, that the days are coming when it will rival in power and grandeur the senate-house of ancient Rome herself. It was built entirely of free-stone, tastefully worked and highly polished.*

Margaret Bayard Smith wrote: *50 men, sailors, and marines, were marched by an officer, silently thro' the avenue, each carrying long pole to which was fixed a ball about the circumference of a large plate,—when arrived at the building* [capitol], *each man was station'd at a window, with his pole and machine of wild-fire against it, at the word of command, at the same instant the windows were broken and this wild-fire thrown in, so that an instantaneous conflagration took place and the whole building was wrapt in flames and smoke. The spectators stood in awful silence, the city was light and the heavens redden'd with the blaze!*

Congreve rockets were fired into the ceiling of the House of Representatives, but they had little effect because the ceiling was covered in sheet iron. Hence, mahogany tables, chairs, desks, and curtains were piled in the middle of the room, rocket powder was heaped on the mound, and rockets fired into it, which set off the blaze. The same method was used to burn the Senate wing of the U.S. Capitol as well as the Treasury building and the President's House.

Benjamin Henry Latrobe wrote: *There was no want of materials for the conflagration, for when the number of members of Congress was increased the old platform was left in its place and another raised over it, giving an additional quantity of dry and loose timber. All the stages and seats of the galleries were of timber and yellow pine. The mahogany desks, table, and chairs were in their places . . . At last they made a great pile in the center of the room of the furniture and, retiring, set fire to a quantity of rocket stuff in the middle. The whole was soon in a blaze, and so intense was the flame that the glass of the lights was melted.*

The Boston *Weekly Messenger* published on September 16, 1814: *The Vandals* [British] *destroyed without remorse this collection of valuable and scarce books* [Library of Congress], *the loss of which is irreparable. If his incendiary hand were not to be arrested by the monument of art exhibited in the South Wing of the Capitol, it could not be expected the enemy would respect what none but Heathens or barbarians ever before wantonly destroyed, a Public Repository of History, Science, and Law.*

British Lt. George Robert Gleig published his memory of the event in 1847: *Unfortunately . . . a noble library, several printing-offices, and all the national archives were likewise committed to the flames, which, though no doubt the property of Government, might better have been spared.* [Actually much of the archives were saved (*see* Saving the Declaration of Independence Tour *in part 1*).]

The vestibule at the entrance to the old Supreme Court chamber in the Senate wing survived the burning.

The U.S. Capitol as it appeared after the British torching in August 1814. (1814 drawing by George Munger; Library of Congress)

Benjamin Henry Latrobe wrote to his wife, Mary Elizabeth Hazlehurst, soon after the burning of Washington: *the ruin of the Capitol, which, I assure you, is a melancholy spectacle . . . However, many important parts are wholly uninjured, and what particularly is gratifying to me, the picturesque entrance of the house of Representatives with its handsome columns, the Corn Capitals of the Senate Vestibule, the Great staircase, and all the Vaults of the Senate chambre, are entirely free from any injury which cannot be easily repaired.*

The only exterior visible wall dating from 1814 is the sandstone wall on the west side of the Senate wing. An exact replica of the original wall was built in 1959–60 when the Senate wing was enlarged on the east side. A plaque, designated to commemorate the original location of the Library of Congress, is placed near the entrance to suite S-230-236.

The British raised the flag of Great Britain on Capitol Hill and British troops bivouacked, just to the east of the U.S. Capitol, during the night of August 24, 1814. A temporary hospital for treating British wounded was also established here. In a room on the ground floor of the House Wing, where President Madison maintained a work space, Rear Adm. George Cockburn took a bound volume of James Madison's personal copy of the 1810 U.S. Government receipts and expenses, stamped on the cover "President of the U. States." Cockburn wrote on the inside cover, "Taken in President's room in the Capitol of Washington 24th. August 1814." The memento was returned by a rare book dealer in 1940. The Library of Congress was reestablished using Thomas Jefferson's personal library as its nucleus. In 1815, Congress paid Jefferson $23,950, which was considered about half the auction value.

Portraits of Louis XVI and Marie Antoinette were also reportedly taken, but the culprit is unknown.

In the U.S. Capitol Visitor Center, on the east side of the U.S. Capitol, there is an exhibition hall that contains numerous items related to the War of 1812. Among them is a model of Capitol Hill from 1789 to 1815 showing the appearance of the capitol building; a letter from Thomas Jefferson to Samuel Harrison Smith dated September 21, 1814, offering his library to replace the congressional library lost in the burning of the capitol; four original books belonging to Jefferson that he sold to the government to replace the library; a facsimile of the "Report of Destroyed House Records" dated September 15, 1814; a reproduction of Benjamin Henry Latrobe's design for corn cob columns; and Latrobe's plan for the rebuilding of the capitol.

Capitol Graffiti

Allegedly the following graffiti was found on the ruined U.S. Capitol walls after the fire, "George Washington founded this city after a seven years' war with England—James Madison lost it after a two years' war." "James Madison is a rascal, a coward and a fool." "Armstrong sold the city for 5,000 dollars." "The capital of the Union lost by cowardice."

The "corncob capitals" designed by Benjamin Henry Latrobe and carved by Giuseppe Franzoni in 1809 survived the fire and still stand in the east entry to the Senate Vestibule. (Library of Congress)

War of 1812–related items in the U.S. Capitol include statues of Maj. Gen. Andrew Jackson in the crypt area of the first floor and congressional War Hawk Henry Clay in Statuary Hall on the second floor. The Old Supreme Court Chamber is a good location to view the original walls of the U.S. Capitol. However, the ceiling in this chamber was replaced after the fire. In the hall just before the chamber entrance, the Senate Vestibule has six original columns depicting corn stalks and ears of corn at the top.

In the stairwell between the second and third floors of the Senate wing is a huge and impressive oil painting by William H. Powell, executed in 1865, entitled "Battle of Lake Erie." It depicts Com. Oliver Hazard Perry on September 10, 1813, transferring from the U.S. brig *Lawrence* to the U.S. brig *Niagara*. After his victory, Perry wrote a message to Maj. Gen. William Henry Harrison: "We have met the enemy and they are ours." Powell took some artistic license in his composition of the painting. Eyewitnesses claimed there were only four men who rowed the craft, not six as depicted by Powell. There would not have been any waves due to light winds on the day of the battle. It is also doubtful that Perry would have been standing or waving his sword. Perry did not take the "colors" as depicted flying on the bow of his craft, but he did take his battle flag which Powell does not show. The young boy pulling at Perry, urging him to sit down, is Perry's thirteen-year old brother Alexander. Alexander did not accompany Perry in the boat during this transfer. Local lore claims that the painting frame was made from the wood of the *Lawrence*, but this is not supported by any contemporary evidence.

When the U.S. Capitol was rebuilt, the copper for the new roof (which survived from the 1820s until about 1861) came from Levi Hollingsworth's Gunpowder Copper Works, located on the Great Gunpowder River near the Baltimore County/Harford County (Maryland) border. Hollingsworth was wounded in the Battle of North Point.

Only two blocks to the northeast of the Capitol is the **SEWALL-BELMONT HOUSE**, also called Alva Belmont House, built by Robert Sewall in 1800 on three city lots. Incorporating part of an earlier house, the current structure dates from 1820 and is one of the oldest buildings in Washington.

SEWALL-BELMONT HOUSE. NRHP. Address: 144 Constitution Ave., NE. **Parking:** parking garages, public transportation recommended. **Hours:** museum open Wednesday through Sunday, noon to 4 p.m. **Fees:** suggested donation $5 per person. **Facilities:** historic house tour, exhibits, museum shop. **Contacts:** 202-546-1210; www.sewallbelmont.org.

As the British marched down Maryland Avenue, some unidentified parties (possibly Chesapeake flotillamen) fired shots from the house and perhaps from Tomlinson's Hotel across the street (no longer standing). Maj. Gen. Robert Ross's horse was shot from under him, and some accounts also claim one British soldier was killed and three others wounded. The British retaliated by setting the house on fire. This was the only private residence deliberately burned by the British during the occupation. Three privately owned rope walks were burned, but these produced war materiel for the government. A rental house that was once owned by George Washington also burned, probably set afire by sparks from the nearby burning U.S. Capitol. A hotel belonging to Daniel Carroll was also apparently unintentionally destroyed. The shots fired from the Sewall-Belmont House were the only resistance offered against the British during their occupation of Washington. Robert Sewall's son William was living in the house at the time, but he had been called into service with the militia.

Slave Michael Shiner wrote in his diary: *Master left a colored man and me sleve with a olde lady by the name of Mrs. Ried on Capitol Hill and as sone as got sight of the British army raising that hill they looked like flames of fier all red coats and the staks of their guns painted with red vermelion and iron work shimered like a Spanish dollar . . . The British army still continued ther march on toward the Capitol ontill they got against a large brick house [Sewall-Belmont] on Capitol Hill fronting Maryland [Avenue] . . . This house now sets to the Northe east of the United States Senate and as the British army approach that house under the command of General [Robert] Ross and his aides, his horse wher shot from under him and in a twinkle of the eye the house wer sorounded by the British army and search all through upstairs an downstairs . . . but no man whar found . . . They put a globe match to the house and then stood oft a sertin distance . . . and those rockets burst until they came to the explosion part they made the rafters fly East and West.*

Sonia Ressman Fuenties wrote in 1819: *On the retreat of the American forces from Bladensburg, on the 24th August, 1814, a party of Commodore [Joshua] Barney's men [Chesapeake flotillamen], then a portion of that force, threw themselves into the house of the petitioner, and made an attack from said [Sewall-Belmont] house upon the advance party of the British army under the command of [Major] General [Robert] Ross; by which attack General Ross's horse was killed, one or two of his men also were killed, and several were wounded. This adventurous and heroic party were immediately overpowered by the British force; three of them were taken prisoners in the house, whilst the remainder made their escape by flight. The house of the petitioner* [Robert Sewall], *thus made a block-house of by this gallant little band, was instantly set on fire by order of General Ross, and destroyed with all its costly furniture. The house had been deserted by its inhabitants, the proprietor having several months before removed to his farm* [Poplar Hill on His Lordship's Kindness] *in Prince George's county* [Maryland] *for the summer; and his son, Mr. William Sewall, in whose care the house had been left by his father, was then employed in the militia, who had been called into service some time before, when the enemy threatened the adjacent country.*

Rear Adm. George Cockburn reported to Vice Adm. Alexander Cochrane on August 27, 1814: *Advancing a short way past the first Houses of the Town without being accompanied by the Troops, the Enemy opened upon us a heavy fire of Musquetry from the Capitol and two other houses* [one was the Sewall-Belmont House], *these were therefore almost immediately Stormed by our People, taken possession of, and set on fire, after which the Town submitted without further resistance.*

A plaque on the house claims "Commodore Joshua Barney and his men, from this house offered the only resistance." This text is misleading. Barney was wounded and left behind at Bladensburg and was not present during the British advance into Washington. However, it is believed that some if not all the resistance came from his flotillamen.

Albert Gallatin, the fourth secretary of the treasury, serving under Thomas Jefferson and James Madison from 1801 to 1814, leased the house, and from here financed the Louisiana Purchase in 1803. Ironically, at the time of the attack, Gallatin was in Ghent, present-day Belgium, serving as one of five American peace commissioners negotiating the end the war. Some believe the kitchen wing of the Sewall-Belmont House may have survived the fire. Blackened bricks around the front door were discovered during a 2002 renovation suggesting parts of the original walls also survive. Robert Sewall was justified in filing a claim for reimbursement for damages to his house and its contents because the British burned the building after it was used for military purposes. After years of legal maneuvering, the Senate Committee of Claims finally awarded compensation in 1847, some twenty-seven years after Sewall's death. The house now serves as the headquarters for the National Woman's Party.

White House and Lafayette Park Area

WHITE HOUSE. NHL. Address: 1600 Pennsylvania Avenue, NW. **Parking:** garage parking, public transportation recommended. **Hours:** see comment. **Fees:** none. **Contacts:** 202-456-7041; www.whitehouse.gov/history/tours. **Comment:** public tours of the White House are available for groups of ten or more people. Requests must be submitted through one's member of Congress and are accepted up to six months in advance. These self-guided tours are available from 7:30 a.m. to 11 a.m. Tuesday through Thursday, 7:30 a.m. to 12 p.m. Friday, and 7:30 a.m. to 1 p.m. Saturday (excluding federal holidays). Tours are scheduled on a first-come, first-served basis approximately two weeks in advance of the requested date.

The **WHITE HOUSE,** also known in 1814 as the President's Mansion, President's House, and Executive Mansion, was begun in 1792 and completed in 1802. It was first occupied by President John Adams in November 1800.

The British burned the mansion about 11 p.m., August 24, 1814, leaving it a roofless shell. The structure was rebuilt in 1815–17. Some scorch marks are still visible on the sandstone blocks forming the entrance arch of the original kitchen. That structure, immediately below the North Portico, facing Pennsylvania Avenue, was added in 1829–30. Scorch marks are also exposed on the wall behind the South Portico, added in 1824 at the level of the second floor on the Truman Balcony.

Dolley Madison wrote to her sister Lucy Payne Todd, in an 1836 after-the-fact recreation of an event that took place after 3 p.m., August 24, 1814: *Will you believe it my sister? We have a battle or skirmish near Bladensburg, and I am still here within sound of the cannon! M^r. [James] Madison comes not; may God protect us! Two messengers covered with dust, come to bid me to fly; but I wait for him.*

British Lt. George Robert Gleig published his remembrance of the event in 1821: *The President's house, . . . though likewise a public building, was remarkable for nothing, except the want of taste exhibited in its structure. It was small, incommodious, and plain; in no respect likely to excite the jealousy of a people peculiarly averse to all pomp or parade, even in their chief magistrate.*

According to British accounts, advance units that included Maj. Gen. Robert Ross and Rear Adm. George Cockburn, found a "victory dinner" for forty persons at the president's mansion during the night of August 24, 1814. Other accounts claim there was no prepared dinner, only such refreshment as was kept in readiness for messengers and officers returning from errands, etc. However, Paul Jennings, an African American who was a slave

The White House as it appeared after being burned by the British. (1814 engraving by William Strickland after drawing by George Munger; Library of Congress)

to President James Madison, said he set the table himself. It is more likely that a table was set as James and Dolley often entertained, but this was probably not a victory dinner. Ross, Cockburn, and nine other officers ate another meal that night at Barbara Suter's Boardinghouse, only a few hundred yards from the President's House. Ross and Cockburn may have eaten some food at the White House but they ate their main evening meal at Suter's. Other officers and possibly troops also may have helped themselves to the food from Madison's table.

> British Capt. James Scott published his remembrance in 1834: *Never was nectar more grateful to the palates of the gods than the crystal goblets of Madeira and water I quaffed off at Mr.* [James] *Madison's expense.*

Dolley Madison is credited with saving the portrait of George Washington attributed to Gilbert Stuart, but she had plenty of help. Paul Jennings claims that while Dolley carried off some silver, Jean Pierre Sioussat (doorkeeper) and Tom Magraw (gardener) took the painting down and sent it off by wagon with some large silver urns, red curtains, papers, and other valuables. Two New Yorkers, Jacob Barker and Robert G. L. De Peyster, either oversaw or helped break apart the gilt frame from the Washington portrait and personally removed the painting still on its stretcher. The painting was not cut out of its stretcher as many claim. Barker returned the painting a few weeks later. The White House has a three-piece silver tea set reportedly given by the Madisons to Jacob Barker for his assistance.

> Dolley Madison wrote to her sister Lucy Payne Todd in an 1836 after-the-fact recreation of an event that took place after 3 p.m., August 24, 1814: *I have ordered the frame to be broken, and the canvas taken out . . . the precious portrait placed in the hands of two gentlemen* [Jacob Barker and Robert G. L. De Peyster] *of New York for safe keeping. And now, dear sister, I must leave this house, or the retreating army will make me a prisoner in it, by filling up the road I am directed to take. When I shall again write to you, or where I shall be tomorrow, I cannot tell!!*

The Washington portrait, which hangs in the East Room, and a small wooden medicine chest in the Map Room are the only objects remaining in the mansion that were there before the conflagration. The medicine chest was returned by a Canadian named Archibald Kains claiming his grandfather, a paymaster on H.M. bomb-vessel *Devastation*, took it.

A "White Wash" Job?

The White House is made of tan-colored sandstone and, according to some accounts, "white washed" to hide scorch marks. However, white washing was a standard method of providing a protective coating, and the President's House was white washed as early as the fall of 1798, sixteen years before the British burning. As early as 1810, the term "White House" was in general use. Some accounts claim George Washington named the mansion after the white house where his wife, Martha Dandridge Custis, was living when he proposed. By the mid-nineteenth century, it became known as the Executive Mansion. In 1901, President Theodore Roosevelt signed an order officially naming the building the "White House." During exterior renovations, 1978–94, some thirty layers of paint and white wash were removed. The carved sill under one first-floor window on the north front, immediately west of the North Portico, has been left unpainted to show the original stone color. Thus while the house was no doubt painted white after being rebuilt in 1817, it was sometimes called the "White House" prior to the war.

The *Devastation,* not present during the capture of Washington, arrived at Alexandria several days after the British land forces had withdrawn from Washington. How Kains acquired the object and whether it is authentic are unknown.

Another account claims that Lt. Beau Colclough Urquhart of the 85th took President Madison's "fine dress sword." A Windsor writing armchair, referred to as the "Madison Chair" and used by the president between August 26 and 27, 1814, at the Caleb Bentley House in Brookeville (*see* First Family Flight Tour *in part 1*), Maryland, is in the White House collection. The executive branch operated briefly from this house immediately after the evacuation of Washington. Also in the collection is a miniature painting of Capt. Richard Shaw of the 4th King's Own Regiment of Foot as well as his regimental belt plate. Engraved on the painting frame are the words "Capt. R. Shaw Honored by Fireing the American Capital 1814." None of these objects is on view to the public. The following portraits, however, may be seen during public tours: James Madison (Blue Room), Dolley Madison (Red Room), James Monroe (Blue Room), William Henry Harrison (Green Room), Andrew Jackson (Green Room), and two sculptures of Henry Clay (statue on ground floor corridor and bust in Red Room).

The President's House doorkeeper (some accounts say Dolley Madison's steward), Jean Pierre Sioussat, known as French John, took the mansion's pet macaw to the Octagon House (*see below*) for safekeeping. A slave, Paul Jennings, later reported that "a rabble, taking advantage of the confusion, ran all over the White House, and stole lots of silver and whatever they could lay their hands on." A receipt in the National Archives, made out to an African American named Nace Rhodes, thanks him for the return of some of the house silver.

LAFAYETTE SQUARE, then known as "President's Square," is immediately north of the White House.

LAFAYETTE SQUARE. NHD. **Location:** bounded on north by H Street, east by Madison Place, south by Pennsylvania Avenue, and west by Jackson Place, just north of White House, NW. **Parking:** garage parking, public transportation recommended. **Contact:** www.nps.gov/history/nr/travel/wash/Dc30.htm.

The **MAJ. GEN. ANDREW JACKSON STATUE,** located in the center of Lafayette Square, is dedicated to U.S. President and War of 1812 hero Maj. Gen. Andrew Jackson, famous for his defeat of the British on January 8, 1815, at the Battle of New Orleans. The equestrian sculpture, dedicated on January 8, 1853, the 38th anniversary of Jackson's victory, depicts him doffing his cocked hat on a rearing horse. This was the first equestrian sculpture cast in the United States. Clark Mills designed the stature, which was cast from melted bronze taken from British cannons captured at the Battle of New Orleans. The four 870-pound cannons at the base of the statue were captured from the Spanish when the United States occupied Florida prior to the signing of the Adams–Onis Treaty in 1819. They are named El Egica, El Aristo, El Apolo, and Witza. Lafayette Square served as an American encampment during the War of 1812 and, for a brief time, as a British camp during their occupation of Washington.

Com. Stephen Decatur, a U.S. Navy War of 1812 hero, lived in the 1817 **DECATUR HOUSE,** the first private house built on the square.

DECATUR HOUSE. NRHP. **Address:** 1610 H Street, NW. **Parking:** garage parking, public transportation recommended. **Hours:** Monday through Saturday, 10 a.m. to 5 p.m., Sunday, noon to 4 p.m.; tours: Friday and Saturday, begin 10:15 a.m. and end 3:15 p.m.; Sunday, begin 12:15 and end 3:15 p.m. **Fees:** guided tours $5 adults, children 12 and under free. **Facilities:** exhibits, house tours, museum shop. **Contacts:** 202-842-0920; www.decaturhouse.org. **Comment:** self-guided tours not offered.

Decatur achieved fame as commander of the U.S. frigate *United States* when on October 25, 1812, he captured the H.M. frigate *Macedonian*. Decatur was later awarded $30,000 in prize money. This was the only British frigate brought to America as a prize of war (*see also* Macedonian Monument, U.S. Naval Academy, Annapolis Tour *in part 2*). With the *United States* blockaded in New London, Connecticut, Decatur took command of the U.S. frigate *President* at New York City in May 1814. He attempted to sail to the open sea but ran aground at Sandy Hook because of a piloting error. Although he freed his ship, Decatur, on January 15, 1815, was captured by three British frigates. Decatur died in a basement room of Decatur House from a wound received in a duel with Capt. James Barron at the Bladensburg Dueling Grounds (*see* Battle of Bladensburg Tour *in part 1*) on March 22, 1820.

In Decatur House is the sword that the Commonwealth of Virginia presented to Decatur in recognition of his capture of the H.M. frigate *Macedonian*. Benjamin Henry Latrobe designed Decatur House as well as the gate house and commandant's house (Tingey House) of the Washington Navy Yard. Latrobe also served as architect for the rebuilding of the U.S. Capitol after the British burning. Sheridan Circle, Massachusetts Avenue and 23rd Street, was originally named Decatur Circle in honor of Stephen Decatur but was changed to Sheridan Circle in 1890 when a statue to the Civil War hero was authorized and completed in 1909.

> ### "Our country, right or wrong"
>
> Tradition holds that in Norfolk on April 4, 1816, at a testimonial dinner held in his honor after his triumphant return from the Barbary States, Com. Stephen Decatur said, "Our Country! In her intercourse with foreign nations, may she always be in the right, but our country right or wrong." But, according to the Norfolk *American Beacon* on April 5, 1816, and the Norfolk *Gazette & Public Ledger* on April 6, 1816, Decatur said: "Our country! In her intercourse with foreign nations, may she always be in the right, and always successful, right or wrong." After dinner and numerous toasts, the guests sang a two-verse song written especially for the occasion to the tune of "To Anacreon in Heaven," the same melody used by Francis Scott Key for "The Star-Spangled Banner."

Southeast Washington Area

Benjamin Stoddert, the first secretary of the navy, authorized the **WASHINGTON NAVY YARD** in 1799. It is the U.S. Navy's oldest shore establishment.

WASHINGTON NAVY YARD. NHD. Address: between 6th and 11th streets and M and O streets, SE. **Parking:** no personal vehicles allowed on base except on weekends; pay parking available adjacent to base at 6th and M streets. **Facilities:** outdoor displays and museum. **Contacts:** 202-433-3738; www.history.navy.mil/about/navy_yard.html. **Comment:** there are three gates to the base. Visitors' gate is located at 11th and O streets. Click "Visit" on Web page for additional information about visitor access and parking.

The U.S. sloop-of-war *Wasp*, built at the Navy Yard, participated in one of the earliest naval engagements of the war. Under the command of Capt. Jacob Jones, *Wasp* captured H.M. brig *Frolic* on October 18, 1812, but on the same day *Wasp* was captured by H.M. ship-of-the-line *Poictiers*. The U.S. sloop *Scorpion* was rebuilt here and became the flagship of the Chesapeake Flotilla. The U.S. schooner *Lynx,* under construction, survived the 1814 burning

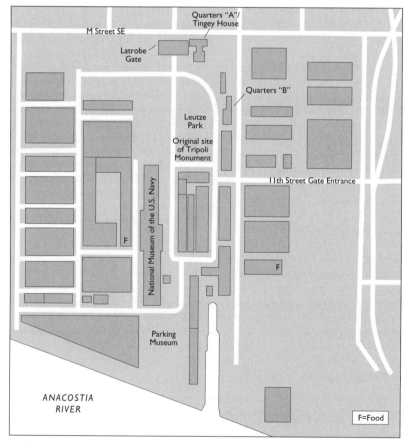

Washington Navy Yard

and later served in the Mediterranean. The U.S. frigate *Constellation* sat in ordinary (laid up in reserve) here prior to the war before being outfitted in early 1813 and then became blockaded on June 22, 1813, in the Elizabeth River, Virginia. Sailors from *Constellation* helped to protect Craney Island at the mouth of the Elizabeth River and thus helped save Norfolk, Portsmouth, the Gosport Navy Yard, and the *Constellation* from British capture.

The Washington Navy Yard served as the base for the defense of the Potomac River and the Potomac Flotilla. In the face of the British advance on August 23, 1814, Brig. Gen. William H. Winder and his troops withdrew from Long Old Fields (*see* British Invasion Tour *in part 1*) to the Eastern Branch Bridge near the Washington Navy Yard. Brigadier General Winder was conferring with President James Madison, Secretary of War John Armstrong, and other cabinet members at the nearby Griffith Coombe house (no longer extant) about 10 a.m. when a scout reported the British were marching for Bladensburg. President Madison, his cabinet, and Winder's troops rode to the Bladensburg battlefield (*see* Bladensburg Battlefield Tour *in part 1*). The nearby Eastern Branch Bridge and much of the Navy Yard were set on fire to keep them out of British hands by orders of Capt. Thomas Tingey at 8:20 p.m. on August 24, 1814.

The British arrived at the Navy Yard the next morning and burned almost everything remaining except the main gate and Quarters "A" and "B." The Tripoli Monument was "slightly injured," reportedly by British officers. The schooner *Lynx* was only slightly damaged. The machinery of the steam engine and boiler survived the fire. Gunpowder and part of the yard's provisions were recovered when a gunboat was retrieved from near Little Falls on the Potomac River. A second gunboat laden with provisions and gunpowder ran aground and was plundered by inhabitants near the Navy Yard.

Capt. Thomas Tingey reported to Secretary of Navy William Jones on August 27, 1814: *It appear'd that they* [British] *had left the Yard, about ½ an hour when we arrived. I found my dwelling house* [Quarters A] *and that of Lieutenant* [Nathaniel] *Haraden* [Quarters B] *untouched by fire—but some of the people of the neighborhood had commenc'd plundering them . . . Could I have stayed another hour, I had probably saved all my furniture and stores—but being advised by some friends that I was not safe . . . I therefore again embark'd in the gig . . . I had no sooner gone, than such a scene of devastation and plunder took place in the houses (by the people of the neighbourhood) as is disgraceful to relate—not a movable article from the cellars to the garrets has been left us—and even some of the fixtures, and locks of the doors, have been shamefully pillaged.*

Captain Thomas Tingey reported to Secretary of Navy William Jones on October 18, 1814: *The buildings destroyed, by the fire . . . were, the Mast-shed, and timber-shed, the joiners & boat-builders shops, and mould loft—all the Offices—the medical store—the plumbers and smiths shops, and block-makers shop—the saw-mill & block mill, with their whole apparatus, tools and machinery—the building for the steam engine, and all the combustible parts of it's machinery and materials; the rigging loft—the apartments for the master, and the boatswain of the yard, with all their furniture—the gun carriage makers and painters shops, with all the materials and tools therein at the time: also the hulls of the old frigates* Boston, New York *and* General Greene.

On September 4 and 5, 1814, a few days after the British land forces withdrew, fire-vessels were readied and launched from the Navy Yard against the British naval squadron that was descending the Potomac River with plunder from Alexandria. The fire-vessels, however, did no damage.

During construction work at the Washington Navy Yard in 1905, the graves of fourteen War of 1812 soldiers and sailors were uncovered. The bodies were interred in Arlington

Eagle and Anchor Rancor

A great eagle and anchor, carved by Giuseppe Franzoni, once stood atop the Latrobe gate, but they were removed when the additions were built. The eagle and anchor, designed by Benjamin Henry Latrobe, were ridiculed by Dr. William Thornton, first architect of the U.S. Capitol. His comments were published in the Washington *Federalist* on April 26, 1808:

such an arch as the inferior one was never made to a Gateway before, and till the extinction of taste will never be made again . . . The eagle, which crowns it, is so disproportionate to the Anchor, that we are reminded of the Rook in the Arabian Nights Entertainments; but on reviewing it the Eagle looks only like a good fat Goose, and the Anchor fitter for a cock-boat than even a gunboat.—If the American hope rested on such an anchor she would soon breathe her exit in a sigh of despair!

Latrobe was so outraged by Thornton's comments that he retained Francis Scott Key as counsel and sued Thornton for libel. After many delays, the case was adjudicated in June 1813, awarding Latrobe one cent in damages and court costs.

National Cemetery. A memorial was dedicated to them by the National Society United States Daughters War of 1812 in April 1976.

The 1806 main gate and flanking guard houses, designed by Benjamin Henry Latrobe and thus known as the **LATROBE GATE** (NRHP), located at 8th and M streets, represent one of the earliest examples of Greek Revival architecture in the United States. The gate is one of the few structures to have survived the 1814 fire. The second-story and Victorian-style guard houses were added between 1880 and 1881, greatly altering and largely hiding the original structure. The Latrobe Gate is the oldest continuously manned U.S. Marine sentry post in the nation.

There is no public access to the 1804 **QUARTERS "A,"** better known as **TINGEY HOUSE** (NRHP). It was occupied by and named for Capt. Thomas Tingey, the first commandant of the Washington Navy Yard, who ordered the yard burned to keep it out of the hands of the British. Tingey House survived the fire. Tingey's 1808 rules for the operation of the Washington Navy Yard were adopted for all American naval stations on the Atlantic Coast. Tingey is buried at Congressional Cemetery, Washington, D.C.

There is no public access to **QUARTERS "B"** (NRHP) located on the northeast side of Leutze Park and built in 1801 as the Navy Yard's second officer's residence. It was occupied by Lt. Nathaniel Haradan during the war. Like Quarters "A," it escaped burning by the British. Subsequent additions and alterations, which have doubled the size of the building, have enclosed the original structure so that little of it is visible today.

TRIPOLI MONUMENT SITE, originally called the Naval Monument, was located at Leutze Park. It was erected by the officers of the U.S. Navy in 1808 to eulogize six American naval officers who fell during the War with Tripoli in 1804. The monument, Washington's first outdoor monument, was reportedly vandalized by British officers during the morning of August 25, 1814. It was moved to the west front terrace of the U.S. Capitol in 1831. In 1960, the monument was moved a second time to the grounds of the U.S. Naval Academy in Annapolis (*see* Annapolis Tour *in part 2 for more details*).

NATIONAL MUSEUM OF THE U.S. NAVY, housed in a six-hundred-foot-long structure that accommodated the Breech Mechanism Shop of the old Naval Gun Factory, contains paintings, artifacts, and interpretive exhibits on the War of 1812.

NATIONAL MUSEUM OF THE U.S. NAVY. Address: 805 Kidder Breese Street, SE; Building No. 76. **Parking:** free, personal vehicles allowed on base only on weekends; pay parking available outside gate at 6th and M streets. **Hours:** Monday through Friday, 9 a.m. to 5 p.m., and weekends, 10 a.m. to 5 p.m. **Fees:** none. **Facilities:** exhibits, museum store, restrooms, picnic tables and eating facilities nearby. **Contacts:** 202-433-4882; www.history.navy.mil/branches/org8-1.htm.

Artifacts include the sword that Midshipman David Glasgow Farragut had onboard the U.S. frigate *Essex* in 1813, a powder horn inscribed "Ship Constellation—44" (number of guns) and dated 1813, a 12 pounder howitzer cannonball recovered from the Battle of Bladensburg, and a presentation dirk given to Lt. William H. Allen of U.S. frigate *Chesapeake* after he was captured by H.M. frigate *Leopard*. It is inscribed "Given to Lieutenant William H. Allan as a token of esteem for his courage & endurance in the action on June 22nd 1807 by the officers of U.S. frigate Chesapeake."

The **U.S. MARINE BARRACKS AND COMMANDANT HOUSE** is located near, but not at, the Washington Navy Yard. Many confuse the Commandant House of the U.S. Marine Barracks with the Tingey House, which is the Commandant's House at the Navy Yard.

U.S. MARINE BARRACKS AND COMMANDANT HOUSE. NHD. Address: 8th and I streets, SE. **Parking:** limited street parking. **Facilities:** tours available Wednesday at 10 a.m. or by appointment. **Contacts:** 202-433-4173; www.mbw.usmc.mil. **Comment:** the exterior of the Commandant House, located on the north side of the barracks quadrangle, can be viewed without entrance into the barracks, which is restricted to military personnel only. However, the public can gain access to the barracks quadrangle during Friday evening summer concerts and parades. For details contact: 202-433-4073; www.mbw.usmc.mil/parades.asp.

The U.S. Marine Corps Commandant House, built in 1806, is probably the oldest public building in continuous use in the nation's capital. It has served as the official residence of eighteen of the twenty commandants who have headed the U.S. Marine Corps. The house was considerably enlarged in 1836 from its original two-story hipped roof design. No one knows why the British did not burn the house during their occupation of Washington. One theory holds that the British used it for their headquarters. Another suggests that Maj. Gen. Robert Ross was so impressed by the stand that the U.S. Marines made at Bladensburg, he ordered the house and barracks untouched as a gesture of soldierly respect. The most logical explanation is that either the British just missed it or the residents of the neighborhood pleaded with the British, pointing out that burning the barracks and house would almost certainly cause damage to adjoining private property. This same argument apparently saved the offices of the *Daily National Intelligencer* and the U.S. Patent Office. Several houses were accidentally set ablaze by sparks from the British burning of the U.S. Capitol and the American and British burning of the Washington Navy Yard.

Captain's Clerk Mordecai Booth wrote to Capt. Thomas Tingey on August 24, 1814: *The British Army were momentarily expected—and as I mounted my horse, was told that the whistling of the balls, had been distinctly heard at the* [U.S.] *Marine Barracks; Which you heard, as well as myself.*

Other Washington Sites

National Museum of American History

The Star-Spangled Banner garrison flag, which flew over Fort McHenry on September 14, 1814, is exhibited in a special gallery at the Smithsonian Institution's **NATIONAL MUSEUM OF AMERICAN HISTORY**. Originally 32 by 40 feet, the flag is significantly shorter because Lt. Col. George Armistead's family gave fabric square samples from the flag to visitors as mementoes. A star from the flag is also missing, but no one knows who received it. A white V-shaped piece of material stitched over the stripes is thought to be part of an "A" for Armistead. Also in this gallery is a British bombshell of the type used during the bombardment of Fort McHenry, a punch bowl in the shape of a thirteen-inch British mortar presented to Lieutenant Colonel Armistead in 1816 by the citizens of Baltimore, and a charred timber from the White House believed to be a result of the August 24, 1814, burning by the British.

NATIONAL MUSEUM OF AMERICAN HISTORY. Address: National Mall at Constitution Avenue and 14th Street, NW. **Parking:** garage parking, public transportation recommended. **Hours:** normal hours are 10 a.m. to 5:30 p.m. daily, but during summer generally open until 7:30 p.m. **Fees:** none. **Facilities:** exhibits, restrooms, cloak room, food, museum shop. **Contacts:** 202-633-1000; www.americanhistory.si.edu.

A Congreve rocket, named after its inventor, William Congreve (1772–1828), is also on exhibit. The rockets were a new and frightening but generally inaccurate weapon of war. At least one of the rockets was presented to the Smithsonian Institution by a delegation of British military officers on March 31, 1967. At the time, Maj. Gen. P. G. Glover, director of Great Britain's Royal Artillery Institution, said: "Now that a century and a half have elapsed, I am sure that the rockets' red glare of your National Anthem refers to Congreve rockets used in the bombardment viewed by Francis Scott Key." A Congreve rocket is also on display at Fort McHenry (*see* Baltimore Tour *in part 2*). Other War of 1812 exhibits can be found in the military and maritime transportation galleries.

Octagon House

The Treaty of Ghent ending the war was signed in the **OCTAGON HOUSE**.

OCTAGON HOUSE. NHL. Address: 1799 New York Avenue, NW. **Parking:** parking garages, public transportation recommended. **Hours:** Monday through Friday, 8 a.m. to 5 p.m. **Fees:** none. **Facilities:** historic house, museum shop, restrooms. **Contacts:** 202-638-3221; www. nps.gov/history/Nr/travel/wash/dc22.htm.

Col. John Tayloe III of Mt. Airy Plantation, Richmond County, Virginia, said to be the wealthiest plantation owner in Virginia at the time, built Octagon House in 1801 as his

The Treaty of Ghent officially ending the war was ratified by President Madison at Octagon House on February 16, 1815, when he signed it on the drum table located in the second-story Round Room also known as the Treaty Room. The table and a dispatch-box in which the treaty arrived are exhibited here. (Jack Boucher 1971 photograph; HABS, Library of Congress)

winter city house. During the British occupation of Washington, Tayloe asked the French Minister Louis Serurier and his wife to occupy the house to spare it from possible looting and burning. A makeshift Bourbon flag flew over the house, signifying that Octagon House was under the French King's protection. Serurier sent a letter to Maj. Gen. Robert Ross, who was then overseeing the burning of the President's House, asking that a guard be placed at his residence for protection. Ross wrote back that the French King's house would be as respected as if His Majesty were there in person. White House doorkeeper or steward Jean Pierre Sioussat, known as French John, took the mansion's pet macaw to Octagon House for safekeeping. A month later, Serurier offered his house to President Madison who occupied it for six months after the President's House had burned. The President's cabinet members met here on several occasions.

Tayloe's son, John Tayloe IV, serving as a midshipman on board U.S. frigate *Constitution* on August 19, 1812, died of wounds he received during the battle against H.M. frigate *Guerriere.*

Following the signing of the Treaty of Ghent, one of the biggest of many social events at the Octagon House took place. Drinks were ordered for all the servants. French John, the White House doorkeeper, was said to be drunk for two days.

Drum Table

During the San Francisco, California, earthquake of 1906, a woman who had bought the drum table on which was signed the Treaty of Ghent was concerned that it might be consumed in the fire started by the quake. She reportedly chopped off the table legs, wrapped it in a blanket, and rolled it to safety (although the flames, ironically, never reached her home). After the American Institute of Architects acquired the Octagon House in 1902, she supposedly returned the table to the house. However, no documentation of this story has been uncovered, and until such proof emerges, it must be considered a folktale.

Joseph Gales, Jr., publisher of the Washington *Daily National Intelligencer,* wrote sometime after the event: *Soon after nightfall, Members of Congress and others . . . presented themselves at the President's* [Octagon] *house, the doors of which stood open. When the writer entered the drawing room . . . it was crowded to its full capacity, Mrs.* [Dolley] *Madison (the President being with the Cabinet) doing the honours of the occasion . . . Among the members present were gentlemen of opposite politics, but lately arrayed against one another in continual conflict and fierce debate, now with elated sprits thanking God, and with softened hearts cordially felicitating with one another upon the joyful intelligence . . . But the most conspicuous object in the room was Mrs. Madison herself, then in the meridian of life and queenly beauty.*

Farragut Square

This square is named after Adm. David Glasgow Farragut who fought as a midshipman onboard the U.S. frigate *Essex* during the War of 1812.

FARRAGUT SQUARE. Address: 1634 I Street, near intersection with 17th Street, NW. **Parking:** garage parking, public transportation recommended. **Hours:** daylight hours. **Fees:** none. **Facilities:** none.

U.S. frigate *Essex* sailed into the Pacific during the war to harass British whaling ships while protecting American whalers. The *Essex* was captured by two British warships on March 28, 1814, near Valparaiso, Chile. Farragut later criticized Capt. David Porter, Jr., for surrendering to the British. Farragut's sword, which he had onboard the *Essex,* is on display at the National Museum of the U.S. Navy, Washington Navy Yard (*see above*). The Farragut Monument, in the square, commemorates Farragut's Civil War exploits and includes mortars cast from the propellor of the U.S. sloop-of-war *Hartford,* on whose deck in 1864 he reportedly uttered the famous words "Damn the torpedoes, full speed ahead." The monument, sculpted by Vinnie Ream, was dedicated on April 25, 1881. A box with documents relating to Farragut's career is in the granite base of the monument.

Francis Scott Key Park

Francis Scott Key Park, Star-Spangled Banner Memorial is located near the site of the now-demolished circa 1803 house that was Francis Scott Key's home along with an adjacent one-story law office.

FRANCIS SCOTT KEY PARK, STAR-SPANGLED BANNER MEMORIAL. Location: 34th and M streets, NW. **Parking:** limited street parking, public transportation recommended. **Facilities:** interpretative panels. **Comment:** traffic is usually very congested.

This small park, featuring interpretive plaques about Francis Scott Key, was dedicated on September 14, 1993. The Francis Scott Key House, also called Key Mansion, was located near 3516–3518 M Street west of the park. Key occupied the house and adjacent one-story law office from 1805 to 1828. Key served from June 19, 1814, to July 1, 1814, as a lieutenant and quartermaster in the Georgetown Light Artillery. Key and his wife, Mary Tayloe Lloyd Key, watched the conflagration of Washington from their home the night after he had served as an aide to Brig. Gen. Walter Smith of the D.C. militia during the Battle of Bladensburg. It was here that Richard E. West, Mary's brother-in-law, came to seek Key's assistance in freeing Dr. William Beanes, who on August 26, 1814, had been seized by the British in Upper Marlboro, Maryland. As a result, Key found himself with the British fleet during the bombardment of Fort McHenry (*see* Upper Marlboro, *and the* Story of "The Star-Spangled

Over the years, the Key House (now demolished) has been used for many purposes: a flag factory, an ice cream parlor, and an awning shop. As shown here, it was simply a tourist attraction. (Circa 1896 photograph; HABS, Library of Congress)

Banner" *sidebar in* British Invasion Tour *in part 1*). This inspired him to write the lyrics that eventually were titled "The Star-Spangled Banner," which became the national anthem in 1931. Key moved to the Maples House, now known as the Friendship House Settlement, at 619 D Street SE, when construction of the Chesapeake and Ohio Canal cut across the back of his property and disturbed his privacy. A subsequent owner removed the gabled roof and added a store front on the first floor. In 1948, the M Street house was demolished in order to connect Whitehurst Freeway with Key Bridge.

Under the leadership of Francis Scott Key-Smith, a direct descendant of F. S. Key, the Francis Scott Key Memorial Association sought to buy the Key House in 1908 but lacked the funds. In 1931, the District of Columbia Historical Society spearheaded a second attempt to buy the building, but this attempt also failed. Mr. Key-Smith noted that most of the original building had been destroyed in late 1912 and early 1913, leaving only the south wall and a portion of the original east wall intact. The house was acquired by the National Park Service, but because of the Great Depression, no funds were authorized to restore it. In 1947, Congress authorized $75,000 for the construction of a replica Key House. Bricks and lumber from the post-Key structure were numbered and stored around the city, some under Key Bridge. But the money was never authorized because President Harry S. Truman pocket-vetoed the bill. Much of the building material was either lost or stolen. This prompted the jibe that "anyone can lose a house key but only Uncle Sam could lose Key's house." A rafter end from the house is exhibited at the Flag House and Star-Spangled Banner Museum (*see under* Baltimore Tour *in part 2*).

Winfield Scott Monument

The **WINFIELD SCOTT MONUMENT,** sculpted by Henry Kirke Brown, was dedicated in 1874.

WINFIELD SCOTT MONUMENT. Address: Scott Circle, intersection of Rhode Island and Massachusetts avenues, NW. **Parking:** parking garages, public transportation recommended. **Facilities:** none.

Although best remembered for his contributions during the Mexican War and Civil War, Gen. Winfield Scott (1786-1866) attained the rank of major general in 1815 as a result of his leadership and heroism during the War of 1812. The bronze statue depicts Scott upon a stallion with a mare's body. Scott preferred to ride mares, but his family objected to him on a mare, so the artist modified the appearance of the horse. The sculpture was cast in bronze from Mexican War cannon captured by Scott.

Tudor Place

TUDOR PLACE was constructed between 1794 and 1816 by Thomas Peter and his wife, Martha Custis Peter, granddaughter of Martha Washington, on the crest of Georgetown Heights. Dr. William Thornton, first architect of the U.S. Capitol and Octagon House, designed the house in the neoclassical style. During the war, interesting letters were penned by Mrs. Peter.

TUDOR PLACE. NRHP. **Address:** 1644 31st Street, NW. **Parking:** street parking. **Hours:** Tuesday through Saturday, 10 a.m. to 4 p.m.; Sunday, noon to 4 p.m. **Fees:** house tours $8 adults, $6 military and seniors 61 and older, $3 students aged 7 to 18, children 6 and under free; self-guided tours of gardens $3 per person. **Facilities:** guided house tours; self-guided garden tours, gift shop. **Contacts:** 202-965-0400; www.tudorplace.org.

Martha Custis Peter wrote to Mrs. Josiah Quincy on July 13, 1813: *We are all on the alert here to give the British a warm reception. An express arrived on Thursday last, saying they were in the river; and, as the wind was fair, we expected every moment to see their white sheets shivering in the breeze. The drums began to beat, the military to parade; and in a moment all was bustle and alarm. Before night, scarcely a man was to be seen in the streets: they were all posted at Fort Warburton* [Washington] *... The Secretaries of War and of the Navy joined the van; and each new-made officer vied with the other who should put on most finery; expecting, no doubt, by their dazzling appearance, to strike the enemy with dismay.*

Anna Marie Brodeau Thornton wrote on August 24, 1814: *We stayed all night at Mrs.* [Martha Custis] *Peter's and there witnessed the conflagration of our poor undefended and devoted city.*

Martha Custis Peter wrote again to Mrs. Josiah Quincy on August 26, 1814, two days after the burning of Washington: *For some weeks the citizens have expected a visit from the British, and repeatedly called upon the Secretary of the War Department and the President for protection. The first laughed at what he called their idle fears. The President said he was*

From Tudor Place during the evening of August 24, 1814, Mrs. Martha Peter, Dr. William Thornton, and his wife, Anna Marie Brodeau Thornton, watched the capital burn. (Unknown Photographer 1962; HABS, Library of Congress)

called on from all quarters for protection; that he could not protect everyone; and the District must take care of itself . . . About three days before the British came, Armstrong acknowledged that he now believed they would be here. The Cabinet then began to make great exertions, and assured the citizens that they would have so large a force, that it would be impossible for the British to penetrate through them. Knowing our Treasury to be much in want of money, the several banks in the District loaned the Cabinet two hundred thousand dollars for their defense. On Friday last, the troops were all ordered to march, as the enemy were landing, in considerable numbers, forty-five miles from Washington. Unfortunately, we never shut the stable-door till the steed is stolen . . . Two cannon were placed opposite the Capitol, two at the offices, and two at the President's house . . . On Wednesday, our troops received information that the enemy were at Bladensburg; and formed themselves in battle array on the ground between the city and that place. From what I can learn, nothing was ever worse ordered. For an hour before the engagement took place, the General was not to be found. The President was on the ground, who, no doubt, had some little curiosity to see what sort of beings those were who dared to approach his Capitol, but I believe he was soon satisfied, as he fled so swiftly, that he has never been heard of since. The whole Cabinet are off, no one knows where. The citizens vow they will hang Armstrong on the walls of the Capitol when he returns.

(*See* First Family Flight Tour *in part 1 for* Dumbarton House, *where Dolley Madison first fled from the White House when the British threatened Washington.*)

This ends the District of Columbia Tour.

ACKNOWLEDGMENTS

This travel guide is an outgrowth of the book I co-authored with Scott Sheads and Donald Hickey entitled *The War of 1812 in the Chesapeake: A Reference Guide to Historic Sites in Maryland, Virginia, and the District of Columbia*. First and foremost I acknowledge the research, opinions, and assistance these colleague have given me in the course of gathering the information in the reference guide, much of which is used in this travel guide. Numerous scholars, archivists, curators, librarians, and local experts have aided in the preparation of this guide, which profited from their knowledge. To all these people a heartfelt thanks.

Christopher George, Ross Kimmel, Larry Leone, Robert Reyes, and Edward Seufert freely shared their knowledge of the Battle of North Point and Carole Herrick her knowledge of the First Family flight and saving the Declaration of Independence and other federal documents. Without their assistance, these tours would have been significantly poorer. The following individuals also deserve special thanks: Gloria Allen, William Allman, Stewart Barroll, Mary Baumann, Paul Berry, Steve Bilicke, Jeff Bossart, Betty Bowen, the late Ronald Bozarth, Nancy Bramucci, Richard Brunkhorst, Stuart Butler, Robert Campbell, Ginger Carter, Ed Chaney, Bill Clark, Wayne Clark, Ann Collins, Gary Collins, Kathy Concannon, Alice Cook, Jane Cox, Don Creveling, R. Thomas Crew, Jr., Ed Day, the late Jon Dean, Mike Dixon, William Dudley, Jim Dunbar, Van Dyke, Jeff Enright, Erich Eshelman, Evelyne Eshelman, Betsy Feiler, John Feiler, William Foote, Ben Ford, Tom Fowler, Laura Galke, Tanya Gossett, Fred Grady, Chris Grazzini, Linda Green, Mary Kay Harper, William Hazel, Keith Heinrich, Fred Hopkins, Dave Howell, Mike Hughes, Maureen Kavanagh, Julia King, Jeffery Korman, Greg R. Krueger, Frank Kubalis, Burt Kummerow, Nancy Kurtz, Peter Kurtz, Susan Langley, Gareth McNair-Lewis, Kathy Lee Erlandson Liston, Rodney Little, James Loewen, David Lowe, Darrin Lowery, Rufus S. Lusk III, Tom Marsh, Phil Michel, H. Bryan Mitchell, Barbara Stewart Mogle, Russell Mogel, Vanessa Moineauz, Janie Morgan, Kent Mountford, Terry Nicholson, Rynell Novak, Patrick O'Neill, Apryl Parcher, Ken Parcher, Susan Pearl, William Pencek, Dwayne Pickett, Anthony Pitch, Jennifer Pollack, John Pousson, the late Stanley Quick, Jessica Reed, Susan Reidy, Linda Reno, Orlando Ridout, Franklin Robinson, Joanne Roland, Robin Roland, Ron Roller, Marci Ross, Warren Rowley, Mary Louise de Sarran, Wayne Schaumburg, Gary Scott, Betty Seifert, Donald Shomette, Debora Silvertson, Hugh Smith, Michael Smolek, James Stein, the late Stephen Strach, Edwin Swann, Peter Tattle, Richard Thomas, Bruce Thompson, Frank Thorton, Mrs. Carmichael Tilghman, Chris Van de Velde, Richard Van Stolk, Louise Velletri, Anna von Lunz, Elaine Ward, Donna Ware, Jenna Watts, John Weiss, Joseph Whitehorne, George Williams, Glenn Williams, James Wood, and Francis Zumbrum.

Anyone who has updated information, corrections, or comments may contact me through the Johns Hopkins University Press.

APPENDIXES

Appendix A

Suggested Walks

Some people don't blink at walking (or hiking) several miles, while others prefer to walk as little as possible. The walks suggested in this appendix are generally intended to be leisurely family strolls, although a few of the routes are more strenuous and geared to the enthusiastic walker (for example, following the British route out of Benedict uphill over three miles to their first encampment site). Even the one mile uphill walk from the American first line, past the second line, to the third line at Bladensburg can be taxing for some. Pick and choose from the following suggestions based on your interest and walking tolerance. A few of these walks are on road shoulders. Always face oncoming traffic and be alert.

MARYLAND

Annapolis (Anne Arundel County): Brick Sidewalks and Plebes

Level of Difficulty: Easy (mostly flat with slight hill from waterfront to the Statehouse). Annapolis is an easy town to walk around, most tourist do. From the visitor center on West Street (there is also one near the harbor area) it is only 0.2 mile south to the Maryland Statehouse and another 0.3 mile east to the Naval Academy via Gate 3. To make a circuit walk, explore the academy and exit Gate 1 (to the south), walk to the waterfront, take a boat ride, get a bite to eat or just watch the people. Depending on how much you explore, the circuit walk is about 1.6 miles plus any deviations. Remember to have your photo ID for entrance to the academy. *See* Annapolis Tour *in part 2 for map and details.*

Baltimore City: Walk It and Boat It

Level of Difficulty: Easy to Moderate (Moderate for those going to Federal Hill due to the many steps. These can be avoided by going to the south side of the park although it is still a walk uphill). From the Inner Harbor Visitor Center, it is 0.5 mile south to Federal Hill for an excellent view of the Inner Harbor and city. Also from the visitor center, it is 0.6 mile north and then east mostly along the Inner Harbor to the Flag House and Star-Spangled Banner Museum. Battle Monument is 0.6 mile north of the visitor center. Hiking enthusiasts can adapt the bike routes to Patterson Park, Francis Scott Key Monument, the Wells and McComas Monument, First Presbyterian Church Burying Ground, and Fort McHenry as walks. Remember that water taxis, with connections to Fells Point and Fort McHenry, can be used to complement your walk. *See* Baltimore Tour *in part 2 for map and details.*

Benedict (Charles County): August Exhaustion Hike

Level of Difficulty: Strenuous. Follow the British invasion route from their first encampment at Benedict to what is known as Patuxent City today. Park at the Indian Creek Hunting Area lot on the south side of Route 231 about 0.5 mile north of Benedict. This is approximately where the British encampment was located August 19 and 20, 1814. Follow Route 231 west approximately 3.5 miles. Pick a summer day (around August 20 is perfect), and imagine being part of an over-4,000-man-strong army invading the United States. Be sure to peer back down the hill to get views of the Patuxent River valley. Use caution as the road shoulders are narrow. Unfortunately there is no interpretation currently posted along this route. Unless you have a second vehicle that can be dropped off at Patuxent City you will need to backtrack to the Indian Creek Hunting Area, a total distance of 7 miles. *See* British Invasion Tour *in part 1 for map and details.*

Bladensburg (Prince George's County): Battlefield Walk

Level of Difficulty: Moderate. Follow the British attack across the Anacostia River, past the first, then the second, and finally the third American line. Stroll around Bladensburg and see the few remaining vestiges of the war. Park at Bladensburg Waterfront Park. It is approximately 0.3 mile across the pedestrian bridge to the American first line, another 0.2 mile to the mill site, another 0.5 to the dueling ground/American second line, another 0.2 mile to the Fort Lincoln Cemetery entrance, another 0.5 mile to the Barney Monument near the Mausoleum, and another 0.2 mile from the cemetery entrance to the Barney battery site on Bladensburg Road at the District of Columbia line. This walk is about 2.5 miles one way. Another option (or add on) is to walk east 0.5 mile from Bladensburg Waterfront Park past the historic Margruder House and Ross House site to the Bostwick House. *See* Bladensburg Battlefield Tour *in part 1 for map and details.*

Frederick (Frederick County): Wartime Refuge

Level of Difficulty: Easy. Frederick served as a refuge for many of the federal cabinet members during the British occupation of Washington. Its pleasant downtown district is filled with historic buildings, shops, museums, and eateries. Begin your tour at the Frederick Visitor Center at 19 East Church Street. The Hessian Barracks are 0.5 mile south of the visitor center and the Francis Scott Key Monument an additional 0.2 mile south of the barracks. *See* Frederick Tour *in part 2 for map and details.*

Havre de Grace (Harford County): Town of Devastation

Level of Difficulty: Easy to Moderate (Moderate for those who choose to go up Angle Hill). The 0.5 mile-long promenade in Millard E. Tydings Memorial Park at Concord Point is a good place to stretch your legs. From Concord Point, it is 0.4 mile north to the east end of Fountain and Bourbon streets, the site of the Potato Battery. Due to land fill and development there are no vestiges of this battery site or any interpretation. It is another 0.2 mile west then north to St. John's Episcopal Church at the intersection of Union and Congress avenues. It is another 0.1 north to the Aveilhe-Goldsborough House at 300 North Union. Both the church and house are among the few structures to survive the British burning of the town. The Rodgers House, set on fire three times, also miraculously survived the flames. It is located a block east of the Aveilhe-Goldsborough House at 226 North Washington Street. The adventurous may want to walk the additional 0.9 mile west and north to Angle Hill Cemetery at the northwest corner of Chapel and Ohio streets. Here war hero John O'Neill is buried near the crest of the hill in the southern portion of the cemetery. *See* Havre de Grace *in part 2* Head of the Chesapeake Tour *for map and details.*

St. Michaels (Talbot County): History and Charm

Level of Difficulty: Easy. St. Michaels is a wonderful town to walk about. A good place to begin your tour is at the St. Michaels Museum at St. Mary's Square (fee). Another option is to park in the free town lot. Nearly all the sites are within about 0.6 mile of the town center. A leisurely stroll around town can be as little as 0.5 mile or as long as several miles, depending on your route. Select and choose what sites you want to see. Highlights include Church Cove Park, St. Mary's Square, St. Michaels Museum, and the Cannonball House. The St. Michaels Museum has produced a nice walking tour available online at http://www.stmichaelsmuseum.com/walkingtour2008.pdf. *See* St. Michaels *in part 2* Maryland Eastern Shore Tour *for map and details.*

Upper Marlboro (Prince George's County): Dr. Beanes Walk

Level of Difficulty: Easy. Visit Darnall's Chance, the home of a man who was tried for treason for releasing some captured British stragglers. See the grave of Dr. William Beanes, whose capture by the British caused a chain of events that led to attorney Francis Scott Key's being aboard a ship during the bombardment of Fort McHenry. Key's lyrics inspired by the event, became the words of our national anthem. Park at Darnall's Chance and tour the house. Then walk 0.3 mile west past a mill pond to the grave of Dr. Beanes (there is also a nice 0.75 mile walk around the mill pond). It is only another 0.3 mile south to Trinity Church (present structure dates from after 1814), where a British soldier tore out pages from the church register. *See* Upper Marlboro *in part 1* British Invasion Tour *for map and details.*

Other Maryland Walks

Short walks are available at several other War of 1812 sites including:

Brookeville (stroll between the Madison House and the Brookeville Academy)
Hampton Mansion (stroll among the cemetery, garden, and numerous outbuildings)
Point Lookout State Park (several options including beach walks)
Sotterley (trail down to water past slave house)
Jefferson Patterson Park and Museum (several trail options)
Fort Washington (stroll down to the river)
Mount Welby

See individual sites for location and facility details.

VIRGINIA

Alexandria: Brick Sidewalks and Shooter's Hill

Level of Difficulty: Easy to Moderate (Moderate for those who choose to walk to Shooter's Hill owing to the distance and numerous steps). Alexandria is a pleasant historic city, well suited for walking. There is a slight rise in the topography as one walks from east to west. There are several parking garages just north of the Lyceum at Prince and King streets. It is five blocks (0.4 mile) north to the Henry Lee House (better known as the Boyhood Home of Robert E. Lee, Henry's son). The muster site (bearing no resemblance to its appearance in 1814) was located on the north side of this location (intersection of North Washington and Cameron streets), then the edge of the city. The Capt. David Porter incident took place about 0.3 mile east and one block south at the east end of Princess Street at the intersection with Union Street (Founders Park). From the Lyceum, it is approximately 1 mile west up King Street to the George Washington Masonic National Memorial on Shooter's Hill (the steps can be avoided by walking the road). From the Lyceum, it is six blocks east on

King Street where the contents of the warehouses were confiscated by the British. *See* Alexandria Tour *in part 2 for map and details.*

Hampton: Little England

Level of Difficulty: Easy. Hampton is a good place to walk around with convenient free parking in the historic district. Start your walk at the Hampton History Museum. Immediately north is the St. John's Episcopal Church. Walk east on Queens Way to King Street and then south to the large battery site at the end of King Street. This area is now a commercial fishing boat docking area. It is a pleasant walk south to Victoria Boulevard. This area was known as Little England during the war. A historic marker about it is located at 4400 Victoria Boulevard. A view of the small battery site can be seen from the east end of Victoria Boulevard at the yacht club. The actual battery site is on private property; please do not trespass. *See* Hampton *under* Greater Norfolk Tour *in part 2 for map and details.*

Norfolk-Portsmouth: Hidden Vestiges of the Past

Level of Difficulty: Easy to Moderate (Moderate for those who choose to walk to Fort Norfolk). Park at one of the garages on Waterside Drive and begin your tour at Nauticus, home of the Hampton Roads Naval Museum. One garage is located at 118 Main Street, site of the British Consul House. It is 0.4 mile to the Allmand-Archer House (327 Duke Street), which served as the American headquarters during the war. For the enthusiasts, it is about 1.3 miles from the Allmand-Archer House north and west to Fort Norfolk. From Nauticus, walk along the waterfront park southeast 0.3 mile to Waterside Festival Market Place and hop aboard the Elizabeth River Ferry to Portsmouth. Visit the Portsmouth Naval Shipyard Museum at 2 High Street. Ball House at 213 Middle Street, used as barracks during the war, is only two blocks west and one block north of the museum. *See* Norfolk *and* Portsmouth *under* Greater Norfolk Tour *in part 2 for map and details.*

Tappahannock (Essex County): Tappahannock on the Rappahannock

Level of Difficulty: Easy. Tappahannock has a small historic district that is compact and well suited for exploration by walking. Start at the Essex County Museum at 218 Water Lane. Street parking is available. From the museum, it is two blocks east on Prince Street to the Custom House, one block south and one block east to the Brockenbrough-McCall House, and two blocks west and one block north to the old courthouse. *See* Tappahannock Tour *under* Virginia *in part 2 for map and details.*

Other Virginia Walks

Short walks are available at several other War of 1812 sites including:

Cape Henry (walk to the old lighthouse and along the beach)
Old Blandford Church and Cemetery, Petersburg (walk around this interesting cemetery)
New Point Comfort Natural Preserve Area (boardwalk)
Organ Cave (easy public tour or strenuous wild cave ramble to "War of 1812 Room," must make reservations in advance)
Pimmet Run walk to Patterson Mill site (on the Potomac River)

Virginia Manufactory of Arms site at the Richmond National Battlefield Civil War
Visitor Center (walk along the James River)

See individual sites for location and facility details.

DISTRICT OF COLUMBIA

Washington City: Washington Walk

Level of Difficulty: Easy. Begin your tour at the Washington D.C. Visitor Information Center at 1300 Pennsylvania Avenue. The White House, Lafayette Square, and Decatur House are three blocks northwest of the Information Center. Farragut Square is another two blocks north on 17th Street. Octagon House is two blocks south and two blocks west of Lafayette Square. The National Museum of American History is located one block south of the information center. Capitol Hill and the Capitol are approximately eight blocks to the east on the National Mall. The Sewall-Belmont House is located one block northeast of the Capitol. *See* District of Columbia, Washington, D.C., Tour *in part 2 for map and details.*

Appendix B

Suggested Bicycling Areas

Although biking enthusiasts are willing to bike nearly anywhere, the suggested routes below are geared more for the casual family or leisure biker. Side trips earmarked for the enthusiasts are more strenuous. Several of these rides are one way. If you do not drop off a second car in advance, or have a pickup arranged, you will need to backtrack, doubling your distance.

There are several useful guides to assist bicyclists. Among them for Maryland are:

Bicycling in Maryland, by the Maryland Department of Transportation (contact 410-333-1663)

Best Bike Routes in Maryland: A County by County Guide, produced by the Maryland Office of Tourism (contact 410-333-1663 X 106)

25 Bicycle Tours in Maryland: From the Allegheny Mountains to the Chesapeake Bay, by Anne H. Oman (Woodstock, VT: Backcountry Guides, 2001)

Among the guides for Virginia is:

Bicyling in Virginia by Virginia Department of Transportation and the Office of Tourism (contact 1-800-847-4882. PDF downloads of a map are available at www .virginiadot.org/bikemap).

MARYLAND

Annapolis (Anne Arundel County): Brick Sidewalks and Plebes

Bicyclists can use the walking itinerary (*see* appendix A *for details*). Remember to bring a photo ID and to wear your bike helmet for entrance to the Naval Academy grounds. Downtown streets can be congested.

Baltimore City: Bike Baltimore

Bicyclists can use the walking itinerary (*see* appendix A *for details*). Battle Monument is 0.6 mile north of the Visitor Center at the Inner Harbor. The enthusiast may wish to travel approximately 0.7 mile west from Battle Monument to the First Presbyterian Church Burying Ground, another 0.8 mile north to the Maryland Historical Society, and another 0.8 mile northwest to the Francis Scott Key Monument. The Flag House and Star-Spangled Banner Museum is 0.6 mile northeast from the Inner Harbor. From the Flag House, it is approximately 1.1 miles to the Wells and McComas Monument. Patterson Park is approximately 1 mile east of the Flag House. Fort McHenry is approximately 2 miles south and east of the Inner Harbor. It is recommended to use Light Street south to Fort Avenue and then follow Fort Avenue east to the fort. This will avoid congested Key Highway (any combination of south and east streets to Fort Avenue will work). A diversion to the Fort Wood site at Leone Riverside Park follows Covington Street south off Fort Avenue. Bikes cannot be accommodated on the water taxis. I recommend that all but the most enthusiastic bikers avoid the congested downtown streets. Instead, bikers are encouraged to transport their bikes by car or transit bus (all outfitted with bike racks) to Fort McHenry and Patterson Park, where bikes can be ridden on paved trails. Be forewarned that Patterson Park is hilly.

Benedict (Charles County): August Exhaustion Ride

Bicyclists may ride from the Indian Creek Hunting area parking lot to and around Benedict. Enthusiasts can follow the British invasion route from the first encampment at Benedict uphill to what is today called Patuxent City. *See* appendix A *for details and the British Invasion Tour in part 1 for map.* Use caution as the road shoulders are narrow and many vehicles speed on this commuter road. This route is not recommended for children or families.

Bladensburg (Prince George's County): Bike the Battlefield

This ride is about 5 miles round trip, the first half uphill and the return downhill. There is another approximately 1-mile side trip to see the historic Margruder House, Bostwick House, and the Ross House site. *See* appendix A *for details and* Bladensburg Battlefield Tour *in part 1 for map.* Use side streets where possible as main streets are usually congested.

Caulks Field (Kent County): Route to the Battlefield

Park at the Caulks Field Battlefield Monument. Go south 0.1 mile on Caulks Field Road and make a sharp right (west) on Tolchester Beach Road. Follow it 2.2 miles across Tolchester Road to Maryland Parkway and turn right (north). Follow it 0.25 mile to the Mitchell House B&B (*See sidebar on p. 155*). The house is privately owned, so please be respectful and do not disturb the occupants. Return to Tolchester Beach Road and turn left (east) and proceed 0.3 mile to Bay Shore Road. Turn left (north) 1.5 miles to the intersection with Chantilly Farm Lane (private).

During the evening of August 30, 1814, a force of about 260 British troops landed near here on a now-private stretch of shoreline on Chesapeake Bay. Continue on Bay Shore Road (east) approximately 1.5 miles to Georgetown Road, following the British route to the battlefield. Turn right (south) on Georgetown Road and proceed 1.5 miles to Caulks Field Road. At this intersection the Americans felled trees to slow the British advance. As the British turned left (southeast) onto Caulks Field Road, advance American forces opened fire and then withdrew to the American line stretched across the field near the battle monument. Envision American cannon on the road ahead and 200 troops supporting each flank and imagine the confusion of a night fight. *See part 2* Maryland Eastern Shore Tour *on p. 154 for details.*

Biking enthusiasts can continue on Caulks Field Road south 0.7 mile to Rock Hall Road, which becomes Sandy Bottom Road. Continue on Sandy Bottom Road about 1 mile to St. Paul's Parish Kent. Legend states the church served as a barracks during the war, that wounded soldiers from the battle were treated on the premises, and that the dead were buried here (*see sidebar* British Soldier Burials Disputed *on p. 155*).

Frederick (Frederick County): Frederick Refuge

Bicyclists can use the walking itinerary (*See* Frederick *in appendix A for details and* Maryland: Frederick Tour *in part 2 for map*). Use side streets where possible as main streets are usually congested.

Havre de Grace (Harford County): Town of Devastation

Bicyclists can use the walking itinerary (*See* Havre de Grace *in* appendix A *for details and* Maryland: Head of the Chesapeake Tour *in part 2 for map*).

North Point (Baltimore County): Battle of North Point Ride

Park at Fort Howard Park and bike 0.6 mile northwest to the Veterans Hospital entrance gate. Inside the gate, follow Gettysburg Avenue 0.3 mile south to the British landing beach. Return to the gate and bike 0.7 mile north to the Todd House. It is another 0.9 mile to the entrance of North Point State Park on right (east), 0.4 mile to the Shaw House site on left (west), another 1.3 miles to the American abandoned entrenchment site, another 1.1 miles to the Aguila Randall Monument on right (east), another 0.7 mile to Battle Acre on left (south), another 0.2 mile to the North Point Battlefield site on right (north), and another 0.3 mile to the Methodist Meeting House site on right (northeast). *See* Battle of North Point Tour *in part 1 for map and details.* For a less-traveled route take a right (east) on Bay Shore Road off North Point Road and then left (north) on the North Point Spur hiking and bike path. A parking area is located here. North Point Spur will cross North Point Road and continue to near the Shaw House site. The park also has other marked bicycling paths.

Nottingham to Thomas Church (Prince George's County): Sunken Road Ride

This is a lovely, although hilly, ride along rural roads. Fenno Road, more than any other road along the British Invasion Route, brings to mind what the conditions must have been like (other than being paved) when the British marched along it to Washington. Where Fenno Road intersects Thomas Church Road, a vestige of an unpaved sunken road continues north. Here one can ponder how it was to travel on such roads in 1814. It is approximately 5.5 miles from Nottingham to Thomas Church and another 1.4 miles to Bellefields where Secretary of State James Monroe spied the British advance from a gable end window. The biking enthusiast can ride another 5 miles to Mount Calvert, where spectacular views of the Patuxent River can be found. *See* British Invasion Tour *in part 1 for map and details.* As of fall of 2010 the bridge over Mataponi Creek is closed on Fenno Road, so be sure to check road conditions before attempting this route from Nottingham. An alternate route is to park near Thomas Church and bike to the north end of Fenno Road where the unpaved vestige section is located. Bellefields and Mount Calvert can also be accessed from the church.

Principio, Charlestown, and Elkton (Cecil County): Head of the Bay Tour

Bicycles are not permitted on the Hatem Memorial Bridge (U.S. Route 40) or Millard E. Tyding Memorial Bridge (I-95) over the Susquehanna River, so start your tour at Principio Iron Works parking lot. After exploring the iron works, follow Route 7 (it briefly joins U.S. 40) approximately 3.5 miles east to Route 267 to Charlestown. After exploring Charlestown, continue east on Route 267 to Route 7 and bike 5.6 miles northeast to Landing Road. Route 7 joins U.S. Route 40 the last 0.7 mile of this stretch. Make a right (south) on Landing Road about 0.5 mile to the Fort Hollingsworth site at the Elk Landing Historical Park. *See* Charlestown, Principio Iron Works *and* Elkton *under* Maryland: Head of the Chesapeake Tour *in part 2 for more details and a map.*

St. Michaels (Talbot County): History and Charm

St. Michaels is a good area to bike. It is flat and, other than Talbot Street, generally not congested. There are numerous sites you may choose to visit. It is about 2 miles northwest of town to the second, lesser-known St. Michaels engagement site. Many bicyclists pedal or go southeast to Oxford via the Oxford Ferry. If you take this route, you will pass the grave of Gen. Perry Benson who was in command of the American forces at St. Michaels during both the first and second engagements. He is buried about 0.25 mile off Royal Oak Road, on the east side of Station Road, off Cedar Grove Road. *See* appendix A *and* Maryland: Maryland Eastern Shore Tour *in part 2 for a map and details.*

Upper Marlboro (Prince George's County): Dr. Beanes Walk

Bicyclists can use the walking itinerary (*see* appendix A *for details and* British Invasion Tour *in part 1 for map*).

VIRGINIA

Alexandria: Brick Sidewalks and Shooter's Hill

Bicyclists can use the walking itinerary (*See* appendix A *for details and* Virginia: Alexandria Tour *in part 2 for map*).

Fort Monroe (city of Hampton): Fort Fun

Bicyclists can park near the lighthouse or the Casemate Museum. From there it is a pleasant ride around and inside the fort and along the road bordering the Bay. Photo ID and bike helmet are required for admittance to the fort. Bike enthusiasts may want to ride to Hampton, approximately 3 miles northwest. Take Route 143 north over Mill Creek bridge and then west over Hampton Creek Bridge to the historic area. *See* appendix A *for details and* Virginia: Greater Norfolk Tour *in part 2 for map.*

Hampton: Little England

Bicyclists can use the walking itinerary. The enthusiast may want to bike to Fort Monroe, approximately 3 miles southeast. Continue east and then south on Route 143 over the Hampton River Bridge and Mill Creek Bridge to the fort. Another option is to bike to Blackbeard Point (posted private property), approximately 1.6 miles from Victoria Boulevard and Bridge Street, or to Hampton University, 1.6 miles for views back to Hampton across Hampton Creek. *See* appendix A *for details and* Virginia: Greater Norfolk Tour *in part 2 for map.*

Norfolk: Hidden Vestiges of the Past

Bicyclists can use the walking itinerary to ride to Fort Norfolk from Nauticus. Enthusiasts could also ride to the sites of Forts Tar and Barbour. *See* appendix A *for details and* Virginia: Greater Norfolk Tour *in part 2 for map.*

Tappahannock (Essex County): Tappahannock on the Rappahannock

Bicyclists can use the walking itinerary. *See* appendix A *for details and* Virginia: Tappahannock Tour *in part 2 for map.*

DISTRICT OF COLUMBIA

Washington: Pedal Power

Bicyclists can use the walking itinerary. In addition, bicyclists may bike southeast on Pennsylvania Avenue and then south on 8th Street, about 1 mile total, to the U.S. Marine Barracks. From the barracks, it is another 0.7 mile to the visitor entrance gate of the Washington Navy Yard. Make sure you have proper ID and wear your biking helmet if you want to enter the Navy Yard. It is about 1.5 miles west from the information center to the Francis Scott Key Park in Georgetown. Tudor Hall and Dumbarton are about 0.5 mile north of M Street. Use side streets where possible as main streets are usually congested. *See* appendix A *for details and* District of Columbia: Washington, D.C., Tour *in part 2 for map.*

Appendix C

Canoe, Kayak, and Small Boating Areas

There are several useful guides to assist small boat enthusiasts. Among them are:

Sea Kayaking Maryland's Chesapeake Bay: Day Trips on the Tidal Tributaries and Coastlines of the Western and Eastern Shore, by Michael Savario and Andrea Nolan (Woodstock, VT: Backcountry Guides, 2003)

Sea Kayaking the Baltimore / Washington, D.C., Area, by Michael Gaaserud (Oakton, VA: Rainmaker Publishing LLC, 2007)

Sea Kayaking Virginia: A Paddler's Guide to Day Trips from Georgetown to Chincoteague, by Andrea Nolan (Woodstock, VT: Backcountry Guides, 2005)

Exploring the Chesapeake in Small Boats, by John Page Williams, Jr. (Centreville, MD: Tidewater Publishers, 2000) (note that historic information about the Chesapeake Flotilla is inaccurate).

For information on Maryland public boat services and ramps call 1-800-688-FINS or visit www.dnr.state.md.us/boating. For similar information on Virginia, call 804-637-1000 or visit www.dgif.state.va.us/boating/access/. This information is also available from regional centers that handle boating registration. Contact the Chesapeake Bay Program (1-800-662-CRIS; www.chesapeakebay.net/publications.aspx?menuitem=16872) for a copy of *The Chesapeake Bay, Susquehanna River, and Tidal Tributaries Public Access Guide.*

MARYLAND

Annapolis (Anne Arundel County): Spa Creek and Severn River

Remarks It is about a 1-mile paddle from Truxton Park to the Annapolis City Dock.
Put-in Sites Truxton Park, head of Spa Creek, beach launch next to boat ramp, no fee for launching watercraft transported via car top.
Rentals Annapolis Canoe and Kayak, 311 Third Street, 410-263-2303, www.annapolis canoeandkayak.com; and Kayak Annapolis, no street address, 443-949-0773, www.kayak annapolistours.com.

Baltimore City and Baltimore County: Patapsco River and Bear Creek

Remarks From the Canton Waterfront Park, it is about a 1-mile paddle south to Fort McHenry or approximately a 2-mile paddle west to the Inner Harbor. From the Inverness Park on Lynch Cove, it is a 2.5-mile paddle to the head of Bear Creek, the approximate right flank of the American line at the Battle of North Point.
Put-in Sites Canton Waterfront Park (take exit 57 off I-895 to Boston Street and turn left on South East Avenue, no fee); Inverness Park boat ramp (take exit 39 south off I-695 onto Merritt Boulevard, left (east) on Wise Avenue, right (south then east) on Lynch Road, right (south) on Jasmine Road and right (west and then south) onto Inverton Road to end.

Bladensburg (Prince George's County): Anacostia River

Remarks It is a short paddle from the Bladensburg Waterfront Park to the site of the Anacostia Bridge over which the British stormed to attack the first American line. The river can be explored only a short distance upstream depending on water-level conditions.
Put-in Site Bladensburg Waterfront Park, 4601 Annapolis Road.
Rentals Bladensburg Waterfront Park: Canoe, kayak, paddleboat, and rowboat rentals, Saturday and Sunday, 10 a.m. to 6 p.m. *Fees* (canoe or kayak): resident, $5/hour, $12/day; nonresident, $6/hour, $15/day; (rowboat and paddleboat): resident, $6/hour, $15/day; nonresident, $7/hour, $20/day.

Centreville (Queen Anne's County): Corsica River

Remarks It is about a 1.2-mile paddle from the Centreville boat landing to Fort Point on the south side of Corsica River. The earthworks here, visible by water only (private property), are among the best preserved in the Mid-Atlantic region. Respect private property and do not trespass.
Put-in Site Centreville boat landing, end of Watson Road, off Spaniard Neck Road, off Church Hill Road, west of Centreville.

Charlestown (Cecil County): Northeast River

Remarks Northeast River is a beautiful boating area. The ruins of the town's stone wharf are visible just below the boat ramp at the end of Conestoga Road. A gun battery was constructed on the hill overlooking the wharf but it was never used.
Put-in Site A boat ramp is located at the intersection of Market and Water streets near the stone wharf at the end of Conestoga Street. Boat trailers must park at lot B and require a Charlestown boat trailer permit. Call 410-287-6173 for details.

Easton (Talbot County): North Fork of Tred Avon River (Fort Stokes)

Remarks Fort Stokes, also spelled Stoakes, a well-preserved earthwork on private property, can only be seen by water. The fort site is located on a point of land on the northwest side of the river, the first major point downriver from Easton Point, on the former Henry Hollyday plantation, Ratcliffe Manor. It was built to protect Easton and named after James Stokes, a local shipbuilder and Methodist preacher whose shipyard workers largely built the earthen redoubt. It mounted six cannons behind breastworks and a structure built to house the fort's garrison. A contemporary account described the fort as "an embankment . . . thrown up, sufficient to effectually shelter 500 men, and entrench a score of pieces of artillery." Although nearby St. Michaels was twice attacked in 1813, Fort Stokes never saw action but was manned again when the British raided up the Choptank River in October 1814. After the war, picnics were held at Fort Stokes.
Put-in Site Boat ramp at end of Port Street, Easton.

Havre de Grace (Harford County): Susquehanna River/Chesapeake Bay

Remarks The head of Chesapeake Bay is wide and can be windy so pick your day wisely to avoid choppy waters. It is a pleasant paddle along the town waterfront to Susquehanna River.

Put-in Sites Jean Roberts Memorial Park landing at intersection of Ostego and Union streets, north end of town ($5 fee on weekends), and marina at Millard E. Tydings Memorial Park off Commerce Street.

Leonardtown (St. Mary's County): Breton Bay

Remarks There are several options for exploring Breton Bay and the Leonardtown waterfront. One may put-in at Leonardtown Wharf, Public Park, Port of Leonardtown Park, Camp Calvert Landing, or Abell's Wharf. The easiest access is either at the public wharf (bit of a carry to the water) or Camp Calvert Landing. But the most interesting and pleasant paddle is putting in at Port of Leonardtown Park and paddling down McIntosh Run approximately 2.4 miles to the public wharf where the British landed on July 19, 1814. Keep in mind you need to paddle back up against the current over the last mile unless you arrange for a shuttle. St. Mary's County has produced a great watertrails guide including McIntosh Run and Breton Bay. It can be downloaded at www.visitstmarysmd.com/docs/WaterTrailsBrochure.pdf. This guide also has a recommended paddle at St. Inigoes Creek where the British conducted raids in 1813 and 1814.

Put-in Site The Leonardtown Wharf Public Park is located at the south end of Washington Street. The McIntosh Run launch site at Port of Leonardtown Park is located on the south side of Route 5 just east of the bridge over the run. The Camp Calvert Landing is at the end of Camp Calvert Road just east of Leonardtown off Route 5. Abell's Wharf is located at the end of Abell Creek Lane of Route 244 south of Leonardtown. For additional information call 301-475-9791.

Patuxent River

Remarks There are several launching spots along the river, many near War of 1812–related sites. Depending on your interest, launch in Anne Arundel, Calvert, Charles, Prince George's, or St. Mary's counties. It is about 0.2 mile downriver from the Benedict Bridge to the approximate British landing site at Benedict. It is about 0.5 mile across the river to Hallowing Point and the Col. Benjamin Mackall House site just north of the bridge on the Calvert County side, about 2.5 miles to Trent Hall Creek on the Charles County side of the river, and about 3 miles south to Sheridan Point on the Calvert side, all sites of British raids. It is about a 2-mile paddle from Greenwell State Park across the river to the head of St. Leonard Creek. Nottingham is about 4 miles downstream from Selby's Landing. It is about 1.7 miles downstream from Patuxent Wetlands Park to Mount Calvert, and about 1.5 miles upstream to the scuttle site of the Chesapeake Flotilla. For river map and landings go to www.patuxentwatertrail.org/navigate.html. *See also* appendix D *for a free boat excursion on the Patuxent.* River currents and tides can make paddling strenuous. Check tide schedules and go with the flow when possible.

Put-in Sites

ANNE ARUNDEL COUNTY
Patuxent Wetlands Park (1598 Southern Maryland Boulevard), no charge, 410-741-9330.
CALVERT COUNTY
Kings Landing Park (3255 Kings Landing Road), 410-535-2661.
CHARLES COUNTY
Benedict Community Park (south side of Benedict Bridge), no charge, 301-932-3470.

PRINCE GEORGE'S COUNTY

There are no fees for launching watercraft transported via car top; permit required for trailer; $5 for resident and $7 for nonresident; call 301-627-6074.

Clyde Watson Boating Area (17901 Magruders Ferry Road), boat ramp and pier, 301-627-6074.

Governor Bridge canoe launch (7600 Governor Bridge Road), no charge, must walk boat down to bank of river, 301-627-6074.

Mount Calvert (end of Mount Calvert Road), 301-627-6074, but note, no put-ins or take-outs are allowed, only landings.

Patuxent River Park (Jackson's Landing and Selby's Landing, 16000 Croom Airport Road), 301-627-6074.

Queen Anne canoe launch (18405 Queen Anne Road), no charge, 301-627-6074.

ST. MARY'S COUNTY

Greenwell State Park (25420 Rosedale Manor Lane), must walk boat to launch beach, park entrance fee of $3 per vehicle, 301-373-9775).

Rentals Patuxent River Park, 1600 Croom Airport Road, Prince George's County. *Fees:* Daily rate: resident, $12, nonresident, $15. Hourly rate: resident, $5, nonresident, $6. *Contact:* 301-627-6074.

Patuxent Riverkeeper, 18600 Queen Anne Road, Prince George's County. *Fees:* Daily kayak rate: members, $25, nonmembers, $35; daily canoe rate: members, $35, nonmembers, $40. *Contact:* 301-249-8200; www.paxriverkeeper.org. *Comment:* boats must be picked up at office. The Queen Anne boat launch is about 0.5 mile away at 18405 Queen Anne Road. Guided day trips and overnight trips on river also offered. Contact 301-249-8200 for details.

Potomac River

Remarks It is about a 2-mile paddle from Piscataway Park to Fort Washington.
Put-in Sites North end of Wharf Road off West Farmington Road, west off Indian Head Highway, Charles County. No fee. One can also put in at Fort Washington Marina on the north side of Piscataway Creek, but there is a $5 launch fee. For general information about the marina visit www.coastal-properties.com/ftwashington.html. Rentals are also available at the marina from Atlantic Kayak. *Fees:* range from $25 for 2-hour rental to $50 for all day for a single open-cockpit kayak to $35 for 2-hour rental to $65 for all day for sea kayaks and tandem open-cockpit kayaks. *Contact:* 301-292-6455; www.atlantickayak.com.

St. Michaels (Talbot County): Harbor and Miles River

Remarks From the landing, it is a pleasant paddle to see all three gun battery and boom sites in the harbor. *See* www.tourtalbot.org/PDFs/StMichaelsWaterTrail.pdf.
Put-in Sites There is a boat ramp and landing at both the west and east ends of Chew Avenue. The ramp at East Chew Avenue puts you in the middle of the War of 1812 sites.

Sassafras River (Kent and Cecil Counties)

Remarks Fredericktown/Georgetown were nearly completely destroyed by fire during the British attack on the two towns. It is about 8.5 miles east from Turner Creek landing to Fredericktown/Georgetown, and about 3.1 miles from Fox Hole landing west to Fredericktown/Georgetown.

Put-in Sites Turner Creek boat landing (end of Turner Creek Road, Kent County, no fee), and Fox Hole Landing (end of Fox Hole Road just east of U.S. Route 302 and Route 290, Kent County, no fee).

VIRGINIA

Alexandria: Potomac River

Remarks It is an approximately 2-mile paddle from Belle Haven Marina to King Street, Alexandria.
Put-in-Site Belle Haven Marina, exit off George Washington Memorial Parkway to Belle Haven Road, just south of Alexandria.
Rentals Belle Haven Marina (canoes, kayaks, sail boats). *Contact:* for hours and fees call 703-768-0018 or go to www.saildc.com/boats/canoes_kayaks.php

Portsmouth: Elizabeth River

Remarks The best way to see the Fort Nelson site and its relationship to Fort Norfolk, Craney Island, and Gosport Navy Yard is by boat.
Put-in Site There is a free boat ramp with ample parking at Portsmouth City Park, off City Park Avenue.

Pungoteague: Underhill Creek

Remarks The Battle of Pungoteague or Rumleys Gut took place on May 30, 1814. Because this battle is not covered elsewhere in the guide, a brief summary follows. A militia camp was established at Waterhouse Point on the south entrance to the creek. Approximately five hundred British troops landed on the opposite side near West Point, then marched east to Rumleys Gut. They engaged a small group of militia on the north side of Underhill Creek. The Americans withdrew into the woods to the north until about a thousand reinforcements arrived from the east and caused the British to withdraw back to their boats. At least six British soldiers were killed and fourteen wounded. No Americans were killed, although two were wounded. The British burned the American barracks. The only way to see this battlefield is by water because of private ownership of the site. The entrance to Underhill Creek can be seen from the northeast across the creek and from the area of Rumsey's Gut still further to the northeast. Waterhouse Point is down the creek on the same side as the ramp. Maps of the battle can be found in *Pungoteague to Petersburg,* by Alton Brooks Parker Barnes (vol. 1, 1988, pp. 155-56). This book is difficult to find but it can be accessed online at www.ghotes.net/parker_barnes/Vol%20I/index.html.
Put-in Site Boat ramp at end of Harborton Road (Route 180), southwest of Onancock, Accomack County.

Tappahannock: Rappahannock River

Remarks Views of the Rappahannock can be seen at the end of Prince Street but, for the boating enthusiast, getting out on the river is the best way to imagine the British raid on Tappahannock in early December 1814.
Put-in Site Boat ramp at end of Prince Street. Limited parking nearby.

DISTRICT OF COLUMBIA

Potomac River

Remarks The Mason's Ferry site, where President Madison fled from the British into Virginia, is immediately downstream from Jack's Boathouse and a 2-mile paddle downstream from Fletcher's Boat House.

Put-in Sites Jack's Boathouse, just northwest of Francis Scott Key Park and bridge, 3500 K Street, NW (www.jacksboathouse.com), and Fletcher's Boat House, 4940 Canal Road, NW (www.fletchersboathouse.com/) (note tunnel clearance 7 feet).

Rentals Jack's Boathouse and Fletcher's Boat House.

Appendix D

Boat Excursions

This appendix does not include all available boat excursions nor does inclusion in the list indicate that the excursions are recommended. For some locations, there is only one company operating. In other areas, such as Baltimore, there are many choices. None of these excursions is specific to the War of 1812, but all pass war-related sites.

MARYLAND

Annapolis

Harbor Queen *Location:* Annapolis City Dock. *Parking:* metered parking at dock, city garages. *Hours:* March 28 through May 8, weekdays, noon to 3 p.m. on hour, weekends, 11 a.m. to 6 p.m. on hour; May 9 through September 7, weekdays, 11 a.m. to 4 p.m. on hour, weekends, 11 a.m. to 7 p.m. on hour; September 8 through October 4, weekdays, noon to 4 p.m., weekends, 11 a.m. to 6 p.m. on hour; October 21 through November 22, as weather permits. *Fees:* $12 adults, $5 children 3 to 11, children under 3 free. *War of 1812–related sights:* U.S. Naval Academy, dome of Maryland Statehouse, distant views of sites of Forts Severn, Madison, Nonsense. *Contacts:* 410-268-7600; www.watermarkcruises.com/cruises40min.htm. *Comment:* 40-minute narrated cruise of Annapolis Harbor and U.S. Naval Academy.

Miss Ann *Location:* Annapolis City Dock. *Parking:* metered parking at dock, city garages. *Hours:* April 17 through May 16, weekdays, 3:30 to 6:30 p.m., every hour on the half hour, weekends, 1:30 to 6:30 p.m., every hour on the half hour; May 17 through September 6, weekdays, 3:30 to 8:30 p.m., every hour on the half hour, weekends, 1:15 to 8:15 p.m., every 30 minutes; September 7 through October 3, weekdays, 3:30 to 6:30 p.m., every hour on the half hour, weekends and holidays, 1:15 to 7:15 p.m., every 30 minutes. *Fees:* $12 adults, $5 children 3 to 11, children under 3 free. *War of 1812–related sights:* U.S. Naval Academy, dome of Maryland Statehouse, distant views of sites of Forts Severn, Madison, Nonsense. *Contacts:* 800-569-9622; www.watermarkcruises.com/cruises40min.htm. *Comment:* narrated tours of Spa Creek and U.S. Naval Academy.

Baltimore Inner Harbor

Spirit *Location:* Inner Harbor, 561 Light Street (near Maryland Science Center). *Parking:* special parking rate with Intercontinental Hotel Garage at 30 East Lee Street. *Hours:* April through October, weather permitting, cruises vary but generally daily, 12:30, 2:30, and 4:30 p.m. *Fees:* $19.82 adults, $10.81 children 3 to 11. *War of 1812–related sights:* Fells Point, Fort McHenry, Francis Scott Key Bridge, Stodder's Shipyard site where U.S. frigate *Constellation* was built. *Contacts:* 886-406-8439; www.spiritcruisesbaltimore.com./bd/sightseeing/indes.jsp. *Comment:* narrated 75-minute cruise.

Bladensburg

Anacostia River Boat Tours *Location:* Bladensburg Waterfront Park. *Parking:* free. *Hours:* Late May through late September, Tuesday through Friday 12 noon, Saturday and Sunday, 5 p.m. *Fees:* free. *Contacts:* 301-779-0371; www.pgparks.com/Things_To_Do/Nature/Bladensburg_Waterfront_Park.htm.; and www.baygateways.net/general.cfm?id=135. *Comment:* 45-minute narrated tours geared toward wildlife, but upon prior request a War of 1812–focused tour can be arranged. No advance reservations possible so sign up as soon as you arrive at the park. Due to limited seating it is first come first served.

Havre de Grace

Martha Lewis *Location:* 352 Commerce Street, Yacht Basin, Millard E. Tydings Memorial Park. *Parking:* free. *Hours:* June through October, days and times vary. *Contacts:* 410-939-4078; www.skipjackmarthalewis.org. *Comment: Martha Lewis* is a 1955 Chesapeake Bay skipjack.

Patuxent River

Pontoon Boat *Location:* Patuxent River Park, 16000 Croom Airport Road, Prince George's County. *Parking:* free. *Hours:* April through October, Sunday, 2 p.m. *Fees:* Free. *Contact:* 301-627-6074. *Comment:* these one-hour naturalist-led trips are geared toward wildlife but they provide an opportunity to experience a portion of the river where the Chesapeake Flotilla and British barges passed. Call for reservations and more information. Trips are weather- and wind-dependent. Sunset cruises are sometimes offered; contact the park for further information.

Solomons

Wm B. Tennison *Location:* Calvert Marine Museum, *Parking:* free. *Hours:* May through October, Wednesday through Sunday, 2 p.m., July and August, Saturday and Sunday additional 12:30 p.m. cruise. *Fees:* $7 adults, $4 children 5 to 12, children under 5 free. *War of 1812–related sights:* mouth of Patuxent River where British blockade occurred; Rousby Hall and Point Patience, raided by British, and Thomas Johnson Bridge near where anchor from H.M. troop ship *Dictator* lost, recovered, and now on display at Mariners' Museum. *Contacts:* 410-326-2043, X15; www.calvertmarinemuseum.com. *Comment:* narrated 60-minute cruise on historic 1899 vessel. The museum occasionally has cruises up to St. Leonard Creek, site of Maryland's largest naval engagement, June 1814. Contact museum for details.

St. Michaels

Patriot *Location:* next to Crab Claw Restaurant. *Parking:* free at Chesapeake Bay Maritime Museum. *Hours:* Cruises offered daily Friday through Sunday, weather permitting, 11 a.m., 2:30, and 4:30 p.m. Generally from April to November additional cruises offered Wednesday and Thursday at 12:30 and 2:30 p.m.; lunch and special evening cruises at additional rates. *Fees:* $24.50 adults, $20.75 seniors 62+, $12.50 children 12 to 17, children under 12 free. *War of 1812–related sights:* Parrott Point gun battery site and location of floating boom. *Contacts:* 410-745-3100; www.patriotcruises.com. *Comment:* narrated 60-minute cruise; 12:30 lunch cruise, 90 minutes. Also contact the Chesapeake Bay Maritime Museum, which has cruises on the *Mister Jim. Contact:* 410-745-2916.

VIRGINIA

Alexandria

Admiral Tilp *Location:* City Marina, Cameron and Union streets. *Parking:* parking garages. *Hours:* hourly departures—April, weekends, noon to 6 p.m.; May 1 through 25, weekends, noon to 8 p.m.; May 26 through September 7, Tuesday through Thursday, 11 a.m. to 2 p.m., Friday, 1 to 2 p.m., Saturday, 11 a.m. to 10 p.m., Sunday, 11 a.m. to 8 p.m.; September 8 through October 12, Saturday, noon to 9 p.m. and Sunday, noon to 7 p.m. *Fees:* $14 adults, $8 children 2 to 11. *Contacts:* 877-511-2628; *Comment:* 40-minute narrated tour. Also consider using the National Harbor ferry for views of Alexandria, Potomac River, and Washington, D.C., but the cost of ferry is more than the cost of the tour boat. Boat excursions to Mount Vernon also available.

Norfolk

American Rover *Location:* 333 Waterside Drive. *Parking:* city garage. *Hours:* 1.5-hour cruise, June through late August, Wednesday through Saturday, 11:30 a.m.; 2-hour cruise mid April through late October, 3 p.m. (except Mondays Spring and Fall). *Fees:* 1.5-hour cruise, $14 adult, $8 children under 13; 2-hour cruise, $16 adult, $10 children. *War of 1812–related sights:* Fort Norfolk, site of Fort Nelson and Craney Island, Lamberts Point. *Contacts:* 757-627-7245; www.americanrover.com. *Comment:* this is a sailing vessel with opportunities to help set sails and take a turn at the helm.

Victory Rover *Location:* 1 Waterside Drive, next to Nauticus. *Parking:* city garage. *Hours:* March, daily except Monday, 2 p.m., April through late May, daily, 11 a.m. and 2 p.m., late May through Labor Day, daily, 11 a.m., 2 p.m., and 5:30 p.m., day after Labor Day through October, daily, 11 a.m. and 2 p.m., November through December, daily except Monday 2 p.m. *Fees:* $16.50 adult, $10.00 children under 13. *War of 1812–related sights:* Fort Norfolk, site of Fort Nelson and Craney Island, Lamberts Point. *Contacts:* 757-627-7406, www .navalbasecruises.com. *Comment:* 2-hour narrated cruise.

Elizabeth River Paddlewheel Ferry *Location:* This ferry runs between Harbor Park, Norfolk and North Landing, Portsmouth. Harbor Park is conveniently located at Waterside, the waterfront hub of Norfolk and North Landing at Olde Town, very near the Naval Shipyard Museum. *Hours:* Memorial Day to Labor Day, weekdays, 7 a.m. to 11:45 p.m., weekends, 10 a.m. to 11:45 p.m., Labor Day to Memorial Day, Monday through Thursday, 7 a.m. to 9:45 p.m., Friday, 7 a.m. to 11:45 p.m., Saturday, 10 a.m. to 11:45 p.m., Sunday, 10 a.m. to 9:45 p.m. *War of 1812–related sights:* Gosport Navy Yard site and approximate anchoring position of U.S. frigate *Constellation*. *Contacts:* 757-222-6100; www.gohrt.com/services/paddlewheel-ferry. *Comment:* this is an economical way to see the area by water but the sites are limited to the upper-river area.

Tappahannock

Capt. Thomas *Location:* 1156 Tappahannock Boulevard. *Parking:* free. *Hours:* Tuesday through Sunday, 10 a.m. to 4:30 p.m. *Fees:* $25 per person, optional $11 lunch buffet; reservations required. *Contacts:* 804-453-BOAT (2628); www.virginia.org/site/description .asp?attrID=28654. *Comment:* cruise on the Rappahannock River to winery and return. Views of Tappahannock from water.

DISTRICT OF COLUMBIA

Nightingale *Location:* 31st and K Street, Georgetown. *Parking:* garage suggested. *Hours:* April through October, Monday through Friday, noon to 7 p.m. on hour; Saturday and Sunday, noon to 9 p.m. on hour. *Fees:* $13 adults, $6 children 3 to 12, discount for tickets purchased online. *Contacts:* 1-800-405-5911; www.capitolrivercruises.com. *War of 1812–related sights:* Mason's Ferry site; skyline of Washington and distant view of Capitol Hill. *Comment:* 45-minute narrated tour.

SUGGESTED READING

Readers are encouraged to consult *The War of 1812 in the Chesapeake: A Reference Guide to Historic Sites in Maryland, Virginia, and the District of Columbia,* by Ralph E. Eshelman, Scott S. Sheads, and Donald R. Hickey (Baltimore: Johns Hopkins University Press, 2010) as it provides a detailed summary of the War of 1812 and the role the Chesapeake played in that war. It also includes complete citations for most of the quotes used in this guide. Included is a complete chronology of the War in the Chesapeake and a thorough bibliographic essay. Although this travel guide has new and updated information, much of it is gleaned from the reference guide.

There are many broad studies of the War of 1812. One of the most detailed and still the most useful is the classic written by Henry Adams, *History of the United States of America [during the Administrations of Jefferson and Madison],* 9 vols. (New York: C. Scribner's Sons, 1889–91). Although Adams's judgments must be treated with caution, volumes 6–7 provide a good overview of the political, diplomatic, and military history of the war. Also indispensable is Benson J. Lossing's remarkable work, *The Pictorial Field-Book of the War of 1812* (New York: Harper & Brothers, 1868), which is based on the author's extensive travels in the 1850s and includes hundreds of sketches of 1812 sites as they appeared some forty years after the war. For a contemporary history of the war from the British perspective, see William James, *A Full and Correct Account of the Military Occurrences of the Late War between Great Britain and the United States of America,* 2 vols. (London: privately printed, 1818). The best American counterparts are two works by Charles J. Ingersoll, *Historical Sketch of the Second War between the United States of America, and Great Britain,* 2 vols. (Philadelphia: Lea and Blanchard, 1845–49), and *History of the Second War between the United States of America and Great Britain,* 2 vols. (Philadelphia: Lippincott, Grambo & Co., 1853). Both James and Ingersoll were witnesses to the war, James as an enemy alien in the United States and then a refugee in Halifax and Ingersoll as a member of Congress from Pennsylvania.

A good overview of the war that focuses on the American side and includes political, diplomatic, and financial as well as military history is *The War of 1812: A Forgotten Conflict,* by Donald R. Hickey (Urbana: University of Illinois Press, 1989). Hickey's companion volume, *Don't Give Up the Ship! Myths of the War of 1812* (Toronto: Robin Brass Studio, and Urbana: University of Illinois Press, 2006) challenges many widely held misconceptions about the war, including a fair number bearing on the Chesapeake.

There are few works devoted exclusively to the War of 1812 in the Chesapeake. *The Dawn's Early Light,* by Walter Lord (New York: W.W. Norton, 1972) is a popular account focusing on the war in Maryland and Washington that is both engaging and generally reliable. *Terror on the Chesapeake: The War of 1812 on the Bay,* by Christopher T. George (Shippensburg, PA: White Mane Publishing Company, 2000), is a more recent account. Like Lord, George focuses on the war in the Upper Chesapeake, although he does include a chapter on the Virginia engagements at Craney Island and Hampton. *The Burning of Washington: The British Invasion of 1814,* by Anthony Pitch (Annapolis, MD: Naval Institute Press, 2000) and *August 24, 1814: Washington in Flames,* by Carole L. Herrick (Falls Church, VA: Higher Education

Publications, Inc., 2005) both cover the British occupation of Washington and the events leading up to that event. Pitch includes many anecdotes that make his work engaging. Herrick makes use of numerous contemporary narratives. She also goes into detail about the First Family's escape to Virginia. Donald G. Shomette has revised and expanded his work, *Flotilla: Battle for the Patuxent* (Solomons, MD: Calvert Marine Museum Press, 1981) in a new edition retitled *Flotilla: The Patuxent Naval Campaign in the War of 1812* (Baltimore: Johns Hopkins University Press, 2009).

Presently there is no comprehensive study on Virginia during the War of 1812, although such a work, tentatively titled *Defending the Old Dominion: Virginia and Its Militia in the War of 1812,* is being undertaken by Stuart Butler. Patrick O'Neill is working on a comprehensive history of the British ascent and descent of the Potomac River in 1814 including the American attempt to attack the squadron from batteries established at White House and Indian Head as well as by fire-ships. It is tentatively titled *"To Annoy or Destroy the Enemy": The Battle of the White House after the Burning of Washington in September 1814.* For an account of the Battle of Craney Island, the largest battle to take place in Virginia during the war, see *The Battle of Craney Island: A Matter of Credit,* by John M. Hallahan (Portsmouth, VA: Saint Michael's Press, 1986). This work also has a chapter on the Battle of Hampton. For an account of the Battle of Pungoteague, the largest battle on Virginia's Eastern Shore, see *Pungoteague to Petersburg,* vol. 1, by Alton Brooks Parker Barnes (A. Lee Howard Books: Bowling Green, VA, 1988; also available online).

INDEX